Thomas Wallace Knox

The boy travellers in the Far East

Adventures of two youths in a journey to Japan and China

Thomas Wallace Knox

The boy travellers in the Far East
Adventures of two youths in a journey to Japan and China

ISBN/EAN: 9783744745093

Printed in Europe, USA, Canada, Australia, Japan

Cover: Foto ©Andreas Hilbeck / pixelio.de

More available books at **www.hansebooks.com**

The Boy Travellers in the Far East

ADVENTURES OF

TWO YOUTHS IN A JOURNEY

TO

JAPAN AND CHINA

BY

THOMAS W. KNOX

AUTHOR OF "CAMP-FIRE AND COTTON-FIELD" "OVERLAND THROUGH ASIA"
"UNDERGROUND" "JOHN" ETC.

Illustrated

NEW YORK

HARPER & BROTHERS, PUBLISHERS

FRANKLIN SQUARE

1880

PREFACE.

To my Young Friends:

Not many years ago, China and Japan were regarded as among the barbarous nations. The rest of the world knew comparatively little about their peoples, and, on the other hand, the inhabitants of those countries had only a slight knowledge of Europe and America. To-day the situation is greatly changed: China and Japan are holding intimate relations with us and with Europe, and there is every prospect that the acquaintance between the East and the West will increase as the years roll on. There is a general desire for information concerning the people of the Far East, and it is especially strong among the youths of America.

The characters in "The Boy Travellers" are fictitious; but the scenes that passed before their eyes, the people they met, and the incidents and accidents that befell them are real. The routes they travelled, the cities they visited, the excursions they made, the observations they recorded—in fact, nearly all that goes to make up this volume—were the actual experiences of the author at a very recent date. In a few instances I have used information obtained from others, but only after careful investigation has convinced me of its entire correctness. I have aimed to give a faithful picture of Japan and China as they appear to-day, and to make such comparisons with the past that the reader can easily comprehend the changes that have occurred in the last twenty years. And I have also endeavored to convey the information in such a way that the story shall not be considered tedious. Miss Effie and "The Mystery" may seem superfluous to some readers, but I am of opinion that the majority of those who peruse the book will not consider them unnecessary to the narrative.

In preparing illustrations for this volume the publishers have kindly allowed me to make use of some engravings that have already appeared in their publications relative to China and Japan. I have made selections from the volumes of Sir Rutherford Alcock and the Rev. Justus Doolittle, and also from the excellent work of Professor Griffis, " The Mikado's Empire." In the episode of a whaling voyage I have been under obligations to the graphic narrative of Mr. Davis entitled " Nimrod of the Sea," not only for illustrations, but for incidents of the chase of the monsters of the deep.

The author is not aware that any book describing China and Japan, and specially addressed to the young, has yet appeared. Consequently he is led to hope that his work will find a welcome among the boys and girls of America. And when the juvenile members of the family have completed its perusal, the children of a larger growth may possibly find the volume not without interest, and may glean from its pages some grains of information hitherto unknown to them.

T. W. K.

New York, *October*, 1879.

CONTENTS.

12 CONTENTS.

ILLUSTRATIONS.

A Japanese Swimming-scene. Reproduced from a Painting by a Japanese Artist....*Frontispiece.*

THE BOY TRAVELLERS.

CHAPTER I.

THE DEPARTURE.

"WELL, Frank," said Mr. Bassett, "the question is decided."

Frank looked up with an expression of anxiety on his handsome face. A twinkle in his father's eyes told him that the decision was a favorable one.

"And you'll let me go with them, won't you, father?" he answered.

"Yes, my boy," said the father, "you can go."

Frank was so full of joy that he couldn't speak for at least a couple of minutes. He threw his arms around Mr. Bassett; then he kissed his mother and his sister Mary, who had just come into the room; next he danced around the table on one foot; then he hugged his dog Nero, who wondered what it was all about; and he ended by again embracing his father, who stood smiling at the boy's delight. By this time Frank had recovered the

MR. BASSETT HAS DECIDED.

use of his tongue, and was able to express his gratitude in words. When the excitement was ended, Mary asked what had happened to make Frank fly around so.

"Why, he's going to Japan," said Mrs. Bassett.

2

"Going to Japan, and leave us all alone at home!" Mary exclaimed, and then her lips and eyes indicated an intention to cry.

Frank was eighteen years old and his sister was fifteen. They were

very fond of each other, and the thought that her brother was to be separated from her for a while was painful to the girl. Frank kissed her again, and said,

"I sha'n't be gone long, Mary, and I'll bring you such lots of nice things when I come back." Then there was another kiss, and Mary concluded she would have her cry some other time.

"But you won't let him go all alone, father, now, will you?" she asked as they sat down to breakfast.

"I think I could go alone," replied Frank, proudly, "and take care of myself without anybody's help; but I'm going with Cousin Fred and Doctor Bronson."

MARY.

"Better say Doctor Bronson and Cousin Fred," Mary answered, with a smile; "the Doctor is Fred's uncle and twenty years older."

Frank corrected the mistake he had made, and said he was too much excited to remember all about the rules of grammar and etiquette. He had even forgotten that he was hungry; at any rate, he had lost his appetite, and hardly touched the juicy steak and steaming potatoes that were before him.

During breakfast, Mr. Bassett explained to Mary the outline of the proposed journey. Doctor Bronson was going to Japan and China, and was to be accompanied by his nephew, Fred Bronson, who was very nearly Frank's age. Frank had asked his father's permission to join them, and Mr. Bassett had been considering the matter. He found that it would be very agreeable to Doctor Bronson and Fred to have Frank's company, and as the opportunity was an excellent one for the youth to see something of foreign lands under the excellent care of the Doctor, it did not take a long time for him to reach a favorable decision.

"Doctor Bronson has been there before, hasn't he, father?" said Mary, when the explanation was ended.

"Certainly, my child," was the reply; "he has been twice around the world, and has seen nearly every civilized and uncivilized country in it.

He speaks three or four languages fluently, and knows something of half a dozen others. Five years ago he was in Japan and China, and he is acquainted with many people living there. Don't you remember how he told us one evening about visiting a Japanese prince, and sitting cross-legged on the floor for half an hour, while they ate a dinner of boiled rice and stewed fish, and drank hot wine from little cups the size of a thimble?"

Mary remembered it all, and then declared she was glad Frank was going to Japan, and also glad that he was going with Doctor Bronson. And she added that the Doctor would know the best places for buying the presents Frank was to bring home.

MARY THINKING WHAT SHE WOULD LIKE FROM JAPAN.

" A crape shawl for mother, and another for me; now don't you forget," said Mary; "and some fans and some ivory combs, and some of those funny little cups and saucers such as Aunt Amelia has, and some nice tea to drink out of them."

" Anything else?" Frank asked.

" I don't know just now," Mary answered; "I'll read all I can about Japan and China before you start, so's I can know all they make, and then I'll write out a list. I want something of everything, you understand."

"If that's the case," Frank retorted, "you'd better wrap your list around a bushel of money. It'll take a good deal to buy the whole of those two countries."

Mary said she would be satisfied with a shawl and a fan and anything else that was pretty. The countries might stay where they were, and there were doubtless a good many things in them that nobody would want anyway. All she wished was to have anything that was nice and pretty.

For the next few days the proposed journey was the theme of conversation in the Bassett family. Mary examined all the books she could find about the countries her brother expected to visit; then she made a list of the things she desired, and the day before his departure she gave him a sealed envelope containing the paper. She explained that he was not to open it until he reached Japan, and that he would find two lists of what she wanted.

"The things marked 'number one' you must get anyway," she said, "and those marked 'number two' you must get if you can."

Frank thought she had shown great self-denial in making two lists

OVERLAND BY STAGE IN THE OLDEN TIME.

instead of one, but intimated that there was not much distinction in the conditions she proposed. He promised to see about the matter when he reached Japan, and so the conversation on that topic came to an end.

It did not take a long time to prepare Frank's wardrobe for the journey. His grandmother had an impression that he was going on a whaling voyage, as her brother had gone on one more than sixty years before. She proposed to give him two heavy jackets, a dozen pairs of woollen stockings, and a tarpaulin hat, and was sure he would need them. She

OVERLAND BY RAIL IN A PULLMAN CAR.

was undeceived when the difference between a sea voyage of to-day and one of half a century ago was explained to her. The housemaid said he would not need any thick clothing if he was going to Japan, as it was close to Jerusalem, and it was very hot there. She thought Japan was a seaport of Palestine, but Mary made it clear to her that Japan and Jaffa were not one and the same place. When satisfied on this point, she expressed the hope that the white bears and elephants wouldn't eat the poor boy up, and that the natives wouldn't roast him, as they did a missionary from her town when she was a little girl. "And, sure," she added, "he won't want any clothes at all, at all, there, as the horrid natives don't wear nothing except a little cocoanut ile which they rubs on their skins."

"What puts that into your head, Kathleen?" said Mary, with a laugh.

"And didn't ye jest tell me," Kathleen replied, "that Japan is an island in the Pacific Oshin? Sure it was an island in that same oshin where Father Mullaly was roasted alive, and the wretched natives drissed theirselves wid cocoannt ile. It was in a place they called Feejee."

Mary kindly explained that the Pacific Ocean was very large, and contained a great many islands, and that the spot where Father Mullaly was cooked was some thousands of miles from Japan.

At breakfast the day before the time fixed for Frank's departure, Mr. Bassett told his son that he must make the most of his journey, enjoy it as much as possible, and bring back a store of useful knowledge. "To accomplish this," he added, "several things will be necessary; let us see what they are."

"Careful observation is one requisite," said Frank, "and a good memory is another."

"Constant remembrance of home," Mrs. Bassett suggested, and Mary nodded in assent to her mother's proposition.

"Courage and perseverance," Frank added.

"A list of the things you are going to buy," Mary remarked.

"A light trunk and a cheerful disposition," said Doctor Bronson, who had entered the room just as this turn of the conversation set in.

"One thing more," Mr. Bassett added.

"I can't think of it," replied Frank; "what is it?"

"Money."

"Oh yes, of course; one couldn't very well go travelling without money. I'm old enough to know that, and to know it is very bad to be away from one's friends without money."

The Doctor said it reminded him of a man who asked another for ten cents to pay his ferriage across the Mississippi River, and explained that he hadn't a single penny. The other man answered, "It's no use throwing ten cents away on you in that fashion. If you haven't any money, you are just as well off on this side of the river as on the other."

"You will need money," said Mr. Bassett, "and here is something that will get it."

He handed Frank a double sheet of paper with some printed and written matter on the first page, and some printed lists on the third and fourth pages. The second page was blank; the first page read as follows :

LETTER OF CREDIT.

New York, *June* 18th, 1878.

To Our Correspondents :

We have the pleasure of introducing to you Mr. Frank Bassett, the bearer of this letter, whose signature you will find in the margin. We beg you to honor his drafts to the amount of two hundred pounds sterling, upon our London house, all deductions and commissions being at his expense.

We have the honor to remain, Gentlemen,

Very truly yours,

Blank & Co.

The printed matter on the third and fourth pages was a list of banking-houses in all the principal cities of the world. Frank observed that every country was included, and there was not a city of any prominence that was not named in the list, and on the same line with the list was the name of a banking-house.

The paper was passed around the table and examined, and finally returned to Frank's hand. Mr. Bassett then explained to his son the uses of the document.

"I obtained that paper," said he, "from the great house of Blank & Company. I paid a thousand dollars for it, but it is made in pounds sterling because the drafts are to be drawn on London, and you know that pounds, shillings, and pence are the currency of England."

"When you want money, you go to any house named on that list, no matter what part of the world it may be, and tell them how much you want. They make out a draft which you sign, and then they pay you the money, and write on the second page the amount you have drawn. You get ten pounds in one place, ten in another, twenty in another, and you continue to draw whenever you wish. Each banker puts down the amount you have received from him on the second page, and you can keep on drawing till the sum total of your drafts equals the figures named on the first page. Then your credit is said to be exhausted, and you can draw no more on that letter."

"How very convenient that is!" said Frank; "you don't have to carry money around with you, but get it when and where you want it."

"You must be very careful not to lose that letter," said Mr. Bassett.

"Would the money be lost altogether?" Frank asked in return.

COOKING-RANGE IN THE OLDEN TIME.

COOKING-RANGE ON A PULLMAN CAR.

"No, the money would not be lost, but your credit would be gone, and of no use. A new letter would be issued in place of the missing one, but only after some months, and when the bankers had satisfied themselves that there was no danger of the old one ever being used again."

"Can I get any kind of money with this letter, father?" Frank inquired, "or must I take it in pounds sterling? That would be very inconvenient sometimes, as I would have to go around and sell my pounds and buy the money of the country."

"They always give you," was the reply, "the money that circulates in the country where you are. Here they would give you dollars; in

Japan you will get Japanese money or Mexican dollars, which are current there; in India they would give you rupees; in Russia, rubles; in Italy, lire; in France, francs; in Spain, pesetas, and so on. They give you the equivalent of the amount you draw on your letter."

This reminded the Doctor of a story, and at the general request he told it.

A traveller stopped one night at a tavern in the interior of Minnesota. On paying his bill in the morning, he received a beaver skin instead of a dollar in change that was due him. The landlord explained that beaver skins were legal tender in that region at a dollar each.

He hid the skin under his coat, walked over the street to a grocery store, and asked the grocer if it was true that beaver skins were legal tender for one dollar each.

CHANGE FOR A DOLLAR—BEFORE AND AFTER.

"Certainly," answered the grocer, "everybody takes them at that rate."

"Then be kind enough to change me a dollar bill," said the stranger, drawing the beaver skin from under his coat and laying it on the counter.

The grocer answered that he was only too happy to oblige a stranger, and passed out four musk-rat skins, which were legal tender, as he said, at twenty-five cents each.

"Please, Doctor," said Mary, "what do you mean by legal tender?"

The Doctor explained that legal tender was the money which the law declares should be the proper tender, or offer, in paying a debt. "If

I owed your father a hundred dollars," said he, " I could not compel him to accept the whole amount in ten-cent pieces, or twenty-five-cent pieces, or even in half-dollars. When the government issues a coin, it places a limit for which that coin can be a legal tender. Thus the ten-cent piece is a legal tender for all debts of one dollar or less, and the half-dollar for debts of five dollars or less."

Mary said that when she was a child, ten cherries were exchanged among her schoolmates for one apple, two apples for one pear, and two pears for one orange. One day she took some oranges to school intending to exchange them for cherries, of which she was very fond ; she left them in Katie Smith's desk, but Katie was hungry and ate one of the oranges at recess.

" Not the first time the director of a bank has appropriated part of the funds," said the Doctor. " Didn't you find that an orange would buy more cherries or apples at one time than at another ?"

" Why, certainly," Mary answered, " and sometimes they wouldn't buy any cherries at all."

" Bankers and merchants call that the fluctuation of exchanges," said

KATHLEEN'S EXPECTATIONS FOR FRANK AND FRED.

Mr. Bassett; and with this remark he rose from the table, and the party broke up.

The next morning a carriage containing Doctor Bronson and his nephew, Fred, drove up in front of Mr. Bassett's house. There were farewell kisses, and hopes for a prosperous journey; and in a few minutes the three travellers were on their way to the railway station. There was a waving of handkerchiefs as the carriage started from the house and rolled away; Nero barked and looked wistfully after his young master, and the warm-hearted Kathleen wiped her eyes with the corner of her apron, and flung an old shoe after the departing vehicle.

" And sure," she said, " and I hope that wretched old Feejee won't be in Japan at all, at all, and the horrid haythens won't roast him."

As they approached the station, Frank appeared a little nervous about something. The cause of his anxiety was apparent when the carriage stopped. He was the first to get out and the first to mount the platform. Somebody was evidently waiting for him.

Doctor Bronson followed him a minute later, and heard something like the following:

" There, now, don't cry. Be a good girl, and I'll bring you the nicest little pigtail, of the most Celestial pattern, from China."

" I tell you, Mr. Frank Bassett, I'm not crying. It's the dust in the road got into my eyes."

"'But you are; there's another big tear. I know you're sorry, and so am I. But I'm coming back."

" I shall be glad to see you when you come back; of course I shall, for your sister's sake. And you'll be writing to Mary, and she'll tell me where you are. And when she's writing to you she'll—"

The bright little face turned suddenly, and its owner saw the Doctor standing near with an amused expression on his features, and, perhaps, a little moisture in his eyes. She uttered a cheery "Good-morning," to which the Doctor returned,

" Good-morning, Miss Effie. This is an unexpected pleasure."

" You see, Doctor" (she blushed and stammered a little as she spoke), " you know I like to take a walk in the morning, and happened to come down to the station."

" Of course, quite accidental," said the Doctor, with a merry twinkle in his eyes.

" Yes, that is, I knew Frank—I mean Mr. Bassett—that is, I knew you were all three going away, and I thought I might come down and see you start."

"Quite proper, Miss Effie," was the reply; "so good-bye: I must look after the tickets and the baggage."

"Good-bye, Doctor Bronson; good-bye, Mr. Fred. *Bon voyage!*"

EFFIE WAITING FOR SOMEBODY.

Frank lingered behind, and the rest of the dialogue has not been recorded.

"She's a nice girl," said Fred to the Doctor as they made their way to the ticket-office. "And she's very fond of Mary Bassett, Frank's sister. Spiteful people say, though, that she's oftener in Frank's company than in Mary's; and I know Frank is ready to punch the head of any other boy that dares to look at her."

"Quite so," answered Dr. Bronson; "I don't think Frank is likely to be forgetful of home."

Soon the whistle sounded, the great train rolled into the station, the conductor shouted "All aboard!" our friends took their seats, the bell rang, and the locomotive coughed asthmatically as it moved on.

Frank looked back as long as the station was in sight. Somebody continued to wave a delicate handkerchief until the train had disappeared; somebody's eyes were full of

GOOD-BYE.

tears, and so were the eyes of somebody else. Somebody's good wishes followed the travellers, and the travellers—Frank especially—wafted back good wishes for that somebody.

CHAPTER II.

OVERLAND TO CALIFORNIA.

OUR three travellers were seated in a Pullman car on the Erie Railway. Frank remarked that they were like the star of empire, as they were taking their way westward.

Fred replied that he thought the star of empire had a much harder time of it, as it had no cushioned seat to rest upon, and no plate-glass window to look from.

WATERING-PLACE ON THE ERIE RAILWAY.

THE COURSE OF EMPIRE.

"And it doesn't go at the rate of thirty miles an hour," the Doctor added.

"I'm not sure that I know exactly what the star of empire means," said Frank. "I used the expression as I have seen it, but can't tell what it comes from."

He looked appealingly at Doctor Bronson. The latter smiled kindly, and then explained the origin of the phrase.

"It is found," said the Doctor, "in a short poem that was written more than a hundred and fifty years ago, by Bishop Berkeley. The last verse is like this:

"Westward the course of empire takes its way;
   The first four acts already past,
A fifth shall close the drama with the day:
   Time's noblest off-spring is the last."

"You see the popular quotation is wrong," he added; "it is the *course* of empire that is mentioned in the poem, and not the *star*."

"I suppose," said Fred, "that the Bishop referred to the discovery of America by Columbus when he sailed to the West, and to the settlement of America which began on the Eastern coast and then went on to the West."

"You are exactly right," was the reply.

Frank added that he thought "star of empire" more poetical than "course of empire."

"But course is more near to the truth," said Fred, "than star. Don't you see that Bishop Berkeley wrote before railways were invented, and before people could travel as they do nowadays? Emigrants, when they went out West, went with wagons, or on horseback, or on foot. They travelled by day and rested at night. Now—don't you see?—they made their course in the daytime; when they couldn't see the stars at all; and when the stars were out, they were asleep, unless the wolves or the Indians kept them awake. They were too tired to waste any time over a twinkling star of empire, but they knew all about the course."

There was a laugh all around at Fred's ingenious defence of the author of the verse in question, and then the attention of the party was turned to the scenery along the route. Although living near the line of

VALLEY OF THE NEVERSINK.

the Erie Railway, neither of the boys had ever been west of his station. Everything was therefore new to the youths, and they took great interest in the panorama that unrolled to their eyes as the train moved on.

They were particularly pleased with the view of the valley of the Neversink, with its background of mountains and the pretty town of Port Jervis in the distance. The railway at one point winds around the edge of a hill, and is far enough above the valley to give a view several miles in extent.

Frank had heard much about the Starucca Viaduct, and so had Fred, and they were all anxiety to see it. Frank thought it would be better to

STARUCCA VIADUCT.

call it a bridge, as it was only a bridge, and nothing more; but Fred inclined to the opinion that "viaduct" sounded larger and higher.

"And remember," said he to Frank, "it is more than twelve hundred feet long, and is a hundred feet above the valley. It is large enough to have a much bigger name than viaduct."

Frank admitted the force of the argument, and added that he didn't care what name it went by, so long as it carried them safely over.

When they were passing the famous place, they looked out and saw the houses and trees far below them. Fred said they seemed to be riding in the air, and he thought he could understand how people must feel in a balloon.

Doctor Bronson said he was reminded of a story about the viaduct.

3

"Oh! tell it, please," said the two boys, in a breath.

"It is this," answered the Doctor. "When the road was first opened, a countryman came to the backwoods to the station near the end of the bridge. He had never seen a railway before, and had much curiosity to look at the cars. When the train came along, he stepped aboard, and before he was aware of it the cars were moving. He felt the floor trem-

NIAGARA FALLS, FROM THE AMERICAN SIDE.

bling, and as he looked from the window the train was just coming upon
the viaduct. He saw the earth falling away, apparently, the tree-tops far
below him, and the cattle very small in the distance. He turned pale as
a sheet, and almost fainted. He had just strength enough to say, in a
troubled voice, to the man nearest him,

"Say, stranger, how far does this thing fly before it lights?"

"I don't wonder at it," said Fred; "you see, I thought of the same
thing when the train was crossing."

The railway brought the party to Niagara, where they spent a day
visiting the famous cataract and the objects of interest in the vicinity.
Frank pronounced the cataract wonderful, and so did Fred; whereupon the
Doctor told them of the man who said Niagara was not at all wonderful,
as any other water put there would run down over the Falls, since there
was nothing to hinder its doing so. The real wonder would be to see it
go up again.

They looked at the Falls from all the points of view. They went under the Canadian side, and they also went under the Central Fall, and into
the Cave of the Winds. They stood for a long time watching the water
tumbling over Horseshoe Fall, and they stood equally long on the American side. When the day was ended, the boys asked the Doctor if he
would not permit them to remain another twenty-four hours.

"Why so?" the Doctor asked.

"Because," said Frank, with a bit of a blush on his cheeks—"because
we want to write home about Niagara and our visit here. Fred wants to
tell his mother about it, and I want to write to my mother and to Mary,
and—and—"

"Miss Effie, perhaps," Fred suggested.

Frank smiled, and said he might drop a line to Miss Effie if he had
time, and he was pretty certain there would be time if they remained another day.

Doctor Bronson listened to the appeal of the boys, and when they were
through he took a toothpick from his pocket and settled back in his chair
in the parlor of the hotel.

"Your request is very natural and proper," he answered; "but there
are several things to consider. Niagara has been described many times,
and those who have never seen it can easily know about it from books
and other accounts. Consequently what you would write about the Falls
would be a repetition of much that has been written before, and even your
personal impressions and experiences would not be far different from
those of others. I advise you not to attempt anything of the kind, and, at

ENTRANCE TO THE CAVE OF THE WINDS.

all events, not to stop here a day for that purpose. Spend the evening in writing brief letters home, but do not undertake a description of the Falls. If you want to stay a day in order to see more, we will stay, but otherwise we will go on."

The boys readily accepted Doctor Bronson's suggestion. They wrote short letters, and Frank did not forget Miss Effie. Then they went out to see the Falls by moonlight, and in good season they went to bed, where they slept admirably. The next day the journey was resumed, and they had a farewell view of Niagara from the windows of the car as they crossed the Suspension Bridge from the American to the Canadian side.

On they went over the Great Western Railway of Canada, and then over the Michigan Central; and on the morning after leaving Niagara they rolled into Chicago. Here they spent a day in visiting the interesting places in the Lake City. An old friend of Doctor Bronson came to see him at the Tremont House, and took the party out for a drive. Under the guidance of this hospitable citizen, they were taken to see the City-hall, the stock-yards, the tunnel under the river, the grain-elevators, and other things with which every one who spends a short time in Chicago is sure to be made familiar. They were shown the traces of the great fire of 1870, and were shown, too, what progress had been made in rebuilding the city and removing the signs of the calamity. Before they finished their tour, they had absorbed much of the enthusiasm of their guide, and were ready to pronounce Chicago the most remarkable city of the present time.

As they were studying the map to lay out their route westward, the boys noticed that the lines of the railways radiated in all directions from Chicago, like the diverging cords of a spider's web. Everywhere they stretched out except over the surface of Lake Michigan, where railway building has thus far been impossible. The Doctor explained that Chicago was one of the most important railway centres in the United States, and owed much of its prosperity to the network they saw on the map.

"I have a question," said Frank, suddenly brightening up.

"Well, what is it?"

"Why is that network we have just been looking at like a crow calling to his mates?"

"Give it up; let's have it."

"Because it makes Chi-ca-go."

"What's that to do with the crow?" Fred asked.

"Why, everything," Frank answered; "the crow makes ye-caw-go, doesn't it?"

"Now, Frank," the Doctor said, as he laughed over the conundrum, "making puns when we're a thousand miles from home and going west! However, that will do for a beginner; but don't try too often."

Fred thought he must say something, but was undecided for a moment. The room was open, and as he looked into the hall, he saw the chambermaid approaching the opposite door with the evident intention

FROM CHICAGO TO SAN FRANCISCO.

of looking through the keyhole. This gave him his opportunity, and he proposed his question.

"Why are we like that chambermaid over there?"

"The Doctor and Frank couldn't tell, and Fred answered, triumphantly,

"Because we're going to Pek-in."

"I think you boys are about even now," said the Doctor, "and may stop for the present." They agreed to call it quits, and resumed their study of the map.

They decided to go by the Northwestern Railway to Omaha. From the latter place they had no choice of route, as there was only a single line of road between Omaha and California.

From Chicago westward they traversed the rich prairies of Illinois and Iowa—a broad expanse of flat country, which wearied them with its monotony. At Omaha they crossed the Missouri River on a long bridge; and while they were crossing, Frank wrote some lines in his note-book to the effect that the Missouri was the longest river in the world, and was sometimes called the "Big Muddy," on account of its color. It looked

OMAHA.

like coffee after milk has been added; and was once said by Senator Benton to be too thick to swim in, but not thick enough to walk on.

Now they had a long ride before them. The Union Pacific Railway begins at Omaha and ends at Ogden, 1016 miles farther west. It connects at Ogden with the Central Pacific Railway, 882 miles long, which terminates at San Francisco. As they rode along they had abundant time to learn the history of the great enterprise that unites the Atlantic and Pacific coasts, and enables one to travel in a single week from New York to San Francisco. The Doctor had been over the route previously; and he had once crossed the Plains before the railway was constructed. Consequently, he was an excellent authority, and had an abundant store of information to draw from.

"The old way of crossing the Plains and the new way of doing the same thing," said Doctor Bronson, "are as different as black and white. My first journey to California was with an ox-wagon, and it took me six months to do it Now we shall make the same distance in four days."

"What a difference, indeed!" the boys remarked.

"We walked by the side of our teams or behind the wagons, we slept on the ground at night, we did our own cooking, we washed our knives by sticking them into the ground rapidly a few times, and we washed our plates with sand and wisps of grass. When we stopped, we arranged our wagons in a circle, and thus formed a 'corral,' or yard, where we drove our oxen to yoke them up. And the corral was often very useful as a fort, or camp, for defending ourselves against the Indians. Do you see that little hollow down there?" he asked, pointing to a depression in the ground a short distance to the right of the train. "Well, in that hollow our wagon-train was kept three days and nights by the Indians. Three days and nights they stayed around, and made several attacks. Two of our men were killed and three were wounded by their arrows, and others had narrow escapes. One arrow hit me on the throat, but I was saved by the knot of my neckerchief, and the point only tore the skin a little. Since that time I have always had a fondness for large neckties. I don't know how many of the Indians we killed, as they carried off their dead and wounded, to save them from being scalped. Next to getting the scalps of their enemies, the most important thing with the Indians is to save their own. We had several fights during our journey, but that one was the worst. Once a little party of us were surrounded in a small 'wallow,' and had a tough time to defend ourselves successfully. Luckily for us, the Indians had no fire-arms then, and their bows and arrows were no match for our rifles. Nowadays they are well armed, but there are

ATTACKED BY INDIANS.

not so many of them, and they are not inclined to trouble the railway
trains. They used to do a great deal of mischief in the old times, and
many a poor fellow has been killed by them."

Frank asked if the Doctor saw any buffaloes in his first journey, and if
he ever went on a buffalo-hunt.

"Of course," was the reply; "buffaloes were far more numerous then
than now, and sometimes the herds were so large that it took an entire day,
or even longer, for one of them to cross the road. Twice we were unable
to go on because the buffaloes were in the way, and so all of us who had
rifles went out for a hunt. I was one of the lucky ones, and we went out
in a party of four. Creeping along behind a ridge of earth, we managed
to get near two buffaloes that were slightly separated from the rest of the
herd. We spread out, and agreed that, at a given signal from the foremost man, we were to fire together—two at one buffalo and two at the
other. We fired as we had agreed. One buffalo fell with a severe
wound, and was soon finished with a bullet through his heart; the other
turned and ran upon us, and, as I was the first man he saw, he ran at me.
Just then I remembered that I had forgotten something at the camp, and,
as I wanted it at once, I started back for it as fast as I could go. It was

a sharp race between the buffalo and me, and, as he had twice as many legs as I could count, he made the best speed. I could hear his heavy breathing close behind me, and his footsteps, as he galloped along, sounded as though somebody were pounding the ground with a large hammer. Just as I began to think he would soon have me on his horns, I heard the report of a rifle at one side. Then the buffalo stumbled and fell, and I ventured to look around. One of the men from camp had fired just in time to save me from a very unpleasant predicament, and I concluded I didn't want any more buffalo-hunting for that day."

Hardly had the Doctor finished his story when there was a long whistle from the locomotive, followed by several short ones. The speed of the train was slackened, and, while the passengers were wondering what was the matter, the conductor came into the car where our friends were seated and told them there was a herd of buffaloes crossing the track.

"We shall run slowly through the herd," the conductor explained, "and you will have a good chance to see the buffalo at home."

They opened the windows and looked out. Sure enough, the plain

HERD OF BUFFALOES MOVING.

was covered, away to the south, with a dark expanse like a forest, but, unlike a forest, it appeared to be in motion. Very soon it was apparent that what seemed to be a forest was a herd of animals.

As the train approached the spot where the herd was crossing the track, the locomotive gave its loudest and shrillest shrieks. The noise

AN OLD SETTLER.

had the effect of frightening the buffaloes sufficiently to stop those which had not crossed, and in the gap thus formed the train moved on. The boys were greatly interested in the appearance of the beasts, and Frank declared he had never seen anything that looked more fierce than one of the old bulls, with his shaggy mane, his humped shoulders, and his sharp, glittering eyes. He was quite contented with the shelter of the railway-car, and said if the buffalo wanted him he must come inside to get him; or give him a good rifle, so that they could meet on equal terms.

Several of the passengers fired at the buffaloes, but Fred was certain he did not see anything drop. In half an hour the train had passed through the herd, and was moving on as fast as ever.

On and on they went. The Doctor pointed out many places of interest, and told them how the road was built through the wilderness.

"It was," said he, "the most remarkable enterprise, in some respects, that has ever been known. The working force was divided into parties like the divisions of an army, and each had its separate duties. Ties were cut and hauled to the line of the road; the ground was broken and made ready for the track; then the ties were placed in position, the rails were brought forward and spiked in place, and so, length by length, the road crept on. On the level, open country, four or five miles of road were built every day, and in one instance they built more than seven miles in a single day. There was a construction-train, where the laborers boarded and lodged, and this train went forward every day with the road. It was a sort of moving city, and was known as the 'End of Track;' there was a post-office in it, and a man who lived there could get his letters the same as though his residence had been stationary. The Union Pacific Com-

"END OF TRACK."

pany built west from Omaha, while the Central Pacific Company built east from Sacramento. They met in the Great Salt Lake valley; and then there was a grand ceremony over the placing of the last rail to connect the East with the West. The continent was spanned by the railway, and our great seaboards were neighbors."

Westward and westward went our travellers. From the Missouri River, the train crept gently up the slope of the Rocky Mountains, till it halted to take breath at the summit of the Pass, more than eight thousand feet above the level of the sea. Then, speeding on over the Laramie Plains, down into the great basin of Utah, winding through the green carpet of Echo Cañon, skirting the shores of Great Salt Lake, shooting like a sunbeam over the wastes of the alkali desert, climbing the Sierra Nevada, darting through the snow-sheds and tunnels, descending the western slope to the level of the Pacific, it came to a halt at Oakland, on the shore of San Francisco Bay. The last morning of their journey our travellers were among the snows on the summit of the Sierras; at noon they were breathing the warm air of the lowlands of California, and before sundown they were looking out through the Golden Gate upon

SNOW-SHEDS ON THE PACIFIC RAILWAY.

VIEW AT CAPE HORN, CENTRAL PACIFIC RAILWAY.

the blue waters of the great Western ocean. Nowhere else in the world does the railway bring all the varieties of climate more closely together.

San Francisco, the City by the Sea, was full of interest for our young adventurers. They walked and rode through its streets; they climbed its steep hill-sides; they gazed at its long lines of magnificent buildings; they went to the Cliff House, and saw the sea-lions by dozens and hundreds, within easy rifle-shot of their breakfast-table; they steamed over the bay, where the navies of the world might find safe anchorage; they had a glimpse of the Flowery Kingdom, in the Chinese quarter; and they wondered at the vegetable products of the Golden State as they found them in the market-place. Long letters were written home, and before they had studied California to their satisfaction it was time for them to set sail for what Fred called "the under-side of the world."

SEAL-ROCKS, SAN FRANCISCO.

CHAPTER III.

ON THE PACIFIC OCEAN.

OFFICERS and men were at their posts, and the good steamer *Oceanic* was ready for departure. It was a few minutes before noon.

As the first note was sounded on the bell, the gangway plank was drawn in. "One," "two," "three," "four," "five," "six," "seven," "eight," rang out from the sonorous metal.

The captain gave the order to cast off the lines. Hardly had the echo of his words ceased before the lines had fallen. Then he rang the signal to the engineer, and the great screw began to revolve beneath the stern of

DEPARTURE FROM SAN FRANCISCO.

the ship.   Promptly at the advertised time the huge craft was under way.
The crowd on the dock cheered as she moved slowly on, and they cheered
again as she gathered speed and ploughed the water into a track of foam.
The cheers grew fainter and fainter; faces and forms were no longer to
be distinguished; the waving of hats and kerchiefs ceased; the long dock
became a speck of black against the hilly shore, and the great city faded
from sight.

DROPPING THE PILOT.

Overhead was the immense blue dome of the sky; beneath and
around were the waters of San Francisco Bay.   On the right was Monte
Diablo, like an advanced sentinel of the Sierras; and on the left were the
sand-hills of the peninsula, covered with the walls and roofs of the great
city of the Pacific Coast.   The steamer moved on and on through the
Golden Gate; and in less than an hour from the time of leaving the dock,
she dropped her pilot, the gangway passage was closed, and her prow
pointed to the westward for a voyage of five thousand miles.

"What a lovely picture!" said the Doctor, as he waved his hand towards the receding shore.

4

THE GOLDEN GATE.

"Why do they call that the Golden Gate?" Fred asked.

"Because," was the reply, "it is, or was, the entrance to the land of gold. It was so named after the discovery of gold in California, and until the completion of the Overland Railway it was the principal pathway to the country where everybody expected to make a fortune."

"It is very wide, and easy of navigation," the Doctor continued, "and yet a stranger might not be aware of its existence, and might sail by it if he did not know where to look for the harbor. A ship must get well in towards the land before the Golden Gate is visible."

"How long shall we be on the voyage, Doctor?"

"If nothing happens," he answered, "we shall see the coast of Japan in about twenty days. We have five thousand miles to go, and I understand the steamer will make two hundred and fifty miles a day in good weather."

"Will we stop anywhere on the way?"

"There is not a stopping-place on the whole route. We are not yet out of sight of the Golden Gate, and already we are steering for Cape King, at the entrance of Yeddo Bay. There's not even an island, or a solitary rock on our course."

"I thought I had read about an island where the steamers intended to stop," Fred remarked.

"So you have," was the reply; "an island was discovered some years ago, and was named Brook's Island, in honor of its discoverer. It was thought at first that the place might be convenient as a coaling station, but it is too far from the track of the steamers, and, besides, it has no harbor where ships can anchor.

"There is a curious story in connection with it. In 1816 a ship, the *Canton*, sailed from Sitka, and was supposed to have been lost at sea, as she never reached her destination. Fifty years later this island was discovered, and upon it was part of the wreck of the *Canton*. There were traces of the huts which were built by the crew during their stay, and it was evident that they constructed a smaller vessel from the fragments of the wreck, and sailed away in it."

"And were lost in it, I suppose?"

"Undoubtedly, as nothing has ever been heard from them. They did not leave any history of themselves on the island, or, at any rate, none was ever found."

At this moment the steward rang the preparatory bell for dinner, and

IN THE FIRE-ROOM.

the conversation ended. Half an hour later dinner was on the table, and the passengers sat down to it.

The company was not a large one, and there was abundant room and abundant food for everybody. The captain was at the head of the table, and the purser at the foot, and between them were the various passengers in the seats which had been reserved for them by the steward. The passengers included an American consul on his way to his post in China, and an American missionary, bound for the same country. There were several merchants, interested in commercial matters between the United States and the Far East; two clerks, going out to appointments in China; two sea-captains, going to take command of ships; a doctor and a mining engineer in the service of the Japanese government; half a dozen "globe-trotters," or tourists; and a very mysterious and nondescript individual, whom we shall know more about as we proceed. The consul and the missionary were accompanied by their families. Their wives and daughters were the only ladies among the passengers, and, according to the usual custom on board steamers, they were seated next to the captain in the places of highest honor. Doctor Bronson and his young companions were seated near the purser, whom they found very amiable, and they had on the opposite side of the table the two sea-captains already mentioned.

Everybody appeared to realize that the voyage was to be a long one, and the sooner the party became acquainted, the better. By the end of dinner they had made excellent progress, and formed several likes and dislikes that increased as time went on. In the evening the passengers sat about the cabin or strolled on deck, continuing to grow in acquaintance, and before the ship had been twenty-four hours at sea it was hard to realize that the company had been assembled so recently. Brotherly friendships as well as brotherly hatreds grew with the rapidity of a beanstalk, and, happily, the friendships were greatly in the majority.

Life on a steamship at sea has many peculiarities. The ship is a world in itself, and its boundaries are narrow. You see the same faces day after day, and on a great ocean like the Pacific there is little to attract the attention outside of the vessel that carries you. You have sea and sky to look upon to-day as you looked upon them yesterday, and will look on them to-morrow. The sky may be clear or cloudy; fogs may envelop you; storms may arise, or a calm may spread over the waters; the great ship goes steadily on and on. The pulsations of the engine seem like those of the human heart; and when you wake at night, your first endeavor, as you collect your thoughts, is to listen for that ceaseless throbbing. One falls into a monotonous way of life, and the days run on one after another, till you find it difficult to distinguish them apart. The hours for meals are the principal hours of the day, and with many persons the table is the place of greatest importance. They wander from deck to saloon, and from saloon to deck again, and hardly has the table been cleared after one meal, before they are thinking what they will have for the next. The managers of our great ocean lines have noted this peculiarity of human nature; some of them give no less than five meals a day, and if a passenger should wish to eat something between times, he could be accommodated.

THE ENGINEER AT HIS POST.

Our young friends were too much absorbed with the novelty of their situation to allow the time to hang heavy on their hands. Everything was new and strange to them, but, of course, it was far otherwise with Doctor Bronson. They had many questions to ask, and he was never weary of answering, as he saw they were endeavoring to remember what they heard, and were not interrogating him from idle curiosity.

"What is the reason they don't strike the hours here as they do on land?" Frank inquired, as they reached the deck after dinner.

The Doctor explained that at sea the time is divided into watches, or periods, of four hours each. The bell strikes once for each half-hour, until four hours, or eight bells, are reached, and then they begin again. One o'clock is designated as "two bells," half-past one is "three bells," and four o'clock is "eight bells." Eight o'clock, noon, and midnight are also signalled by eight strokes on the bell, and after a little while a traveller accustoms himself to the new mode of keeping time.

Fred remembered that when they left San Francisco at noon, the bell struck eight times, instead of twelve, as he thought it should have struck. The Doctor's explanation made it clear to him.

The second day out the boys began to repeat all the poetry they could remember about the sea, and were surprised at the stock they had on hand. Fred recalled something he had read in *Harper's Magazine*, which ran as follows:

> "Far upon the unknown deep,
>   'Mid the billows circling round,
> Where the tireless sea-birds sweep;
>   Outward bound.
> Nothing but a speck we seem,
>   In the waste of waters round,
> Floating, floating like a dream;
>   Outward bound."

Frank was less sentimental, and repeated these lines:

> "Two things break the monotony
>   Of a great ocean trip:
> Sometimes, alas! you ship a sea,
>   And sometimes see a ship."

Then they called upon the Doctor for a contribution, original or selected, with this result:

> "The praises of the ocean grand,
>   'Tis very well to sing on land.
> 'Tis very fine to hear them carolled
> By Thomas Campbell or Childe Harold;
> But sad, indeed, to see that ocean
> From east to west in wild commotion."

The wind had been freshening since noon, and the rolling motion of the ship was not altogether agreeable to the inexperienced boys. They were about to have their first acquaintance with sea-sickness; and though they held on manfully and remained on deck through the afternoon, the ocean proved too much for them, and they had no appetite for dinner or supper. But their malady did not last long, and by the next morning they were as merry as ever, and laughed over the event. They asked the Doctor to explain the cause of their trouble, but he shook his head, and said the whole thing was a great puzzle.

THE WIND RISING.

"Sea-sickness is a mystery," said he, "and the more you study it, the less you seem to understand it. Some persons are never disturbed by the motion of a ship, no matter how violent it may be, while others cannot endure the slightest rocking. Most of the sufferers recover in a short time, and after two or three days at sea are as well as ever, and continue so. On the other hand, there are some who never outlive its effects, and though their voyage may last a year or more, they are no better sailors at the end than at the beginning.

"I knew a young man," he continued, "who entered the Naval Academy, and graduated. When he was appointed to service on board a ship, he found himself perpetually sick on the water; after an experience of two years, and finding no improvement, he resigned. Such occurrences are by no means rare. I once travelled with a gentleman who was a splendid sailor in fine weather; but when it became rough, he was all wrong, and went to bed."

"Were you ever sea-sick, Doctor?" queried Frank.

"Never," was the reply, "and I had a funny incident growing out of this fact on my first voyage. We were going out of New York harbor, and I made the acquaintance of the man who was to share my room. As he looked me over, he asked me if I had ever been to sea.

"I told him I never had, and then he remarked that I was certain to be sea-sick, he could see it in my face. He said he was an old traveller, and rarely suffered, and then he gave me some advice as to what I should do when I began to feel badly. I thanked him and went on deck.

"As the ship left the harbor, and went outside to the open Atlantic, she encountered a heavy sea. It was so rough that the majority of the passengers disappeared below. I didn't suffer in the least, and didn't go to the cabin for two or three hours. There I found that my new friend was in his bed with the very malady he had predicted for me."

"What did you do then, Doctor?"

"Well, I repeated to him the advice he had given me, and told him I saw in his face that he was sure to be sea-sick. He didn't recover during the whole voyage, and I never suffered a moment."

The laugh that followed the story of the Doctor's experience was interrupted by the breakfast-bell, and the party went below. There was a light attendance, and the purser explained that several passengers had gone ashore.

"Which is a polite way of saying that they are not inclined to come out," the Doctor remarked.

"Exactly so," replied the purser, "they think they would make the best appearance alone."

Captain Spofford, who sat opposite to Frank, remarked that he knew an excellent preventive of sea-sickness. Frank asked what it was.

"Always stay at home," was the reply.

"Yes," answered Frank, "and to escape drowning you should never go near the water."

Fred said the best thing to prevent a horse running away was to sell him off.

Everybody had a joke of some kind to propose, and the breakfast party was a merry one. Suddenly Captain Spofford called out, "There she blows!" and pointed through the cabin window. Before the others could look, the rolling of the ship had brought the window so far above the water that they saw nothing.

"What is it?" Fred asked.

"A whale," Captain Spofford answered. "What he is doing here, I don't know. This isn't a whaling-ground."

They went on deck soon after, and, sure enough, several whales were in sight. Every little while a column of spray was thrown into the air,

SPOUTS.

and indicated there was a whale beneath it.

Frank asked why it was the whale "spouted," or blew up, the column of spray. Captain Spofford explained that the whale is not, properly speaking, a fish, but an animal. "He has warm blood, like a cow or horse," said the Captain, "and he must come to the surface to breathe. He takes a certain amount of water into his lungs along with the air, and when he throws it out, it makes the spray you have seen, and which the sailors call a spout."

It turned out that the Captain was an old whaleman. The boys wanted to hear some whaling stories, and their new friend promised to tell them some during the evening. When the time came for the narration, the boys were ready, and so was the old mariner. The Doctor joined the party, and the four found a snug corner in the cabin where they were not likely to be disturbed. The Captain settled himself as comfortably as possible, and then began the account of his adventures in pursuit of the monsters of the deep.

WHALE-SHIP OUTWARD BOUND.

CHAPTER IV.

INCIDENTS OF A WHALING VOYAGE.

CAPTAIN SPOFFORD was a weather-beaten veteran who gave little attention to fine clothes, and greatly preferred his rough jacket and

CAPTAIN SPOFFORD TELLING HIS STORY.

soft hat to what he called "Sunday gear." He was much attached to his
telescope, which he had carried nearly a quarter of a century, and on the
present occasion he brought it into the cabin, and held it in his hand
while he narrated his whaling experiences. He explained that he could
talk better in the company of his old spy-glass, as it would remind him
of things he might forget without its aid, and also check him if he went
beyond the truth.

"There are very few men in the whaling business now," said he,
"compared to the number twenty-five years ago. Whales are growing
scarcer every year, and petroleum has taken the place of whale-oil. Consequently, the price of the latter is not in proportion to the difficulty of
getting it. New Bedford used to be an important seaport, and did an
enormous business. It is played out now, and is as dull and sleepy as
a cemetery. It was once the great centre of the whaling business, and
made fortunes for a good many men; but you don't hear of fortunes in
whaling nowadays.

"I went to sea from New Bedford when I was twelve years old, and
kept at whaling for near on to twenty-seven years. From cabin-boy, I
crept up through all the ranks, till I became captain and part owner, and
it was a good deal of satisfaction to me to be boss of a ship, I can tell you.
When I thought I had had enough of it I retired, and bought a small
farm. I stocked and ran it after my own fashion, called one of my oxen

NEW BEDFORD.

'Port' and the other 'Starboard,' had a little mound like my old quar-ter-deck built in my garden, and used to go there to take my walks. I had a mast with cross-trees fixed in this mound, and used to go up there, and stay for hours, and call out 'There she blows!' whenever I saw a bird fly by, or anything moving anywhere. I slept in a hammock under a tent, and when I got real nervous I had one of my farm-hands rock me to sleep in the hammock, and throw buckets of water against the sides of the tent, so's I could imagine I was on the sea again. But 'twasn't no use, and I couldn't cure myself of wanting to be on blue water once more. So I left my farm in my wife's hands, and am going out to Shanghai to command a ship whose captain died at Hong-Kong five months ago.

"So much for history. Now we'll talk about whales.

"There are several kinds of them—sperm-whales, right-whales, bow-heads; and a whaleman can tell one from the other as easy as a farmer can tell a cart-horse from a Shetland pony. The most valuable is the sperm-whale, as his oil is much better, and brings more money; and then we get spermaceti from him to make candles of, which we don't get from the others. He's a funny-looking brute, as his head is a third of his whole length; and when you've cut it off, there doesn't seem to be much whale left of him.

SPERM-WHALE.

"I sailed for years in a sperm-whaler in the South Pacific, and had a good many lively times. The sperm-whale is the most dangerous of all, and the hardest to kill; he fights with his tail and his mouth, while the oth-ers fight only with their tails. A right-whale or a bow-head will lash the water and churn it up into foam; and if he hits a boat with his tail, he crushes it as if it was an egg-shell. A sperm-whale will do all this, and more too; he takes a boat in his mouth, and chews it, which the others never do. And when he chews it, he makes fine work of it, I can tell you, and short work, too.

"Sometimes he takes a shy at a ship, and rushes at it, head on. Two ships are known to have been sunk in this way; one of them was the *Essex*, which the whale ran into three times, and broke her timbers so that she filled. The crew took to the boats, and made for the coast of South America. One boat was never heard from, one reached the coast,

"THERE SHE BLOWS!"

and the third was picked up near Valparaiso with everybody dead but two, and those barely alive. Provisions and water had given out, and another day would have finished the poor fellows. Another ship was the *Union*, which was stove right under the bows by a single blow from a sperm-whale, and went down in half an hour.

"I was fifteen years old when I pulled my first oar in a whale-boat; I was boat-steerer at eighteen, and second mate at twenty, and before I was twenty-one I had known what it was to be in the month of a sperm-whale. It is hardly necessary to say that I got out of it as fast as I could, and didn't stop to see if my hair was combed and my shirt-collar buttoned. A man has no time to put on frills under such circumstances.

"The way of it was this. The lookout in the cross-trees—we always keep a man up aloft to look out for whales when we're on cruising ground—the man had called out, 'There she blows!' and everybody was on his feet in an instant.

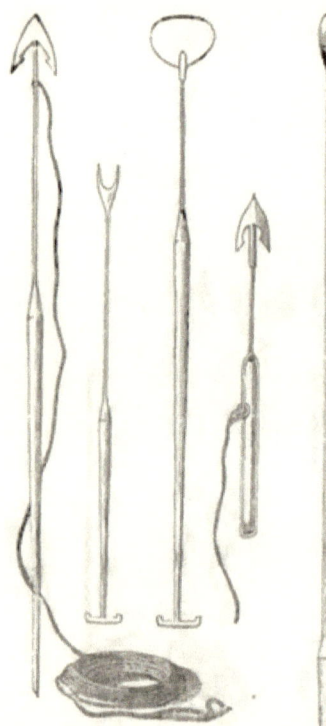

"'Where away?' shouted the first mate.

"'Two points on the weather bow.'

"And before the words had done echoing he called out 'There she blows' again, and a moment after again. That meant that he had seen two more whales.

"We put two boats into the water, the first mate's and mine, and away we went. We pulled our best, and the boats fairly bounced through the waves. It was a race to see who could strike the first whale; we had a good half mile to go, and we went like race-horses.

"Each boat has six men in her—a boat-steerer, as he is called, and five at the oars. The boat-steerer handles the harpoon and lance and directs the whole movement; in fact, for the time he is captain of the boat.

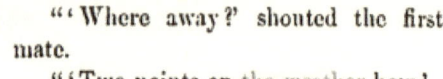

"The first mate's boat headed me a little, and made for a big fellow on the starboard. I went for another, and we struck almost at the same instant. With-

IMPLEMENTS USED IN WHALING.

in three boat-lengths, I stood up, braced my feet firmly, poised my harpoon, and made ready to strike. The whale didn't know we were about, and was taking it very easy. The bow of the boat was about ten feet from his black skin when I sent the iron spinning and whizzing away, and buried it deep in his flesh. Didn't he give a jump! You can bet he did.

"'Starn all! starn all! for your lives!' I yelled.

"There wasn't a moment lost, and the boat went back by the force of the strong arms of the men."

"The whale lashed about and then 'breached;' that is, he threw his great body out of the water, giving me a chance to get in a second harpoon. Then he sounded—that is, he went down—and the lines ran out so fast that the side of the boat fairly smoked when they went over. He ran off two hundred fathoms of line before he stopped, and then we felt the line slack and knew he would soon be up again.

"Up he came not a hundred yards from where he went down, and as he came up he caught sight of the boat. He went for it as a cat goes for a mouse.

"The sperm-whale can't see straight ahead, as his eyes are set far back, and seem to be almost on his sides. He turns partly round to get a glimpse of a boat, then ports his helm, drops his jaw, calculates his distance, and

WHALE "BREACHING."

goes ahead at full speed. His jaw is set very low, and sometimes he turns over, or partly over, to strike his blow.

"This time he whirled and took the bow of the boat in his mouth, crushing it as though it had been made of paper. We jumped out, the oars flew all around us, the sea was a mass of foam, and the whale chewed the boat as though it was a piece of sugar-candy and he hadn't seen any for a month.

"We were all in the water, and nobody hurt. The first mate's boat had killed its whale inside of ten minutes, and before he tried to sound. They left the whale and came to pick us up; then they hurried and made fast to him, as another ship was coming up alongside of ours, and we might lose our game. It is a rule of the sea that you lose your claim to a whale when you let go, even though you may have killed him. Hang on to him and he's yours, though you may hang with only a trout-line and a minnow-hook. It's been so decided in the courts.

"The captain sent another boat from the ship, and we soon had the satisfaction of seeing my whale dead on the water. He got the lance right in his vitals, and went into his 'flurry,' as we call it. The flurry is

IN THE WHALE'S JAW.

the whale's convulsive movements just before. death, and sometimes he does great damage as he thrashes about."

Frank wished to know how large the whale was, and how large whales are generally.

"We don't reckon whales by their length," Captain Spofford answered, "but by the number of barrels of oil they make. Ask any old captain how long the largest whale was that he ever took, and the chances are he'll begin to estimate by the length of his ship, and frankly tell you he never measured one. I measured the largest sperm-whale I ever took, and found him seventy-nine feet long; he made a hundred and seven barrels of oil. Here's the figures of him: nose to neck, twenty-six feet; neck to hump, twenty-nine feet; hump to tail, seventeen feet; tail, seven feet. His tail was sixteen feet across, and he was forty-one feet six inches around the body. He had fifty-one teeth, and the heaviest weighed twenty-five ounces. We took nineteen barrels of oil from his case, the inside of the head, where we dipped it out with a bucket. I know one captain that captured a sperm-whale ninety feet long, that made a hundred and thirty-seven barrels, and there was another sperm taken by the ship *Monka*, of New Bedford, that made a hundred and forty-five barrels. I don't know how long he was.

"There's a wonderful deal of excitement in fastening to a whale, and having a fight with him. You have the largest game that a hunter could ask for; you have the cool pure air of the ocean, and the blue waters all about you. A thrill goes through every nerve as you rise to throw the sharp iron into the monster's side, and the thrill continues when he plunges wildly about, and sends the line whistling over. He sinks, and he rises again; he dashes away to windward, and struggles to escape; you hold him fast, and, large as he is in proportion to yourself, you feel that he must yield to you, though, perhaps, not till after a hard battle. At length he lies exhausted, and you approach for the final blow with the lance. Another thrilling moment, another, and another; and if fortune is in your favor, your prize is soon motionless before you. And the man who cannot feel an extra beat of his pulse at such a time must be made of cooler stuff than the most of us.

"But you don't get all the whales you see, by a long shot. Many a whale gets away before you can fasten to him, and many another whale, after you have laid on and fastened, will escape you. He sinks, and tears the iron loose; he runs away to windward ten or twenty miles an hour, and you must cut the line to save your lives; he smashes the boat, and perhaps kills some of his assailants; he dies below the surface, and when he dies there he stays below, and you lose him; and sometimes he shows

5

such an amount of toughness that he seems to bear a charmed life. We fight him with harpoon and lance, and in these later days they have an invention called the bomb-lance or whaling-gun. A bomb-shell is thrown into him with a gun like a large musket, and it explodes down among his vitals. There's another gun that is fastened to the shaft of a harpoon, and goes off when the whale tightens the line; and there's another that throws a lance half-way through him. Well, there are whales that can stand all these things and live.

"Captain Hunting, of New Bedford, had the worst fight that I know of, while he was on a cruise in the South Atlantic. When he struck the fellow—it was a tough old bull that had been through fights before, I reckon—the whale didn't try to escape, but turned on the boat, bit her in two, and kept on thrashing the wreck till he broke it up completely. Another boat picked up the men and took them to the ship, and then two other boats went in on him. Each of them got in two irons, and that made him mad; he turned around and chewed those boats, and he stuck closely to business until there wasn't a mouthful left. The twelve swimmers

CAPTAIN HUNTING'S FIGHT.

A GAME FELLOW.

were picked up by the boat which had taken the first lot to the ship; two of the men had climbed on his back, and he didn't seem to mind them. He kept on chewing away at the oars, sails, masts, planks, and other fragments of the boats; and whenever anything touched his body, he turned and munched away at it. There he was with six harpoons in him, and each harpoon had three hundred fathoms of line attached to it. Captain Hunting got out two spare boats, and started with them and the saved boat to renew the fight. He got alongside and sent a bomb-lance charged with six inches of powder right into the whale's vitals, just back of his fin. When the lance was fired, he turned and tore through the boat like a hurricane, scattering everything. The sun was setting, four boats were gone with all their gear and twelve hundred fathoms of line, the spare boats were poorly provided, the men were wearied and discouraged, and Captain Hunting hauled off and admitted himself beaten by a whale."

The nondescript individual whom we saw among the passengers early in the voyage had joined the party, and heard the story of Captain Hunting's whale. When it was ended, he ventured to say something on the subject of whaling.

"That wasn't a circumstance," he remarked, "to the great whale that used to hang around the Philippine Islands. He was reckoned to be a king, as all the other whales took off their hats to him, and used to get down on their front knees when he came around. His skin was like leather, and he was stuck so full of harpoons that he looked like a porcupine under a magnifying-glass. Every ship that saw him used to put an iron into him, and I reckon you could get up a good history of the whale-fishery if you could read the ships' names on all of them irons. Lots of whalers fought with him, but he always came out first best. Captain Sammis of the *Ananias* had the closest acquaintance with him, and the way he tells it is this:

"'We'd laid into him, and his old jaw came up and bit off the bow of the boat. As he bit he gave a fling, like, and sent me up in the air; and when I came down, there was the whale, end up and mouth open waiting for me. His throat looked like a whitewashed cellar-door; but I saw his teeth were wore smooth down to the gums, and that gave me some consolation. When I struck his throat he snapped for me, but I had good headway, and disappeared like a piece of cake in a family of children. When I was splashing against the soft sides of his stomach, I heard his jaws snapping like the flapping of a mainsail.

"'I was rather used up and tired out, and a little bewildered, and so I sat down on the southwest corner of his liver, and crossed my legs while I got my wits together. It wasn't dark down there, as there was ten thou-

A FREE RIDE.

sand of them little sea jellies shinin' there, like second-hand stars, in the wrinkles of his stomach, and then there was lots of room too. By-an'-by, while I was lookin' round, I saw a black patch on the starboard side of his stomach, and went over to examine it. There I found printed in injey ink, in big letters, "Jonah, B.C. 1607." Then I knew where I was, and I began to feel real bad.

"'I opened my tobacco-box to take a mouthful of fine-cut to steady my nerves. I suppose my hand was a little unsteady; anyhow, I dropped some of the tobacco on the floor of the whale's stomach. It gave a convulsive jump, and I saw at once the whale wasn't used to it. I picked up a jack-knife I saw layin' on the floor, and cut a plug of tobacco into fine snuff, and scattered it around in the little wrinkles in the stomach. You should have seen how the medicine worked. The stomach began to heave as though a young earthquake had opened up under it, and then it squirmed and twisted, and finally turned wrong side out, and flopped me into the sea. The mate's boat was there picking up the men from the smashed boat, and just as they had given me up for lost they saw me and took me in. They laughed when I told them of the inside of the whale, and the printin' I saw there; but when I showed them the old jack-knife with the American eagle on one side and Jonah's name on the other, they stopped laughin' and looked serious. It is always well to have something on hand when you are tellin' a true story, and that knife was enough.'

"That same captain," he continued, "was once out for a whale, but when they killed him, they were ten miles from the ship. The captain got on the dead whale, and sent the boat back to let the ship know where they were. After they had gone, a storm came on and drove the ship away, and there the captain stayed three weeks. He stuck an oar into the whale to hang on to, and the third week a ship hove in sight. As he didn't know what she was, he hoisted the American flag, which he happened to have a picture of on his pocket-handkerchief; and pretty soon the ship hung out her colors, and her captain came on board. Captain Sammis was tired of the monotony of life on a whale, and so he sold out his interest to the visitor. He got half the oil and a passage to Honolulu, where he found his own craft all right."

"You say he remained three weeks on the back of that whale," said one of the listeners.

"Yes, I said three weeks."

"Well, how did he live all that time?"

"How can I tell?" was the reply; "that's none of my business. Probably he took his meals at the nearest restaurant and slept at home.

CAPTAIN SAMMIS SELLING OUT.

And if you don't believe my story, I can't help it—I've done the best I can."

With this remark he rose and walked away. It was agreed that there was a certain air of improbability about his narrations, and Frank ventured the suggestion that the stranger would never get into trouble on account of telling too much truth.

They had a curiosity to know something about the man. Doctor Bronson questioned the purser and ascertained that he was entered on the passenger-list as Mr. A. of America; but whence he came, or what was his business, no one could tell. He had spoken to but few persons since they left port, and the bulk of his conversation had been devoted to stories like those about the whaling business.

In short, he was a riddle no one could make out; and very soon he received from the other passengers the nickname of "The Mystery." Fred suggested that Mystery and Mr. A. were so nearly alike that the one name was as good as the other.

While they were discussing him, he returned suddenly and said:

"The Captain says there are indications of a water-spout to-morrow; and perhaps we may be destroyed by it."

SHOOTING AT A WATER-SPOUT.

With these words he withdrew, and was not seen any more that evening. Fred wished to know what a water-spout was like, and was promptly set at rest by the Doctor.

"A water-spout," the latter remarked, "is often seen in the tropics, but rarely in this latitude. The clouds lie quite close to the water, and there appears to be a whirling motion to the latter; then the cloud and the sea beneath it become united by a column of water, and this column is what we call a water-spout. It is generally believed that the water rises, through this spout, from the sea to the clouds, and sailors are fearful of coming near them lest their ships may be deluged and sunk. They usually endeavor to destroy them by firing guns at them, and this was done on board a ship where I was once a passenger. When the ball struck the spout, there was a fall of water sufficient to have sunk us if we had been beneath it, and we all felt thankful that we had escaped the danger."

CHAPTER V.

ARRIVAL IN JAPAN.

THE great ship steamed onward, day after day and night after night. There was no storm to break the monotony; no sail showed itself on the horizon; no one left the steamer, and no new-comers appeared; nobody saw fit to quarrel with any one else; and there was not a passenger who showed a disposition to quarrel with his surroundings. Stories were told and songs were sung, to while away the time; and, finally, on the twentieth day, the captain announced that they were approaching land, and the voyage would soon be over.

Our young travellers had found a daily interest in the instruments by which a mariner ascertains his ship's position. Frank had gone so far as to borrow the captain's extra copy of "Bowditch's Navigator" and study it at odd intervals, and after a little while he comprehended the uses of the various instruments employed in finding a way over the trackless ocean. He gave Fred a short lecture on the subject, which was something like the following:

"Of course, you know, Fred, all about the mariner's compass, which points towards the north, and always tells where north is. Now, if we know where north is, we can find south, east, and west without much trouble."

Fred admitted the claim, and repeated the formula he had learned at school: Face towards the north, and back towards the south; the right hand east, and the left hand west.

"Now," continued Frank, "there are thirty-two points of the compass; do you know them?"

Fred shook his head; and then Frank explained that the four he had named were the cardinal points, while the other twenty-eight were the divisions between the cardinal points. One of the first duties of a sailor was to "box the compass," that is, to be able to name all these divisions.

"Let me hear you box the compass, Frank," said Doctor Bronson, who was standing near.

FRANK STUDYING NAVIGATION.

"Certainly, I can," Frank answered, and then began: "North, north by east, north-northeast, northeast by north, northeast, northeast by east, east-northeast, east by north, east—"

"That will do," said the Doctor; "you have given one quadrant, or a quarter of the circle; I'm sure you can do the rest easily, for it goes on in the same way."

"You see," Frank continued, "that you know by the compass exactly in what direction you are going; then, if you know how many miles you go in a day or an hour, you can calculate your place at sea.

"That mode of calculation is called 'dead-reckoning,' and is quite simple, but it isn't very safe."

"Why so?" Fred asked.

"Because it is impossible to steer a ship with absolute accuracy when she is rolling and pitching about, and, besides, the winds make her drift a little to one side. Then there are currents that take her off her course, and sometimes they are very strong."

"Yes, I know," Fred replied; "there's the Gulf Stream, in the Atlantic Ocean, everybody has heard of; it is a great river in the sea, and flows north at the rate of three or four miles an hour."

"There's another river like it in the Pacific Ocean," Frank explained; "it is called the Japan Current, because it flows close to the coast of Japan. It goes through Behring Strait into the Arctic Ocean, and then it comes south by the coast of Greenland, and down by Newfoundland. That's what brings the icebergs south in the Atlantic, and puts them in the way of the steamers between New York and Liverpool.

"On account of the uncertainty of dead-reckoning, the captain doesn't rely on it except when the fog is so thick that he can't get an observation."

"What is that?"

"Observing the positions of the sun and moon, and of certain stars with relation to each other. That is done with the quadrant and sextant; and then they use a chronometer, or clock, that tells exactly what the time is at Greenwich. Then, you see, this book is full of figures that look like multiplication-tables; and with these figures they 'work out their position;' that is, they find out where they are. Greenwich is near London, and all the tables are calculated from there."

"But suppose a sailor was dropped down here suddenly, without knowing what ocean he was in; could he find out where he was without anybody telling him?"

"Certainly; with the instruments I have named, the tables of figures, and a clear sky, so as to give good observations, he could determine his position with absolute accuracy. He gets his latitude by observing the sun at noon, and he gets his longitude by the chronometer and by observations of the moon. When he knows his latitude and longitude, he knows where he is, and can mark the place on the map."

Fred opened his eyes with an expression of astonishment, and said he thought the science of navigation was something wonderful.

The others agreed with him; and while they were discussing the advantages which it had given to the world, there was a call that sent them on deck at once.

"Land, ho!" from the lookout forward.

"Land, ho!" from the officer near the wheel-house.

WORKING UP A RECKONING.

"Land, ho!" from the captain, as he emerged from his room, just aft of the wheel. "Where away?"

"Dead ahead, sir," replied the officer. "'Tis Fusiyama, sir."

The boys looked in the direction indicated, but could see nothing. This is not surprising, when we remember that sailors' eyes are accustomed to great distances, and can frequently see objects distinctly long before landsmen can make them out.

But by-and-by they could distinguish the outline of a cone, white as a cloud and nearly as shadowy. It was the Holy Mountain of Japan, and they recognized the picture they had seen so many times upon Japanese fans and other objects. As they watched it, the form grew more and more distinct, and after a time they no longer doubted that they looked at Fusiyama.

"Just to think," Fred exclaimed, "when we left San Francisco, we steered for this mountain, five thousand miles away, and here it is, right before us. Navigation is a wonderful science, and no mistake."

As the ship went on, the mountain grew more and more distinct, and by-and-by other features of Japanese scenery were brought into view. The western horizon became a serrated line, that formed an agreeable contrast to the unbroken curve they had looked upon so many days; and as the sun went down, it no longer dipped into the sea and sank beneath the waves. All on board the ship were fully aware they were approaching land.

During the night they passed Cape King and entered Yeddo bay. The great light-house that watches the entrance shot its rays far out over the waters and beamed a kindly welcome to the strangers. Slowly they steamed onward, keeping a careful lookout for the numerous boats and junks that abound there, and watching the hundreds of lights that gleamed along the shore and dotted the sloping hill-sides. Sixty miles from

VIEW IN THE BAY OF YEDDO.

Cape King, they were in front of Yokohama; the engines stopped, the anchor fell, the chain rattled through the hawse-hole, and the ship was at rest, after her long journey from San Francisco. Our young adventurers were in Japan.

With the first streak of dawn the boys were on deck, where they were joined by Doctor Bronson. The sun was just rising when the steamer dropped her anchor, and, consequently, their first day in the new country was begun very early. There was an abundance of sights for the young eyes, and no lack of subjects for conversation.

Hardly was the anchor down before the steamer was surrounded by a swarm of little boats, and Frank thought they were the funniest boats he had ever seen.

JAPANESE JUNK AND BOATS.

"They are called 'sampans,'" Doctor Bronson explained, "and are made entirely of wood. Of late years the Japanese sometimes use copper or iron nails for fastenings; but formerly you found them without a particle of metal about them."

"They don't look as if they could stand rough weather," said Fred. "See; they are low and square at the stern, and high and sharp at the bow; and they sit very low in the water."

"They are not in accordance with our notions," replied the Doctor; "but they are excellent sea-boats, and I have known them to ride safely where an American boat would have been swamped. You observe how easily they go through the water. They can be handled very readily, and, certainly, the Japanese have no occasion to be ashamed of their craft."

A JAPANESE IMPERIAL BARGE.

Frank had his eye on a sampan that was darting about like an active fish, first in one direction and then in another. It was propelled by a single oar in the hands of a brown-skinned boatman, who was not encumbered with a large amount of superfluous clothing. The oar was in two pieces—a blade and a handle—lashed together in such a way that they did not form a straight line. At first Frank thought there was something wrong about it; but he soon observed that the oars in all the boats were of the same pattern, and made in the same way. They were worked like sculls rather than like oars. The man kept the oar constantly beneath the water; and, as he moved it forwards and back, he turned it partly around. A rope near his hand regulated the distance the oar could be turned, and also kept it from rising out of the water or going too far below the surface.

Nearly every boat contained a funny little furnace, only a few inches square, where the boatman boiled his tea and cooked the rice and fish that composed his food. Each boat had a deck of boards which were so placed as to be readily removed; but, at the same time, were secured against being washed away. Every one of these craft was perfectly clean, and while they were waiting around the ship, several of the boatmen occupied themselves by giving their decks a fresh scrubbing, which was not at all necessary. The Doctor took the occasion to say something about the cleanliness of the Japanese houses, and of the neat habits of the people generally, and added, "You will see it as you go among them, and cannot fail to be impressed by it. You will never hesitate to eat Japanese food through fear that it may not be clean; and this is more than you can say of every table in our own country."

The steamer was anchored nearly half a mile from shore. English, French, German, and other ships were in the harbor; tenders and steam-launches were moving about; row - boats were coming and going; and, altogether, the port of Yokohama presented a lively appearance. Shore-

JAPANESE GOVERNMENT BOAT.

ward the picture was interesting. At the water's edge there was a stone quay or embankment, with two inner harbors, where small boats might enter and find shelter from occasional storms. This quay was the front of a street where carriages and pedestrians were moving back and forth. The farther side of the street was a row of buildings, and as nearly every one of these buildings had a yard in front filled with shade-trees, the effect was pretty.

Away to the right was the Japanese part of Yokohama, while on the left was the foreign section. The latter included the row of buildings mentioned above; they stood on a level space which was only a few feet above the level of the bay. Back of this was a range of steep hills, which were covered nearly everywhere with a dense growth of trees and bushes, with little patches of gardens here and there. On the summits of the hills, and occasionally on their sides, were houses with wide verandas, and with great windows capable of affording liberal ventilation. Many of the merchants and other foreigners living in Yokohama had their residences in these houses, which were far more comfortable than the buildings near the water. Doctor Bronson explained that the lower part of Yokohama was called the "Bund," while the upper was known as the "Bluff." Business was transacted in the Bund, and many persons lived there; but the Bluff was the favorite place for a residence, and a great deal of money had been expended in beautifying it.

The quarantine officials visited the steamer, and after a brief inspection she was pronounced healthy, and permission was given for the passengers to go on shore. Runners from the hotels came in search of patrons, and clerks from several of the prominent business houses came on board to ask for letters and news. Nearly every commercial establishment in Yokohama has its own boat and a special uniform for its rowers; so that they can be readily distinguished. One of the clerks who visited the ship seemed to be in search of somebody among the passengers, and that somebody proved to be our friend, The Mystery.

The two had a brief conversation when they met, and it was in a tone so low that nobody could hear what was said. When it was over, The Mystery went below, and soon reappeared with a small satchel. Without a word of farewell to anybody, he entered the boat and was rowed to the shore at a very rapid rate.

There was great activity at the forward gangway. The steerage passengers comprised about four hundred Chinese who were bound for Hong-Kong; but, as the steamer would lie a whole day at Yokohama, many of them were preparing to spend the day on shore. The boats crowded at the foot of the gangway, and there was a great contention among the boatmen to secure the patronage of the passengers. Occasionally one of the men fell into the water, owing to some unguarded movement; but he was soon out again, and clamoring as earnestly as ever. In spite of the excitement and activity, there was the most perfect good-nature. Nobody was inclined to fight with any one else, and all the competitors were entirely friendly. The Chinese made very close bargains with the boatmen, and were taken to and from the shore at prices which astonished the boys when they heard them.

The Doctor explained that the tariff for a boat to take one person from ship to shore and back again, including an hour's waiting, was ten cents, with five cents added for every hour beyond one. In the present instance the Chinese passengers bargained to be taken on shore in the morning and back again at night for five cents each, and not more than four of them were to go in one boat. Fred thought it would require a long time for any of the boatmen to become millionnaires at this rate.

Our travellers were not obliged to bargain for their conveyance, as they went ashore in the boat belonging to the hotel where they intended to stay. The runner of the hotel took charge of their baggage and placed it in the boat; and when all was ready, they shook hands with the captain and purser of the steamer, and wished them prosperous voyages in future. Several other passengers went ashore at the same time. Among them was Captain Spofford, who was anxious to compare the Yokohama of to-day with the one he had visited twenty years before.

He explained to the boys that when the American fleet came to Japan in 1854, there was only a small fishing village where the city now stands. Yoko-hama means "across the strand," and the city is opposite, or across

YOKOHAMA IN 1854.

the strand from, Kanagawa, which was established as the official port. The consuls formerly had their offices in Kanagawa, and continued to date their official documents there long after they had moved to the newer and more prosperous town. Yokohama was found much more agreeable, as there was a large open space there for erecting buildings, while the high bluffs gave a cooling shelter from the hot, stifling air of summer. Commercial prosperity caused it to grow rapidly, and made it the city we now find it.

They reached the shore. Their baggage was placed on a large hand-cart, and they passed through the gateway of the Custom-house. A polite official, who spoke English, made a brief survey of their trunks; and, on their assurance that no dutiable goods were within, he did not delay them any further. The Japanese duties are only five per cent. on the value of the goods, and, consequently, a traveller could not perpetrate much fraud upon the revenue, even if he were disposed to do so.

"Here you are in Japan," said the Doctor, as they passed through the gate.

"Yes, here we are," Frank replied; "let's give three cheers for Japan."

"Agreed," answered Fred, "and here we go—Hip! hip! hurrah!"

The boys swung their hats and gave the three cheers.

"And three more for friends at home!" Fred added.

"Certainly," Frank responded. "Here we go again;" and there was another "Hip! hip! hurrah!"

"And a cheer from you, Frank," remarked the Doctor, "for somebody we saw at the railway station."

Frank gave another swing of his hat and another cheer. The Doctor and Fred united their voices to his, and with a hearty shout all around, they concluded the ceremony connected with their arrival in Japan.

CHAPTER VI.

FIRST DAY IN JAPAN.

THEY had no difficulty in reaching the hotel, as they were in the hands of the runner of the establishment, who took good care that they did not go astray and fall into the clutches of the representative of the rival concern. The publicans of the open ports of Japan have a watchful eye for their interests, and the stranger does not have to wander long in the streets to find accommodation. The Doctor had been there before, and took great pains to have his bargain made with the utmost exactness, lest there might be a mistake at the time of his departure. "In Europe and Asia," he remarked to Frank, "a traveller soon learns that he cannot be too explicit in making his contracts at hotels; if he neglects this little formality, he will often find that his negligence has cost him something. The last time I was in Yokohama I had a very warm discussion with my landlord when I settled my bill, and I don't propose to have a repetition of it."

The hotel was much like an American house in its general characteristics, both in the arrangement of the rooms and the style of furniture. The proprietors and managers were foreigners, but the servants were native and were dressed in Japanese costume. The latter were very quiet and orderly in their manners, and made a favorable impression on the young visitors. Frank was so pleased with the one in charge of his room that he wished he could take him home with him, and have a Japanese servant in America. Testimony as to the excellent character of servants in Japan is nearly universal on the part of those who have employed them. Of course there will be an occasional lazy, inattentive, or dishonest fellow, but one finds them much more rarely than in Europe or America. In general, they are very keen observers, and learn the ways and peculiarities of their masters in a remarkably short time. And once having learned them, they never forget.

"When I was last here," said the Doctor, "I was in this very hotel, and had one of the regular servants of the establishment to wait on me. The evening after my arrival, I told him to have my bath ready at seven o'clock in the morning, and to bring a glass of ice-water when he

A JAPANESE STREET SCENE.

waked me. Exactly at seven he was at my bedside with the water, and told me the bath was waiting; and as long as I remained here he came at precisely the same hour in the morning, offered me the glass of water, and announced the readiness of the bath. I never had occasion to tell him the same thing twice, no matter what it was. Occasionally I went to Tokio to spend two or three days. The first time I went, I showed him what clothes I wished to take, and he packed them in my valise; and afterwards I had only to say I was going to Tokio, when he would immediately proceed to pack up exactly the same things I had taken the first time, or their equivalents. He never made the slightest error, and was a trifle more exact than I wished him to be. On my first journey I carried a bottle of cough-mixture to relieve a cold from which I happened to be suffering. The cold had disappeared, and the bottle was empty before my second trip to Tokio; but my faithful servant wrapped it carefully in paper, and put it in a safe corner of my valise, and continued to do so every time I repeated the excursion."

The boys were all anxiety to take a walk through the streets of Yoko-hama, and could hardly wait for the Doctor to arrange matters with the hotel-keeper. In a little while everything was determined, and the party went out for a stroll. The Doctor led the way, and took them to the Japanese portion of the city, where they were soon in the midst of sights that were very curious to them. They stopped at several shops, and looked at a great variety of Japanese goods, but followed the advice of the Doctor in deferring their purchases to another time. Frank thought of the things he was to buy for his sister Mary, and also for Miss Effie; but as they were not to do any shopping on their first day in Japan, he did not see any occasion for opening the precious paper that Mary had confided to him previous to his departure.

They had a walk of several hours, and on their return to the hotel were quite weary enough to rest awhile. Frank and Fred had a whispered conversation while the Doctor was talking with an old acquaintance; and as soon as he was at liberty they told him what they had been conversing about.

"We think we want to write home now, Doctor," said Frank, "and wish to know if you approve of our doing so to-day."

"By all means," replied the Doctor, with a smile; "it is time to begin at once. You are in a foreign country and there are plenty of things to write about. Your information will be to a great extent new and interesting to your friends, and the reasons that I gave you for not writing a long letter from Niagara do not exist here."

"I thought you would say so," responded Fred, his eyes sparkling with animation, "and I want to write while everything is fresh in my mind. I am going to write at once."

"And so am I," echoed Frank; "here goes for a letter to friends at home."

Off the boys ran for their writing materials, and in a little while they were seated on the balcony of the hotel, and making their pens fairly fly over the paper.

Here is the letter from Frank to his mother:

"Yokohama, *August 4th,* 1878.

"My Dear Mother:

"I wish you could see me just now. I am sitting on the veranda of the hotel, and Fred is at the table with me. If we look up from our paper, we can see out upon the bay, where lots of ships are at anchor, and where a whole fleet of Japanese fishing-boats are coming up and dragging their nets along after them. Down in the street in front of us there are some funny-looking men with trousers as tight as their skins, and making the

JAPANESE MUSICIANS.

men look a great deal smaller than they are. They have hats like small umbrellas, and made of plaited straw, to keep the sun off, and they have them tied down under the chin with cords as big as a clothes-line. Doctor Bronson says these are the lower class of Japanese, and that we haven't seen the fine people yet. There are three musicians, at least they are called so, but I can't see that they make much that I should call music. One of them has on one of those great broad hats, another has his head covered with a sort of small cap, while the third has his skull shaven as smooth as a door-knob. The man with the hat on is blowing a whistle and ringing a small bell, the second is beating on a brass plate with a tiny drumstick, while the third has a pair of clappers which he knocks together, and he sings at the same time. Each of them seems to pay no attention to the rest, but I suppose they think they are playing a tune. Two of them have their legs bare, but they have sandals on their feet, held in place by cords or thongs. The man with the hat must be the leader, as he is the only one that wears trousers, and, besides, he has a pocket-book hung to his girdle. I wonder if they make much money out of the music they are playing?

" A couple of fishermen just stopped to look at the musicians and hear the music. One had a spear and a net with a basket at the end, and the other carried a small rod and line such as I used to have when I went out for trout. They didn't have much clothing, though — nothing but a jacket of coarse cloth and a kilt made of reeds. Only one had a hat, and that didn't seem to amount to much. The bareheaded one scowled at me, and I think he can't be very fond of foreigners. Perhaps the foreigners deserve to be scowled at, or, at any rate, some of them do.

JAPANESE FISHERMEN.

"We have seen such lots of things to-day—lots and lots. I can't begin to tell you all in this letter, and there is so much that I don't know where to commence. Well, we went into some shops and looked at the things they had to sell, but didn't buy anything, as we thought it was too soon. One of the shops I liked very much was where they sold silk. It wasn't much like a silk-shop at home, where you sit on a stool in front of a counter and have the clerks spread the things out before you. In this shop the silk was in boxes out of sight, and they only showed you what you asked for. There was a platform in the middle of the shop, and the clerks squatted down on this platform, and unrolled their goods. Two women were there, buying some bright-colored stuff, for making a dress, I suppose, but I don't know. One man sat in the corner with a yardstick ready to measure off what was wanted, and another sat close by him looking on to see that everything was all right. Back of him there were a lot of boxes piled up with the goods in them ; and whenever anything was wanted, he passed it out. You should have seen how solemn they all looked, and how one woman counted on her fingers to see how much it was all coming to, just as folks do at home. In a corner opposite the man with the yardstick there was a man who kept the accounts. He was squatted on the floor like the rest, and had his books all round him ; and when a sale was made, he put it down in figures that I couldn't read in a week.

"Then it was ever so funny to see the men bowing to each other; they did it with so much dignity, as if they had all been princes, or something of the sort. They rest their hands on their knees, and then bend the body forward ; and sometimes they bend so low that their backs are level

" SAYONARA."

JAPANESE SILK-SHOP.

enough to set out a tea-service on and use them for a table. When they want to bid good-bye, they say 'Sayonara,' just·as we say 'Good-bye,' and it means exactly the same thing. They are not satisfied with one bow, but keep on several times, until you begin to wonder when they will get through. Everybody says they are the politest people in the world, and I can readily believe it if what I have seen is a fair sample.

"There have been several men around the hotel trying to sell things to us, and we have been looking at them. One thing I am going to get and send in this letter is a box of Japanese pictures. They are not photographs, but real drawings by Japanese artists, and printed on Japanese paper. You will see how soft and nice the paper is; and though the pictures look rough, they are very good, and, above all things, they are truthful. I am going to get as many different ones as I can, and so I think you will be able to get a good idea of the country as the natives see it themselves. They have these pictures showing all their ways of life—how they cook their food, how they eat it, how they work, how they play—in fact, how everything is done in this very curious country. The Japanese make their drawings with very few lines, and it will astonish you to see how much they can express with a few strokes of a pencil. Here is a

SEVEN-STROKE HORSE.

picture of a horse drawn with seven strokes of the artist's finger-nail dipped in ink, and with a few touches of a wide brush for the mane and tail. Do you think my old drawing-master at home could do the same thing?

"The pillows they sleep on would never do for us. A Japanese pillow is a block of wood with a rest for the head, or rather for the neck, as the head doesn't touch it at all, except just below the ear. It is only a few inches long and high, and is perfectly hard, as the little piece of paper they put on it is intended for cleanliness, and not to make the pillow soft. You can't turn over on one of them, and as for doubling them up to throw at another boy, it is quite out of the question. I shall put in a picture of a Japanese woman lying down with her head on one of these curious things. The women have their hair done up so elaborately that they must sleep on something that does not disturb it, as they can't afford the time and trouble for fixing it every morning. You'll find a picture of their head-dress in the lot I send with this; but it is from a sketch by a foreigner, and not by a native.

FEMALE HEAD-DRESS.

"Perhaps you will want to know something about the weather in Japan. It is very warm in the middle of the day, but the mornings and evenings

THE SIESTA.

are delightful. Around where we are the ground is flat, and the heat is greater than back among the hills. People remain as quiet as possible during the middle of the day; and if you go around the shops at that time, you find nearly everybody asleep who can afford to be so. The Japanese houses are all so open that you see everything that is going on, and they think nothing of lying down in full sight of the street. Since the foreigners came to Yokohama, the natives are somewhat more particular about their houses than they used to be; at any rate, it is said so by those who ought to know. The weather is so warm in summer that the natives do not need to wear much clothing, and I suppose that is the reason why they are so careless about their appearance. In the last few years the government has become very particular about having the people properly dressed, and has issued orders compelling them to put on sufficient clothing to cover them whenever they go out of doors. They enforce these orders very rigidly in the cities and large towns; but in the country the people go around pretty much as they used to. Of course, you understand I am speaking of the lower classes only, and not of the aristocracy. The latter are as careful about their garments as the best people in any other part of the world, and they often spend hours over their toilets. A Japanese noble gotten up in fine old style is a sight worth going a long distance to see, and he knows it too. He has a lot of stiff silks and heavy robes that cost a great deal of money, and they must be arranged with the greatest care, as the least displacement is a serious affair. I haven't seen one of them yet, and Doctor Bronson says we may not see any during our stay in Japan, as the government has abolished the old dress, and adopted that of Western Europe. It is too bad that they have done so, as the Japanese dress is very becoming to the people—ever so much more so than the new one they have taken. Japan

A JAPANESE AT HIS TOILET FOR A VISIT OF CEREMONY.

is fast losing its national characteristics, through the eagerness of the government to follow Western fashions. What a pity! I do hope I shall be able to see one of those old-fashioned dresses, and won't mind how far I have to go for it.

"Now, mother, this letter is addressed to you, but it is intended for everybody; and I know you'll read it to everybody, and have it handed round, so that all can know where I am and what I have told you about Japan. When I don't write to each one of you, I know you will understand why it is,—because I am so busy, and trying to learn all I can. Give my love to each and every one in the family, and tell Mary she knows somebody outside of it that wants a share. Tell her I often think of the morning we left, and how a handkerchief waved from the railway station when we came away. And tell Mary, too, that I haven't yet opened her list of things I am to get for her; but I haven't forgotten it, and have it all safe and right. There are lots of pretty things to buy here; and if she has made a full catalogue of Japanese curiosities, she has given me enough to do for the present—and the presents.

"Good-night, dear mother, and look for another letter by the next mail.

"Your loving son,

"FRANK."

Fred finished his letter almost at the same moment that Frank affixed the signature to his own. By the time they were through it was late in the evening, and the hour for retiring to bed. Their sleeping-places were exactly such as they might have found in any American hotel, and they longed for a view of a Japanese bed. Frank was inclined to ask Doctor Bronson to describe one to them, but Fred thought it would be time enough when they went into the interior of the country and saw one.

They were up early the next morning, but not as early as the Japanese.

"I tell you what," said Frank, "I have made a discovery."

"What is it?"

"I have been thinking of something to introduce into the United States, and make everybody get up early in the morning."

"Something Japanese?"

"Yes. Something that interested us yesterday when we saw it."

"Well, we saw so many things that I couldn't begin to guess in half an hour. What was it?"

"It was a pillow."

"You mean those little things the Japanese sleep on?"

"Yes; they are so uncomfortable that we couldn't use them with any sort of pleasure. Nobody would want to lie in bed after he had waked up, if he had such a pillow under his head. He would be out in a minute, and wouldn't think of turning over for another doze.

"Now, if our Congress will pass a law abolishing the feather pillow all over the United States, and commanding everybody to sleep on the Japanese one, it would make every man, woman, and child get up at least an hour earlier every day. For forty millions of people this would make a gain of forty million hours daily, and that would be equal to forty-five thousand years. Just think what an advantage that would be to the country, and how much more we could accomplish than we do now. Isn't it a grand idea?"

Fred thought it might be grand and profitable to the country, but it would be necessary to make the pillows for the people; and from what he had heard of Congress, he didn't think they would vote away the public money for anything of the sort. Besides, the members of Congress would not wish to deprive themselves of the privilege of sleeping on feather pillows, and therefore they wouldn't vote away their liberties. So he advised Frank to study Japan a little longer before he suggested the adoption of the Japanese pillow in America.

This conversation occurred while the boys were in front of the hotel, and waiting for the Doctor, whom they expected every moment. When he came, the three went out for a stroll, and returned in good season for breakfast. While they were out they took a peep into a Japanese house, where the family were at their morning meal, and thus the boys had an opportunity of comparing their own ways with those of the country they were in.

A dignified native, with the fore part of his head closely shaven, was squatted on the floor in front of a little box about a foot high, which served as a table. Opposite was his wife, and at the moment our party looked in she was engaged in pouring something from a bottle into a small cup the size of a thimble. Directly under her hand was a bowl filled with freshly boiled rice, from which the steam was slowly rising; and at the side of the table was another and smaller one, holding some plates and chopsticks. A tiny cup and a bowl constituted the rest of the breakfast equipment. The master was waited upon by his wife, who was not supposed to attend to her own wants until his had been fully met. She sat with her back to the window, which was covered with paper in small squares pasted to the frame, and at her right was a screen, such as one

A JAPANESE BREAKFAST.

finds in nearly all Eastern countries. On her left was a chest of drawers with curious locks and handles, which doubtless contained the family wealth of linen.

As they went on, after their view of a Japanese interior, Frank asked what was the name and character of the liquid the woman was pouring into the glass or cup for her husband.

"That was probably sa-kee," replied the Doctor.

"And what is sa-kee, please?"

"It is," answered the Doctor, "a sort of wine distilled from rice. Foreigners generally call it rice wine, but, more properly speaking, it is rice whiskey, as it partakes more of the nature of spirit than of wine. It is very strong, and will intoxicate if taken in any considerable quantity. The Japanese usually drink it hot, and take it from the little cups that you saw. The cups hold so small a quantity that a great many fillings are necessary to produce any unpleasant effect. The Japanese rarely drink to intoxication, and, on the whole, they are a very temperate people."

Fred thereupon began to moralize on the policy of introducing Japanese customs into America. He thought more practicable good could be done by the adoption of the Japanese cup—which would teach our people to drink more lightly than at present—than by Frank's plan of introducing the Japanese pillow. He thought there would be some drawbacks to Frank's enterprise, which would offset the good it could do. Thus a great number of people whom the pillow might bring up at an early hour would spend the time in ways that would not be any benefit to society, and they might as well be asleep, and in many cases better, too. But the tiny drinking-cup would moderate the quantity of stimulants many persons would take, and thus a great good might be accomplished.

While thus talking, and trying to conjure up absurd things, they reached the hotel, and soon were seated at breakfast.

During breakfast Doctor Bronson unfolded some of the plans he had made for the disposal of their time, so that they might see as much as possible of Japan.

"We have taken a look at Yokohama since we arrived," said he, "but there is still a great deal to see. We can study the place at our leisure, as I think it best to make this our headquarters while in this part of the empire, and then we will make excursions from here to the points of interest in the vicinity. To-day we will go to Tokio."

"Can't we go first to Yeddo?" said Fred; "I want so much to see that city, and it is said to be very large."

Doctor Bronson laughed slightly as he replied,

"Tokio and Yeddo are one and the same thing. Tokio means the Eastern capital, while Yeddo means the Great City. Both names have long been in use; but the city was first known to foreigners as Yeddo. Hence it was called so in all the books that were written prior to a few years ago, when it was officially announced to be Tokio. It was considered the capital at the time Japan was opened to foreigners; but there were political complications not understood by the strangers, and the true relations of the city we are talking about and Kioto, which is the Western capital, were not explained until some time after. It was believed that there were two emperors or kings, the one in Yeddo and the other in Kioto, and that the one here was highest in authority. The real fact was that the Shogoon, or Tycoon (as he was called by the foreigners), at Yeddo was subordinate to the real emperor at Kioto; and the action of the former led to a war which resulted in the complete overthrow of the Tycoon, and the establishment of the Mikado's authority through the entire country."

"Then the emperor is called the Mikado, is he not?"

"Yes; that is his official title. Formerly he was quite secluded, as his person was considered too sacred to be seen by ordinary eyes; but since the rebellion and revolution he has come out from his seclusion, and takes

MUTSUHITO, MIKADO OF JAPAN.

part in public ceremonials, receives visitors, and does other things like the monarchs of European countries. He is enlightened and progressive, and is doing all he can for the good of his country and its people.

"The curious feature of the revolution which established the Mikado on his throne, and made him the ruler of the whole country is this—that

7

the movement was undertaken to prevent the very things it has brought about."

"How was that?" Frank asked.

"Down to 1853 Japan was in a condition of exclusiveness in regard to other nations. There was a Dutch trading-post at Nagasaki, on the western coast; but it was confined to a little island, about six hundred feet square, and the people that lived there were not allowed to go out of their enclosure except at rare intervals, and under restrictions that amounted to practical imprisonment. In the year I mentioned Commodore Perry came here with a fleet of American ships, left some presents that had been sent

LANDING OF PERRY'S EXPEDITION.

by the President of the United States, and sailed away. Before he left he laid the foundation for the present commercial intercourse between Japan and the United States; and on his return in the following year the privileges were considerably enlarged. Then came the English, and secured similar concessions; and thus Japan has reached her present standing among the nations.

"Having been exclusive so long, and having been compelled against her will to open her ports to strangers, there was naturally a good deal of opposition to foreigners even after the treaty was signed. The government endeavored to carry out the terms of the treaty faithfully; but there was a large party opposed to it, and anxious to have the treaties torn up and the foreigners expelled. This party was so powerful that it seemed to include almost a majority of the nation, and the Kioto government took the Yeddo section to task for what it had done in admitting the foreigners. One thing led to another, and finally came the war between the Mikado and the Tycoon. The latter was overthrown, as I have already told you, and the Mikado was the supreme ruler of the land.

"The Mikado's party was opposed to the presence of foreigners in the country, and their war-cry was 'Death to the strangers!' When the war was over, there was a general expectation that measures would be adopted looking to the expulsion of the hated intruder. But, to the surprise of many, the government became even more progressive than its predecessor had been, and made concessions to the foreigners that the others had never granted. It was a curious spectacle to see the conservative government doing more for the introduction of the foreigner than the very men they had put down because of their making a treaty with the Americans.

"The opponents of the Mikado's government accuse it of acting in bad faith, but I do not see that the charge is just. As I understand the situation, the government acted honestly, and with good intent to expel the foreigner in case it should obtain power. But when the power was obtained, they found the foreigner could not be expelled so easily; he was here, and intended to remain, and the only thing the government could do was to make the best of it. The foreign nations who had treaties with Japan would not tear them up, and the government found that what it had intended at the time of the revolution could not be accomplished. Foreign intercourse went on, and the Japanese began to instruct themselves in Western ways. They sent their young men to America and other countries to be

THE LAST SHOGOON OF JAPAN.

educated. They hired teachers to take charge of schools in Japan, and
in every way tried to turn the presence of the foreigner to their advantage. There is an old adage that what can't be cured must be endured,
and Japan seems to have acted upon it. The foreigner was here as an
evil, and they couldn't cure him out. So they set about finding the best
way of enduring him.

"But it is time we were getting ready for a start for Tokio, and so
we'll suspend our discussion of Japanese political history. It's a dry subject, and I hesitate to talk to you about it lest I may weary you."

Both the boys declared the topic was interesting, and they would consider their study of Japan incomplete without some of its history. The
Doctor promised to return to the subject at some future occasion; and
with this understanding they separated to prepare for their journey to
the capital.

CHAPTER VII.

FROM YOKOHAMA TO TOKIO.

ONE of the innovations in Japan since the arrival of the foreigners is the railway. Among the presents carried to the country by Commodore Perry were a miniature locomotive and some cars, and several miles of railway track. The track was set up, and the new toy was regarded with much interest by the Japanese. For some years after the country was opened there was considerable opposition to the introduction of the new mode of travel, but by degrees all hostility vanished, and the government entered into contracts for the construction of a line from Yokohama to Tokio. The distance is about seventeen miles, and the route follows the shore of the bay, where there are no engineering difficulties of consequence. In spite of the ease of construction and the low price of labor in Japan, the cost of the work was very great, and would have astonished a railway engineer in America. The work was done under English supervision and by English contractors, and from all accounts there is no reason to suppose that they lost anything by the operation.

Doctor Bronson and our young friends went from Yokohama to the capital by the railway, and found the ride a pleasant one of about an hour's duration. They found that the conductors, ticket-sellers, brakemen, and all others with whom they came in contact were Japanese. For some time after the line was opened the management was in the hands of foreigners; but by degrees they were removed, and the Japanese took charge of the business, for which they had paid a liberal price. They have shown themselves fully competent to manage it, and the new system of travel is quite popular with the people. Three kinds of carriages are run on most of the trains; the first class is patronized by the high officials and the foreigners who have plenty of money; the second by the middle-class natives—official and otherwise—and foreigners whose purses are not plethoric; and the third class by the peasantry, and common people generally. Frank observed that there were few passengers in the first-class carriages, more in the second, and that the third class attracted a crowd,

THIRD-CLASS PASSENGERS.

and was evidently popular. The Doctor told him that the railway had
been well patronized since the day it was first opened, and that the facilities of steam locomotion have not been confined to the eastern end of the
empire. The experiment on the shores of Yeddo Bay proved so satisfactory that a line has since been opened from Kobe to Osaka and Kioto,
in the West—a distance of a little more than fifty miles. The people
take to it as kindly as did those of the East, and the third-class carriages
are generally well filled.

At the station in Yokohama the boys found a news-stand, the same as
they might find one in a station in America, but with the difference
against them that they were unable to read the papers that were sold
there. They bought some, however, to send· home as curiosities, and
found them very cheap. Newspapers existed in Japan before the foreigners went there; but since the advent of the latter the number of publications has increased, as the Japanese can hardly fail to observe the great
influence on public opinion which is exercised by the daily press. They
have introduced metal types after the foreign system, instead of printing
from wooden blocks, as they formerly did, and, but for the difference in
the character, one of their sheets might be taken for a paper printed in
Europe or America. Some of the papers have large circulations, and the
newsboys sell them in the streets, in the same way as the urchins of New

York engage in the kindred business.   There is this difference, however,
that the Japanese newsboys are generally men, and as they walk along
they read in a monotonous tone the news which the paper they are selling
contains.

The train started promptly on the advertised time, and the boys found
that there were half a dozen trains each way daily, some of them running
through, like express trains in other countries, while others were slower,
and halted at every station.   The line ran through a succession of fields
and villages, the former bearing evidence of careful cultivation, while the
latter were thickly populated, and gave indications of a good deal of taste
in their arrangement.   Shade-trees were numerous, and Frank readily
accepted as correct the statement he had somewhere read, that a Japanese
would rather move his house than cut down a tree in case the one interfered with the other.   The rice harvest was nearly at hand, and the fields
were thickly burdened with the waving rice-plants.   Men were working
in the fields, and moving slowly to and fro, and everywhere there was an
activity that did not betoken a lazy people.   The Doctor explained that if
they had been there a month earlier, they would have witnessed the process of hoeing the rice-plants to keep down the weeds, but that now the
hoeing was over, and there was little to do beyond keeping the fields
properly flooded with water, so that the ripening plants should have the

JAPANESE PLOUGHING.

necessary nourishment. He pointed out an irrigating-machine, which was in operation close to the railway, and the boys looked at it with much interest. A wheel was so fixed in a small trough that when it was turned the water was raised from a little pool, and flowed over the land it was desirable to irrigate. The turning process was performed by a man who stood above the wheel, and stepped from one float to another. The machinery was very simple, and had the merit of cheapness, as its cost could not have been large at the price of labor in Japan.

In another place a man was engaged in ploughing. He had a primi-

JAPANESE ROLLER.

tive-looking instrument with a blade like that of a large hatchet, a beam set at right angles, and a single handle which he grasped with both hands. It was propelled by a horse which required some one to lead him, but he did not seem to regard the labor of dragging the plough as anything serious, as he walked off very much as though nothing were behind him. Just beyond the ploughman there was a man with a roller, engaged in covering some seed that had been put in for a late crop. He was using a common roller, which closely resembled the one we employ for smoothing our garden walks and beds, with the exception that it was rougher in construction, and did not appear as round as one naturally expects a roller to be.

MANURING PROCESS.

Fred saw a man dipping something from a hole in the ground, and asked the Doctor what he was doing.

The Doctor explained that the hole was a cask set in the ground, and that it probably contained liquid manure. The Japanese use it for enriching their fields. They keep it in these holes, covered with a slight roof to prevent its evaporation as much as possible, and they spread it around where wanted by means of buckets. The great drawback to a walk in a Japanese field is the frequency of the manure deposits, as the odor arising from them is anything but agreeable. Particularly is this so in the early part of the season, when the young plants require a great deal of attention

HOW THEY USE MANURE.

and nourishment. A nose at such times is an organ of great inconvenience.

The Doctor went on to explain that the Japanese farmers were very watchful of their crops, and that men were employed to scare away the birds, that sometimes dug up the seed after it was planted, and also ate the grain while it was ripening. The watchmen had pieces of board which they put on frames suspended in the air, and so arranged that they rattled in the wind, and performed a service similar to that of the scarecrow in America. In addition to this mode of making a noise, the watchmen had whistles and clappers, and sometimes they carried small bells which they rang as they walked about. It was the duty of a watchman to keep constantly on the alert, as the birds were full of mischief, and, from being rarely shot at, their boldness and impudence were quite astonishing to one freshly arrived from America, where the use of fire-arms is so general.

While Doctor Bronson was explaining about the birds, Fred suddenly gave an exclamation of delight.

"Look, look!" said he; "what are those beautiful white birds?"

MODE OF PROTECTING LAND FROM BIRDS.

"Oh, I know," answered Frank; "they are storks. I recognize them from the pictures I have seen on fans and screens. I'm sure they are storks."

STORKS, DRAWN BY A NATIVE ARTIST.

The decision was appealed to Doctor Bronson, who decided that the birds in question were storks, and nothing else. There was no mistaking their beautiful figures; whether standing in the fields or flying in the air, the stork is one of the handsomest birds known to the ornithologist.

"You see," said Doctor Bronson, "that the stork justifies the homage that is paid to him so far as a graceful figure is concerned, and the Japanese have shown an eye for beauty when they selected him for a prominent place in their pictures. You see him everywhere in Japanese art—

in bronzes, on costly paintings, embroidered on silk, printed on fans, and on nearly every article of household use. He has a sacred character, and it would not be easy to find a Japanese who would willingly inflict an injury upon one of these birds."

There are probably no other artists in the world who can equal the Japanese in drawing the stork in all the ways and attitudes he assumes. These are almost countless; but, not satisfied with this, there are some of the native artists who are accused of representing him in attitudes he was never known to take. Admitting this to be the case, it cannot be disputed that the Japanese are masters of their profession in delineating this bird, and that one is never weary of looking at his portrait as they draw it. They have nearly equal skill in drawing other birds, and a few strokes of the brush or pencil will accomplish marvels in the way of pictorial representation. A flock of geese, some on the ground and others in flight, can be drawn in a few moments by a native designer, and the most exacting critic will not find anything wanting.

FLOCK OF GEESE.

The train sped onward, and in an hour from the time of leaving the station at Yokohama it was nearing Tokio. It passed in full view of the forts of Shinagawa, which were made memorable during the days of Perry and Lord Elgin, as the foreign ships were not allowed to pass them, and

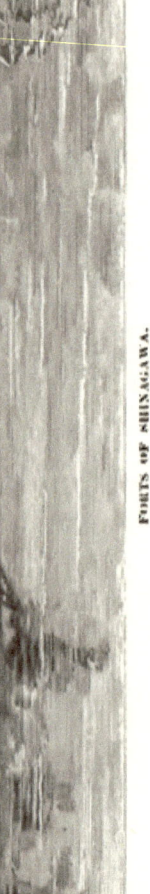

FORTS OF SHINAGAWA.

there was at one time a prospect that they would open fire upon the intruders. Near one of the forts, a boat containing three fishermen was pulling slowly along, one man handling the oar, while the other two were lifting a net. Whether any fish were contained in it the boys did not ascertain, as the train would not stop long enough to permit an investigation. The fort rose from the water like a huge warehouse; it might resist a Chinese junk, or a whole fleet of the rude craft of the East, but could not hold out an hour against the artillery of the Western nations. In recent years the forts of Tokio have been strengthened, but they are yet far from what an American or English admiral would hold in high respect. The Japanese have made commendable progress in army organization; but, so far as one can learn generally, they have not done much in the way of constructing and manning fortifications.

On their arrival in Tokio, our young friends looked around to discover in what the city differed from Yokohama. They saw the same kind of people at the station that they had left in Yokohama, and heard pretty nearly the same sounds. Porters, and others who hoped to serve them and thereby earn something, gathered around; and they found in the open

A JIN-RIKI-SHA.

space in front of the station a liberal number of conveyances ready to take them wherever they wanted to go. There were carriages and jin-riki-shas from which they could choose, and it did not take them long to decide in favor of the jin-riki-sha. It was a novelty to them, though not altogether so, as they had seen it in Yokohama, and had tried its qualities in their journey from the hotel to the station in the morning.

"What is the jin-riki-sha?" the reader naturally asks.

Its name comes from three words, "jin," meaning man; "riki," power; and "sha," carriage: altogether it amounts to "man-power-carriage." It is a little vehicle like an exaggerated baby-cart or diminutive one-horse chaise, and has comfortable seating capacity for only one person, though it will hold two if they are not too large. It was introduced into Japan in 1870, and is said to have been the invention of an American. At all events, the first of them came from San Francisco; but the Japanese soon set about making them, and now there are none imported. It is said that there are nearly a hundred thousand of them in use, and, judging by the abundance of them everywhere, it is easy to believe that the estimate is not too high. The streets are full of them, and, no matter where you go, you are rarely at a loss to find one. As their name indicates, they are carriages drawn by men. For a short distance, or where it is not required to keep up a high speed, one man is sufficient; but otherwise two, or even three, men are needed. They go at a good trot, except when ascending a hill or where the roads are bad. They easily make four and a half or five miles an hour, and in emergencies can do better than the last-named rate.

Frank and Fred were of opinion that the jin-riki-sha would be a slow vehicle to travel in, but asked the Doctor for his experience of one in his previous visit to the country.

"On my first visit to Japan," replied Doctor Bronson, "this little carriage was not in use. We went around on foot or on horseback, or in norimons and cangos."

"And what are norimons and cangos?"

"They are the vehicles in which the Japanese used to travel, and which are still much employed in various parts of the country. We shall see them before long, and then we shall have an excellent opportunity to know what they are. We shall probably be travelling in them in a few days, and I will then have your opinion concerning them.

"As to the jin-riki-sha," he continued, "my experience with it in my last visit to Japan since its introduction gives me a high opinion of the Japanese power of endurance. A few days after my arrival, I had occasion to go a distance of about forty miles on the great road along the coast, from Yokohama to Odiwara. I had three men to draw the carriage, and the journey was made in twelve hours, with three halts of fifteen minutes each. You could not have done better than this with a horse and carriage in place of the man-power vehicle. On another occasion I went from Osaka to Nara, a distance of thirty miles, between ten in the morning and five in the afternoon, and halted an hour for lunch at a Japanese inn on the road. Part of the way the road was through fields, where it was necessary to go slowly, and quite frequently the men were obliged to lift the vehicle over water-courses and gullies, and a good deal of time was lost by these detentions."

Both the boys declared that the travel under such circumstances was excellent, and that it was fully up to what the average horse could accomplish in America.

JAPANESE ON FOOT.

"The next day," said the Doctor, "I went on from Nara to Kioto, which was another thirty miles, in about the same time and with a similar halt for dinner. I had the same men as on the day before, and they raced merrily along without the least sign of fatigue, although there was a pouring rain all day that made the roads very heavy. Frequently there were steep little hills to ascend where the road passed over the water-courses or canals. You will find, as you travel in Japan, that the canals are above the general level of the country, in order to afford the proper fall for irrigation. Where the road crosses one of these canals, there is a sharp rise on one side, and an equally sharp descent on the other. You can manage the descent, but the rise is difficult. In the present instance the rain had softened the road, and made the pulling very hard indeed; and, to add to the trouble, I had injured my foot and was unable to walk, so that I could not lighten the burden of the men by getting out of the carriage at the bad places.

"I was able on this journey, and partly in consequence of my lameness, to have an opportunity to see the great kindness of the Japanese to each other. I had my servant with me (a Japanese boy who spoke English), and he was in a jin-riki-sha with two men to pull it, the same as mine. When we came to a bad spot in the road, the men with his carriage dropped it and came to the aid of mine; and as soon as they had brought it through its troubles, the whole four went back to bring up the other. I did not hear a single expression of anger during the whole day, but everything was done with the utmost good-nature. In some other countries it is quite possible that the men with the lighter burden would adhere to the principle that everybody should look out for himself, and decline to assist unless paid extra for their trouble.

"You will find, the more you know the Japanese, that they cannot be excelled in their kindnesses to each other. They have great reverence and respect for their parents; and their affection for brothers and sisters, cousins, aunts, and all relatives, is worthy of admiration. If you inquire into the circumstances of the laboring-men, whose daily earnings are very small, and with whom life is a most earnest struggle, you will find that nearly every one of them is supporting somebody besides himself, and that many

AN EXPRESS RUNNER.

of their families are inconveniently large. Yet they accept all their burdens cheerfully, and are always smiling, and apparently happy. Whether they are really so has been doubted; but I see no good reason to call their cheerfulness in question.

"But I will tell you a still more remarkable story of the endurance of these Japanese runners. While I was at Kioto, an English clergyman came there with his wife; and after they had seen the city, they were very anxious to go to Nara. They had only a day to spare, as they were obliged to be at Kobe at a certain date to meet the steamer for Shanghai. They made arrangements to be taken to Nara and back in that time—a distance, going and coming, of sixty miles. They had three men to each jin-riki-sha, and they kept the same men through the entire trip. They left the hotel at Kioto at four o'clock in the morning, and were back again at half-past eight in the evening. You couldn't do better than this with a horse, unless he were an exceptionally good one."

Frank thought that he should not enjoy the jin-riki-sha, as he would be constantly thinking of the poor fellows who were pulling him, and of how much they were suffering on his account. He could not bear to see them tugging away and perspiring while he was reclining in a comfortable seat.

"I readily understand you," Doctor Bronson answered, "as I had the same feeling myself, and every American has it when he first comes to the country. He has a great deal of sympathy for the men, and I have known some strangers to refuse to ride in a jin-riki-sha on that account. But if you will apply reason to the matter, you will soon get over the feeling. Remember that the man gets his living by pulling his little carriage, and that he regards it as a great favor when you patronize him. You do him a kindness when you employ him; and the more you employ him, the more will he regard you as his friend. He was born to toil, and expects to toil as long as he lives. He does not regard it as a hardship, but cheerfully accepts his lot; and the more work he obtains, the better is he satisfied. And when you pay him for his services, you will win his most heart-felt affection if you add a trifle by way of gratuity. If you give only the exact wages prescribed by law, he does not complain, and you have only to add a few cents to make his eyes glisten with gratitude. In my experience of laboring-men in all parts of the world, I have found that the Japanese coolie is the most patient, and has the warmest heart, the most thankful for honest pay for honest work, and the most appreciative of the trifles that his employer gives him in the way of presents."

A JAPANESE COOLIE.

When the Doctor had finished his eulogy upon the Japanese, the boys clapped their hands, and were evidently touched with his enthusiasm. From the little they had seen since their arrival in the country, they coincided with him in opinion, and were ready to endorse what he said. And if they had been in any doubt, they had only to refer to the great majority of foreigners who reside in Japan for the confirmation of what the Doctor had declared. Testimony in this matter is as nearly unanimous as it is generally possible to find it on any subject, and some of the foreign residents are ready to go much further in their laudations of the kindly spirit of the natives than did Doctor Bronson.

PITY FOR THE BLIND.

CHAPTER VIII.

SIGHTS IN THE EASTERN CAPITAL OF JAPAN.

TO see the whole of Tokio is a matter of no small moment, as the area of the city is very great. There seems to have been no stint of ground when the place was laid out, and in riding through it you find whole fields and gardens so widely spread that you can readily imagine yourself to be in the rural districts, and are rather surprised when told that you are yet in the city limits. The city is divided into two unequal portions by the Sumida River, and over this river is the Nihon Bashi, or

VIEW OF TOKIO, FROM THE SOUTH.

Nihon Bridge, which is often called the centre of Japan, for the reason that all the roads were formerly measured from it. It has the same relation to Japan as the famous "London Stone" has to England, or, rather, as the London Stone had a hundred years ago.

From the railway station our travellers went to the Nihon Bashi, in order to begin their journey from the centre of the empire. A more practical reason was a desire to see the river, and the great street leading to it, as they would get a good idea of the extent of the city by taking this route, and would obtain numerous glimpses of Japanese street life. They found the streets full of people, and it seemed to the boys that the whole population must be out for an airing. But the Doctor informed them that the sight they were witnessing was an every-day affair, as the Japanese were essentially an outdoor people, and that many of the industries which in other countries would be conducted under a roof were here

seen in progress out of doors. The fronts of the Japanese houses are quite open to the view of the public, and there is hardly anything of what we call privacy. It was formerly no uncommon sight to see people bathing in tubs placed in front of their door-steps; and even at the present time one has only to go into the villages, or away from the usual haunts of foreigners, to see that spectacle which would be unknown in the United States. The bath-houses are now closed in front in all the cities, but remain pretty much as before in the smaller towns. Year by year the country is adopting Western ideas, and coming to understand the Western views of propriety.

JAPANESE LADY COMING FROM THE BATH.

As the boys rode along, their attention was drawn to some tall ladders that rose above the buildings, and they eagerly asked the Doctor what those ladders were for. They could not see the use of climbing up in the air and then coming down again; and, altogether, the things were a mystery to them. A few words explained the matter. The ladders were nothing more nor less than fire-lookouts, and were elevated above the buildings so that the watchmen could have an unobstructed view. A bell was attached to each ladder, and by means of it a warning-signal was given in case of a threatened conflagration. Fires are frequent in Tokio, and some of them have done immense damage. The city is mostly built of wood; and when a fire breaks out and a high wind is blowing, the result is often disastrous to an enormous extent.

After the great fires of the last twenty years, the burned districts have been rebuilt of stone, or largely so; and precautions that were hitherto unknown are now taken for the prevention of fresh disasters. Some of the new quarters are quite substantial, but they resemble too strongly the edifices of a city in Europe to be characteristic of Japan.

A portion of the way took our friends through the grounds of some of the castles, and the boys were rather astonished at the extent of these residences of princes. Doctor Bronson explained that Tokio was formerly a city of princes, and that the residences of the Daimios, as these great men were called, were of more consequence at one time than all the rest of the city. The palace of a Daimio was known as a *yashiki*, and the

FIRE-LOOKOUTS IN TOKIO.

yashikis were capable, in some instances, of lodging five or ten thousand men. Under the present government the power of the princes has been taken away, and their troops of retainers have been disbanded. The government has converted the most of the yashikis into offices and barracks and schools, and one at least has been turned into a manufactory.

The original plan of Tokio was that of a vast camp, and from that the city grew into its present condition. The best locations were occupied by the castles and yashikis, and the principal castle in the centre has the best place of all. Frank observed as they crossed the bridge leading into the castle-yard that the broad moat was full of lotos flowers in full bloom, and he longed to gather some of them so that he might send them home as a souvenir of the country. He had heard of the lotos as a sort of water-lily, similar in general appearance to the pond-lily of his native land. He was surprised to find a flower, eight or ten inches in diameter, growing on a strong stalk that did not float on the water, but held itself erect and far above it. The Doctor explained the matter by telling him that the Japanese lotos is unlike the Egyptian lotos, from which our ideas of that flower are derived. But the Japanese one is highly prized by the people of all ranks and classes, and it grows in abundance in all the castle-moats, and in marshy ground generally.

Near the entrance of one of the castle-yards they met a couple that attracted their attention.   It was a respectable-appearing citizen

who had evidently partaken too freely of the cup that cheers and also inebriates, as his steps were unsteady, and he would have fallen to the ground had it not been for the assistance of his wife, who was leading him and guiding him in the way he should go. As the strangers went past him he raised his hand to his head; but Frank could not determine whether it was a movement of salutation or of dazed inquiry. The Doctor suggested that it was more likely to have been the latter than the former, since the Japanese do not salute in our manner, and the man was too much

TOO MUCH SA-KEE.

under the influence of the "sa-kee" he had swallowed to adopt any foreign modes of politeness. Sights like this are not unknown in the great cities of Japan, but they are far less frequent than in New York or London. The Japanese say that drunkenness is on the decrease in the past few years, owing to the abolition of the Samurai class, who have been compelled to work for a living, instead of being supported out of the revenues of the state, as formerly. They have less time and money for dissipation now than they had in the olden days, and, consequently, their necessities have made them temperate.

For an Oriental city Tokio has remarkably wide streets, and some of them are laid out with all the care of Western engineering. In the course of their morning ride the party came to Sakuradu Avenue, which Fred recognized from a drawing by a native artist, who had taken pains to preserve the architecture of the buildings on each side with complete fidelity. The foundations of the houses were of irregular stones cut in the form of lozenges, but not with mathematical accuracy. The boys had already noticed this form of hewing stone in the walls of the castles, where some very large blocks were piled. They were reported to have been brought from distant parts of the empire, and the cost of their transpor-

SAKURADU AVENUE IN TOKIO.

tation must have been **very great**. **Few of the** houses were of more than **two stories, and the** great majority were of **only one**. **Along** Sakuradu Avenue **they were** of two stories, and had long and **low windows** with paper screens, so that it was impossible **for** a person in the **street to see** what was going on inside. The eaves projected far over the upright **sides,** and thus formed a shelter that was very acceptable in the **heat of sum-** mer, while in rainy weather it had many advantages. These yashikis **were** formerly the property of Daimios, but **are now** occupied by the Foreign **Office** and the **War** Department. Inside the enclosure there are many **shade-trees,** and they make a cooling contrast to the plain walls of the buildings. The Japanese rarely paint the interior or the exterior of **their** buildings. Nearly everything is finished in the natural color of the wood, and very **pretty the** wood is **too**. It is something like oak in appearance, but **a trifle** darker, and is susceptible of a high **polish**. It admits of a **great variety of uses, and is very** easily wrought. It **is known as** keyaki- **wood; and, in spite of the immense quantity that is annually used, it is** cheap and **abundant**.

Some of the **Daimios expended** immense amounts **of money in** the decoration of **their palaces by means of** bronzes, embroideries on silk, fine lacquer, and **the like**. **Art in Japan** was nourished by the Daimios, and we have much **to thank them for in the way** of household **adorn-** ment.

Since the adoption **of Western ideas in** decoration and household fur- niture, **the** Japanese dwellings have lost somewhat in point of attractive- ness. Our carpets **and** furniture are out of place in a Japanese room, and so are our pictures and statuary. It **is** a pity that the people should ever abandon **their** domestic customs for ours, whatever they might do in the matter of military equipment, machinery, and other things that are more **or** less commercial. Japanese men and women are far more attractive in **their native dress** than in ours, and a Japanese house loses its charm **when** the neat mattings give way to European carpets, and chairs and tables are spread around in place of the simple adornments to which the people **were** accustomed.

After **an interesting** ride, in which their eyes were in constant use, the boys reached the Temple **of** Asakusa, which is one of the great points of attraction to a stranger in **Tokio**. The street which led up to the temple was lined with booths, in which a great variety of things were offered for sale. Nearly **all of** these things were of a cheap class, and evidently the **patrons of** the temple were not of the wealthier sort. Toys were numer- **ous,** and as our party alighted they saw some children gazing wistfully at a collection of dolls; Frank and Fred suggested the propriety of making the little people happy by expending something for them. The Doctor gave his approval; so the boys invested a sum equal to about twenty cents of our money, and were astonished at the number of dolls they were able to procure for their outlay. The little Japs were delighted, and danced around in their glee, just as any children might have done in another country. A few paces away some boys were endeavoring to walk on bamboo poles, and evidently they were having a jolly time, to judge by their laughter. Two boys were hanging by their hands from a pole, and endeavoring to turn somersets; while two others were trying to walk on a pole close by them. One of the walkers fell off, and was laughed at by his companions; but he was speedily up again, determined not to give up till he had accomplished his task.

Japanese children are well supplied with dolls and other playthings, and there are certain festivals in which the whole family devotes itself to the preparation or purchase of dolls to amuse the little ones. The greatest of these festivals is known as the "Hina Matsuri," or Feast of Dolls, *hina* meaning doll, and *matsuri* being applicable to any kind of feast. It occurs on the third day of the third month, and for several days before the appointed time the shops are filled with dolls just as they are filled among us at Christmas. In fact, the whole business in this line is transacted at this period, and at other times it is next to impossible to procure the things that are so abundant at the Matsuri. Every family that can afford the outlay buys a quantity of images made of wood or enamelled clay, and dressed to represent various imperial, noble, or mythological characters, either of the present time or of some former period in Japanese history. In this way the children are taught a good deal of history, and their delight at the receipt of their presents is quite equal to that of children in Christian lands. Not only dolls, but a great variety of other things, are given to the girls; for the

THE FEAST OF DOLLS ("HINA MATSURI") IN A JAPANESE HOUSE.

Hina Matsuri is more particularly a festival for girls rather than for boys. The presents are arranged on tables, and there is general rejoicing in the household. Miniature tea and toilet sets, miniature bureaus and wardrobes, and miniature houses are among the things that fall to the lot of a Japanese girl at the time of the Hina Matsuri.

Fred thought the Japanese had queer notions when compared with ours about the location of a temple in the midst of all sorts of entertainments. He was surprised to find the temple surrounded with booths for singing and dancing and other amusements, and was very sure that such a thing would not be allowed in America. Doctor Bronson answered that the subject had been discussed before by people who had visited Japan, and various opinions had been formed concerning it. He thought it was not unlike some of the customs in Europe, especially in the more Catholic countries, where the people go to church in the forenoon and devote the afternoon to amusement. A Japanese does not see any wrong in going to his worship through an avenue of entertainments, and then returning to them. He says his prayers as a matter of devotion, and then applies himself to innocent pleasure. He is firmly attached to his religious faith, and his recreations are a part of his religion. What he does is all well enough for him, but whether it would answer for us is a question which cannot be decided in a moment.

Men of various trades were working in the shops at Asakusa, and their way of operating was of much interest to our young friends. A barber was engaged in arranging the hair of a customer; the forehead had been shaven, and the hair at the back of the head was gathered into a knot and thickly plastered, so as to make it stick and remain in place when turned over into a short cue. The customer knelt on the ground in front of a box that contained the tools of the operator's trade, and by his side was a portable furnace for heating water. The whole equipment was of very little value, and the expense of fitting up a fashionable barber's shop in New York would send hundreds of Japanese barbers on their way rejoicing.

A BARBER AT WORK.

Close by was a clothes-merchant, to whom a customer was making an offer, while the dealer was rubbing his head and vowing he could not possibly part with the garment at that price. Frank watched him to see how the affair terminated, and found it was very much as though the transaction had been in New York instead of Tokio: the merchant, whispering he would ne'er consent, consented, and the customer obtained the garment at his own figures when the vender found he could not obtain his own price. It is the same all the earth over, and Frank thought he

A TRANSACTION IN CLOTHES.

saw in this tale of a coat the touch of nature that makes the whole world kin.

Hundreds of pigeons were circling around the temple, or walking among the people that thronged the street. Nobody showed the slightest intention of harming them, and the consequence was they were very tame. Several stands were devoted to the sale of grain for the birds; and the sharp-eyed pigeons knew, when they saw the three strangers halt in front of one of the stands, that there was good prospect of a free breakfast. The Doctor bought a quart or more of the grain and threw it out upon the ground. Instantly there was a whirring of wings in the air, and in less time than it takes to say so the grain was devoured. The birds were rather shy of the visitors, and possibly it had been whispered to them that the foreigner likes his pigeons broiled or served up in pies. But they did not display any such timidity when the natives approached them. Some of the Japanese temples are the homes of a great number of pigeons, and in this respect they resemble the mosques at Constantinople and other Moslem cities.

Close at hand is a stable where two beautiful ponies are kept. They are snowy white, and are consecrated to the goddess Ku-wanon, the deity of mercy, who is the presiding genius of the temple. They are in the care of a young girl, and it is considered a pious duty to feed them. Pease and beans are for sale outside, and many devotees contribute a few cash for the benefit of the sacred animals. If the poor beasts should eat a quarter of what is offered to them, or, rather, of what is paid for, they would soon die of overfeeding. It is shrewdly suspected that the grain is sold many times over, in consequence of a collusion between the dealers and the keeper of the horses. At all events, the health of the animals is regarded, and it would never do to give them all that is presented.

Frank found the air full of odors more or less heavy, and some of them the reverse of agreeable. They arose from numerous sticks of incense burned in honor of the gods, and which are irreverently called joss-sticks by foreigners. The incense is supposed to be agreeable to the god, and the smoke is thought to waft the supplicant's prayer to heaven. The same idea obtains in the burning of a paper on which a prayer has been printed, the flame carrying the petition as it flies upward. Traces of a

BALL-PLAYING IN JAPAN.

similar faith are found in the Roman Catholic and Greek churches, where candles have a prominent place in religious worship; and the Doctor insisted to his young companions that the Christian and the Pagan are not so very far apart, after all. In addition to the odor of incense, there was that of oil, in which a keeper of a tiny restaurant was frying some cuttle-fish. The oil was of the sort known as "sesame," or barley, and the smell was of a kind that does not touch the Western nostril as agreeably as does that of lavender or Cologne water. Men were tossing balls in the air in front of the restaurant, quite unmindful of the strong odors, and seeming to enjoy the sport, and a woman and a boy were so busy over a game of battledoor and shuttlecock that they did not observe the presence of the strangers.

SPORT AT ASAKUSA.

Through this active scene of refreshment and recreation, our party strolled along, and at length came to the gateway of the temple, an enormous structure of wood like a house with triple eaves, and raised on pillars resembling the piers of a bridge. This is similar to the gateway that is found in front of nearly every Japanese temple, and is an imposing ornament. On either hand, as we pass through, we find two statues of demons, who guard the entrance, and are gotten up in the superlative degree of hideousness. When the Japanese give their attention to the preparation of an image of surpassing ugliness, they generally succeed, and the same is the case when they search after the beautiful. Nothing can be more ugly in feature than the giants at Asakusa, and what is there more gracefully beautiful than the Japanese bronzes that were shown in the great exhibitions at Philadelphia and Paris? *Les extrêmes se touchent.*

Fred thought he would propitiate the demons in a roundabout way, and so he gave a few pennies to some old beggars that were sitting near the gateway. The most of them were far from handsome, and none were beautiful; some were even so repulsive in features as to draw from Frank the suggestion that they were relatives of the statues, and therefore entitled to charity.

Near the gateway was a pagoda or tower in seven stories, and it is said to be one of the finest in Japan. The Japanese pagoda is always built in

an odd number of stories, three, five, seven, or nine, and it usually terminates, as does the one we are now contemplating, with a spire that resembles an enormous corkscrew more than anything else. It is of copper or bronze, and is a very beautiful ornament, quite in keeping with the edifice that it crowns. On its pinnacle there is a jewel, or something supposed to be one, a sacred emblem that appears very frequently in Japanese paintings or bronze-work. The edges of the little roofs projecting from each story were hung with bells that rang in the wind, but their noise was not sufficiently loud to render any inconvenience to the visitor, and for the greater part of the time they do not ring at all. The architecture of the pagoda is in

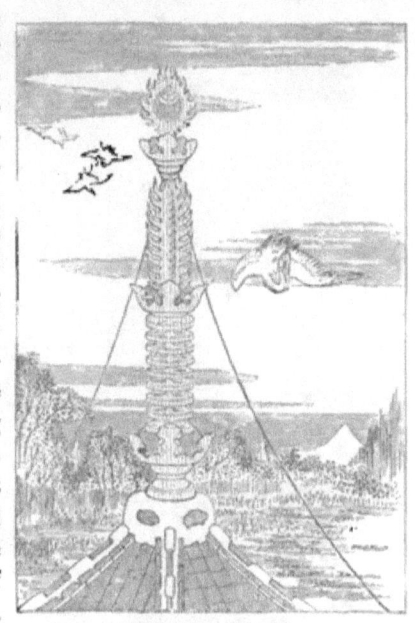

SPIRE OF A PAGODA.

keeping with that of the surrounding buildings, and thoroughly Oriental in all its features.

They passed the gateway and entered the temple. The huge building towered above them with its curved roof covered with enormous tiles, and its eaves projecting so far that they suggested an umbrella or the overhanging sides of a mushroom. Frank admired the graceful curves of the roof, and wondered why nobody had ever introduced them into architecture in America. The Doctor told him that the plan had been tried in a few instances, but that architects were generally timid about innovations, and, above all, they did not like to borrow from the Eastern barbarians. Fred thought they ought to be willing to take anything that was good, no matter where they found it, and Frank echoed his sentiment.

BELFRY IN COURT-YARD OF TEMPLE, SHOWING THE STYLE OF A JAPANESE ROOF.

"When I build a house," said Fred, "I will have a roof on it after the Japanese style, or, at any rate, something suggestive of it. The Japanese roof is pretty and graceful, and would look well in our landscape, I am sure. I don't see why we shouldn't have it in our country, and I'll take home some photographs so that I can have something to work from."

Frank hinted that for the present the house that Fred intended to build was a castle in the air, and he was afraid it would be some time before it assumed a more substantial form.

"Perhaps so," Fred answered, "but you wait awhile, and see if I don't do something that will astonish our neighbors. I think it will do more practical good to introduce the Japanese roof into America than the Japanese pillow."

They agreed to this, and then Frank said it was not the place to waste their time in discussions; they could talk these matters over in the evening, and meanwhile they would look further at the temple and its surroundings.

The boys were somewhat disappointed at the appearance of the interior of the temple. They had expected an imposing edifice like a cathedral, with stately columns supporting a high roof, and with an air of solemn stillness pervading the entire building. They ascended a row of broad steps, and entered a doorway that extended to half the width of the front of the building. The place was full of worshippers mingled with a liberal quantity of pigeons, votive offerings, and dirt. Knowing the Japanese love for cleanliness in their domestic life, it was a surprise to the youths to find the temple so much neglected as it appeared to be. They mentioned the matter to Doctor Bronson, who replied that it probably arose from the fact that the business of everybody was the business of nobody, and that the priests in charge of the temple were not inclined to work very hard in such commonplace affairs as keeping the edifice properly swept out. Thousands of visitors came there daily, and after it was swept in the morning the place soon became soiled, and a renewal of the cleansing process would be a serious inconvenience to the devotees.

People of all classes and kinds were coming and going, and saying their prayers, without regard to each other. The floor was crowded with worshippers, some in rags and others in silks, some in youth and others in old age, some just learning to talk and others trembling with the weight of years; beggars, soldiers, officers, merchants, women, and children knelt together before the shrine of the goddess whom they reverenced, and whose mercy and watchful care they implored. The boys were impressed with the scene of devotion, and reverently paused as they moved among

9

SHRINE OF THE GODDESS KU-WANON.

the pious Japanese. They respected the unquestioning faith of the people in the power of their goddess, and had no inclination to the feeling of derision that is sometimes shown by visitors to places whose sanctity is not in accord with their own views.

But very soon Frank had occasion to bite his lip to suppress a smile when he saw one of the Japanese throw what an American schoolboy would call a "spit-ball" at the head of the great image that stood behind the altar. Then he observed that the whole figure of the god was covered with these balls, and he knew there must be some meaning to the action that he at first thought so funny. He called Fred's attention to the matter, and then asked the Doctor what it meant.

"It is a way they have," replied the Doctor, "of addressing their petitions to the deity. A Japanese writes his prayer on a piece of paper, or buys one already written; then he chews it to a pulp, and throws it at the god. If the ball sticks, the omen is a good one, and the prayer will be answered; if it rebounds or falls, the sign is unlucky, and the petitioner must begin over again. I have been told," continued Doctor Bronson, "that some of the dealers in printed prayers apply a small quantity of glue to them so as to insure their sticking when thrown at the divinity."

In front of the great altar stood a box like a large trough, and into this box each worshipper threw a handful of copper cash or small coin before saying his prayers. There were two or three bushels of this coin in the trough, and it is said that frequently the contributions amount to a hundred dollars' worth in a single day. The money thus obtained is expended in repairing and preserving the building, and goes to support the priests attached to the temple.

CHAPTER IX.

ASAKUSA AND YUYENO.—FIRST NATIONAL FAIR AT TOKIO.

ALL around the shrine of the temple there were prayers fastened, wherever there was a place for fastening them. On the left of the altar there was a large lattice, and this lattice had hundreds of prayers attached to it, some of them folded and others open. Several old men and women were leaning against this lattice, or squatted on the floor in front of it, engaged in selling prayers; and they appeared to be doing a thriving business. The boys bought some of these prayers to send home as curiosities; and they also bought some charms and beads, the latter not unlike those used by Catholics, and having a prominent place in the Japanese worship. Then there were votive tablets on the walls, generally in the form of pictures painted on paper or silk, or cut out of thin paper, like silhouettes. One of them represents a ship on the water in the midst of a storm, and is probably the offering of a merchant who had a marine venture that he wished to have the goddess take under her protection. Shoes and top-knots of men and women were among the offerings, and the most of them were labelled with the names of the donors. These valueless articles are never disturbed, but remain in their places for years, while costly treasures of silver or gold are generally removed in a few days to the private sanctuary of the goddess for fear of accidents. Even in a temple, all the visitors cannot be trusted to keep their hands in check. It is intimated that the priests are sometimes guilty of appropriating valuable things to their own use. But then what could you expect of a lot of heathens like the Japanese? Nothing of the kind could happen in a Christian land.

There were more attractions outside the temple than in it for our young visitors, and, after a hasty glance at the shrines in the neighborhood of the great altar, they went again into the open air.

Not far from the entrance of the temple Frank came upon a stone wheel set in a post of the same material. He looked it over with the greatest care, and wondered what kind of labor-saving machine it was. A quantity of letters and figures on the sides of the post increased his thirst for knowledge, and he longed to be able to read Japanese, so that he might know the name of the inventor of this piece of mechanism, and what it was made for.

He turned to the Doctor and asked what was the use of the post, and how it was operated.

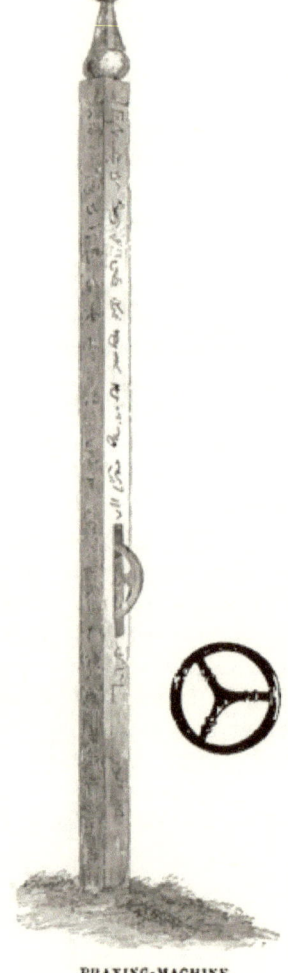

PRAYING-MACHINE.

Just as he spoke, a man passed near the machine and gave the wheel a blow that sent it spinning around with great rapidity. The man gave a glance at it to see that it was turning well, and then moved on in the direction of the temple.

"I know what that is," said Fred, who came along at the moment Frank expressed his wonder to Doctor Bronson.

"Well, what is it?"

"It's a praying-machine; I read about it the other day in a book on Japan."

"Quite right," responded the Doctor; "it is a machine used in every country where Buddhism is the religion."

Then he went on to explain that there is a formula of prayers on the sides of the post, and sometimes on the wheel, and that for each revolution of the wheel these prayers are supposed to be uttered. A devotee passes, and, as he does so, he revolves the wheel; and for each time it turns around a prayer is recorded in heaven to his credit. It follows that a man with strong arms, and possessing a knack of making the wheel spin around, can do a great deal more petitioning to Heaven than the weak and clumsy one.

Fred thought that it would be a good thing to attach these prayer-wheels to mills propelled by water, wind, or steam, and thus secure a steady and continuous revolution. The Doctor told him that this was actually done in some of the Buddhist countries, and a good many of the pious people said their prayers by machinery.

They strolled along to where there were some black-eyed girls in charge of booths, where, for a small consideration, a visitor can practise shooting with bows and arrows. The bows were very small, and the arrows were blunt at the ends. The target was a drum, and consequently the marksman's ear, rather than the eye, told when a shot was successful. The drums were generally square, and in front of each there was a little block of wood. A click on the wood showed that a shot was of more value than when it was followed by the dull boom of the drum. The girls brought tea to the boys, and endeavored to engage them in conversation, but, as there was no common language in which they could talk, the dialogue was not particularly interesting. The boys patronized the archery business, and tried a few shots with the Japanese equipments; but they found the little arrows rather difficult to handle, on account of their diminutive size. An arrow six inches long is hardly heavy enough to allow of a steady aim, and both of the youths declared they would prefer something more weighty.

Near the archery grounds there was a collection of so-called wax-works, and the Doctor paid the entrance-fees for the party to the show. These wax-works consist of thirty-six tableaux with life-size figures, and are intended to represent miracles wrought by Ku-wanon, the goddess of the temple. They are the production of one artist, who had visited the temples devoted to Ku-wanon in various parts of Japan, and determined to represent her miracles in such a way as to instruct those who were unable to make the pilgrimage, as he had done. One of the tableaux shows the goddess restoring to health a young lady who has prayed to her; another shows a woman saved from shipwreck, in consequence of having prayed to the goddess; in another a woman is falling from a ladder, but the goddess saves her from injury; in another a pious man is saved from robbers by his dog; and in another a true believer is overcoming and killing a serpent that sought to do him harm. Several of the groups represent demons and fairies, and the Japanese skill in depicting the hideous is well illustrated. One of them shows a robber desecrating the temple of the goddess; and the result of his action is hinted at by a group of demons who are about to carry him away in a cart of iron, which has been heated red-hot, and has wheels and axles of flaming fire. He does not appear overjoyed with the free ride that is in prospect for him. These figures are considered the most remarkable in all Japan, and many foreign visitors have pronounced them superior to the celebrated collection of Madame Tussaud in London. Ku-wanon is represented as a beautiful lady, and in some of the figures there is a wonderfully gentle expression to her features.

ARCHERY ATTENDANT.

Asakusa is famous for its flower-shows, which occur at frequent intervals, and, luckily for our visitors, one was in progress at the time of their pilgrimage to the temple. The Japanese are great lovers of flowers, and frequently a man will deprive himself of things of which he stands in actual need in order to purchase his favorite blossoms. As in all other countries, the women are more passionately fond of floral productions than the men; and when a flower-show is in progress, there is sure to be a large attendance of the fairer sex. Many of these exhibitions are held at night, as a great portion of the public are unable to come in the day-time on account of their occupations. At night the place is lighted up by means of torches stuck in the ground among the flowers, and the scene is quite picturesque.

A JAPANESE FLOWER-SHOW.   NIGHT SCENE.

Frank and Fred were greatly interested to find the love which the Japanese have for dwarfed plants and for plants in fantastic shapes. The native florists are wonderfully skilful in this kind of work, and some of their accomplishments would seem impossible to American gardeners. For example, they will make representations of mountains, houses, men, women, cats, dogs, boats, carts, ships under full sail, and a hundred other things—all in plants growing in pots or in the ground. To do this they take a frame of wire or bamboo in the shape of the article they wish to represent, and then compel the plant to grow around it. Day by day the plant is trained, bent a little here and a little there, and in course of time it assumes the desired form and is ready for the market. If an animal is represented, it is made more life-like by the addition of a pair of porcelain eyes; but there is rarely any other part of his figure that is formed of anything else than the living green. Our boys had a merry time among the treasures of the gardener in picking out the animate and inanimate forms that were represented, and both regretted that they could not send home some of the curious things that they found. Frank discovered a model of a house that he knew would please his sister; and he was quite sure that Miss Effie would dance with delight if she could feast her eyes on a figure of a dog, with the short nose for which the dogs of Japan are famous, and with sharp little eyes of porcelain.

Fred cared less for the models in green than he did for some dwarf trees that seemed to strike his fancy particularly. There were pines, oaks, and other trees familiar to our eyes, only an inch or two in height, but as perfectly formed as though they were of the natural size in which we see them in their native forests. Then there were bamboo, cactus, and a great many other plants that grow in Japan, but with which we are not familiar. There was such a quantity of them as to leave no doubt that the dwarfing of plants is thoroughly understood in Japan and has received much attention. Doctor Bronson told the boys that the profession of florist, like many other professions and trades, was hereditary, and that the knowledge descended from father to son. The dwarfing of plants, and their training into unnatural shapes and forms, have been practised for thousands of years, and the present state of the florist's art is the result of centuries of development.

In the flower-show and among the tea-booths the party remained at their leisure until it was time to think of going away from Asakusa and seeing something else. As they came out of the temple grounds they met a wedding party going in, and a few paces farther on they encountered a christening party proceeding in the same direction. The wedding procession consisted of three persons, and the other of four; but the principal member of the latter group was so young that he was carried in the arms of one of his companions, and had very little to say of the performances in which he was to take a prominent part. Frank observed that he did not cry, as any well-regulated baby would have done in America, and remarked upon the oddity of the circumstance. The Doctor informed him that it was not the fashion for babies to cry in Japan, unless they belonged to foreign parents.

Frank opened his eyes with astonishment. Fred did likewise.

"And is it really the case," said Frank, "that a Japanese baby never cries?"

"I could hardly say that," the Doctor answered; "but you may live a long time in Japan, and see lots of babies without hearing a cry from one of them. An American or English baby will make more noise and trouble than fifty Japanese ones. You have seen a great many small children since you landed in

A CHRISTENING IN JAPAN.

Japan, and now stop and think if you have heard one of them cry."

The boys considered a moment, and were forced to admit that, as Frank expressed it, they hadn't heard a whimper from a native infant. And they added that they were not anxious to hear any either.

The child that they saw was probably an urchin of about four weeks, as it is the custom to shave the head of an infant on the thirtieth day, or very near that date, and take him to the temple. There the priest performs a ceremonial very much like a christening with us, and for the same object. The party in the present instance consisted of a nurse carrying the child, a servant holding an umbrella to shield the nurse and child from the sun, and lastly the father of the youngster. The mother does not accompany the infant on this journey, or, at all events, it is not necessary that she should do so.

The wedding procession that our boys encountered consisted of the bride and her mother, with a servant to hold an umbrella to protect them

A WEDDING PARTY.

from the sun. Mother and daughter were richly attired, and their heads were covered with shawls heavily embroidered. Weddings in Japan do not take place in the temples, as might naturally be expected, but a part of the ceremonial is performed at the house of the bride, and the remainder at that of the bridegroom. After the wedding the bride accompanies her mother to the temple to say her prayers for a happy life, and this was the occasion which our young adventurers happened to witness.

There are many other temples in Tokio besides Asakusa, and the stranger who wishes to devote his time to the study of Japanese temples can have his wishes gratified to the fullest degree. After our party had finished the sights of Asakusa, they went to another quarter where they spent an hour among temples that were less popular, though more elegant, than those of the locality we have just described. The beauty of the architecture and the general elegance of the interior of the structures captivated them, and they unhesitatingly pronounced the religious edifices of Japan the finest they had ever seen.

They were hungry, and the Doctor suggested Uyeno. The boys did not know what Uyeno was, but concluded they would like some. Fred asked if it was really good.

The Doctor told them that Uyeno was excellent, and Frank asked how it was prepared. He was somewhat taken aback when he learned that Uyeno was not an article of food, but a place where food was to be obtained.

They went there and found a pretty park on a hill that overlooked

STROLLING SINGERS AT ASAKUSA.

a considerable portion of the city. At one side of the park there was an enclosure containing several tombs of the shogoons, or tycoons, of Japan, and there was a neat little temple that is held in great reverence, and receives annually many thousands of visitors. On an edge of the hill, where a wide view was to be had over the houses of the great capital, an enterprising Japanese had erected a restaurant, which he managed after the European manner, and was driving a profitable business. He was patronized by the foreign visitors and residents, and also by many of the Japanese officials, who had learned to like foreign cookery and customs during their journeys abroad, or were endeavoring to familiarize themselves with its peculiarities. Our friends found the restaurant quite satisfactory, and complimented the proprietor on the success of his management. It is no easy matter for a native to introduce foreign customs into his hotel in such a way as to give satisfaction to the people of the country from which the customs are taken.

Uyeno is not by any means the only elevation in Tokio from which a good view can be had of the city and surrounding country. There are several elevations where such views are obtainable, and in nearly all of them the holy mountain, Fusiyama, has a prominent place. A famous view is that of Atago Yama, and another is from Suruga Dai. Both these places are popular resorts, and abound in tea-houses, refreshment booths, swings, and other public attractions. On pleasant afternoons there is always a large attendance of the populace, and it is interesting to see them amusing themselves. There are old people, middle-aged people, youths, and infants,

VIEW FROM SURUGA DAI IN TOKIO.

the latter on the backs of their nurses, where they hang patiently on, and

A CHILD'S NURSE.

seem to enjoy their share of the fun. The quantity of tea that the natives consume in one of these afternoon entertainments is something prodigious; but they do not seem to suffer any injury from what some of us would consider a wild dissipation.

Not far from where the Doctor and his young friends were seated was an enclosure where was held the First National Fair of Tokio in 1877. The enclosure was still standing, and it was the intention of the government to hold a fair there annually, as it fully recognized the advantages of these exhibitions as educators of the people. The Japanese are not generally well informed as to the products of their own country outside of the provinces where they happen to live. A native can tell you what his own district or province produces, but he is often lamentably ignorant of the resources of other parts of the country. It is to break up this ignorance, and also to stimulate improvements in the various industries, that these national fairs have been established.

As the description of the First National Fair at Tokio may not be uninteresting, we will copy from a letter to a New York paper, by one of its correspondents who was in Japan at the time. After describing the opening ceremonies, which were attended by the emperor and empress, together with many high dignitaries of the government, he wrote as follows:

" The buildings are arranged to enclose an octagonal space, and consequently a visitor finds himself at the starting-point when he has made the rounds. The affair is in the hands of the gentlemen who controlled the

Japanese department of the Philadelphia Exhibition in 1876, and many of the features of our Centennial have been reproduced. They have Agricultural Hall, Machinery Hall, Horticultural Hall, and Fine Arts Gallery, as at the Centennial; and then they have Eastern Hall and Western Hall, which the Quaker City did not have. They have restaurants and refreshment booths, and likewise stands for the sale of small articles, such as are most likely to tempt strangers. In many respects the exhibition is quite similar to an affair of the same kind in America; and with a few changes of costume, language, and articles displayed, it might pass for a state or county fair in Maine or Minnesota.

"The display of manufactured articles is much like that in the Japanese section at Philadelphia, but is not nearly so large, the reason being that the merchants do not see as good chances for business as they did at the Centennial, and consequently they have not taken so much trouble to come in. Many of the articles shown were actually at Philadelphia, but did not find a market, and

LOVERS BEHIND A SCREEN.   A PAINTING ON SILK EXHIBITED AT THE TOKIO FAIR.

have been brought out again in the hope that they may have better luck. The bronzes are magnificent, and some of them surpass anything that was shown at the Centennial, or has ever been publicly exhibited outside of Japan. The Japanese seem determined to maintain their reputation of being the foremost workers of bronze in the world. They have also some beautiful work in lacquered ware, but their old lacquer is better than the new.

"In their Machinery Hall they have a very creditable exhibit, considering how recently they have opened the country to the Western world, and how little they had before the opening in the way of Western ideas. There is a small steam-engine of Japanese make; there are two or three looms, some rice-mills, winnowing-machines, an apparatus for winding and spinning silk, some pumps, a hay-cutter, and a fire-engine worked by hand. Then there are several agricultural machines, platform scales, pumps, and a wood-working apparatus from American makers, and there are two or three of English production. In the Agricultural Hall there are horse-rakes, mowers, reapers, and ploughs from America, and there are also some well-made ploughs from Japanese hands. In the Eastern Hall there are some delicate balances for weighing coin and the precious metals; they were made for the mint at Osaka, and look wonderfully like the best French or German balances. The Japanese have been quite successful in copying these instruments, more so than in imitating the heavier scales from America. Fairbanks's scales have been adopted as the standard of the Japanese postal and customs departments. Some of the skilful workmen in Japan thought they could make their own scales, and so they set about copying the American one. They made a scale that looked just as well, but was not accurate as a weighing-machine. As the chief use of a scale is to weigh correctly, they concluded to quit their experiments and stick to Fairbanks's.

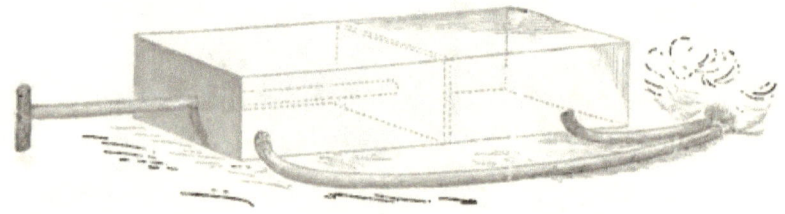

BLACKSMITH'S BELLOWS.

"There is an interesting display of the natural products of Japan, and it is exceedingly instructive to a stranger. The Japanese are studying these things with great attention, and the fair will undoubtedly prove an excellent school for the people by adding to their stock of information about themselves. Each section bears over its entrance the name of the city, province, or district it represents, and as these names are displayed in English as well as in Japanese, a stranger has no difficulty in finding out the products of the different parts of the empire. The result is that many articles are repeated in the exhibition, and you meet with them again and again. Such, for example, are raw silks, which come from various localities, as likewise do articles of leather, wood, and iron. Porcelain of various kinds appears repeatedly, and so do the woods used for making furniture. There is an excellent show of porcelain, and some of the pieces are of enormous size. Kaga, Satsuma, Hizen, Kioto, Nagasaki, and other wares are in abundance, and a student of ceramics will find enough to interest him for many hours.

"In cordage and material for ship-building there is a good exhibit, and there are two well-made models of gun-boats. Wheat, rice, millet, and other grains are represented by numerous samples, and there are several specimens of Indian-corn, or maize, grown on Japanese soil. There is a goodly array of canned fruits and meats, mostly the former, some in tin and the rest in glass. Vinegars, rice-whiskey, soy, and the like are abundant, and so is dried fish of several kinds. There is a good display of tea and tobacco, the former being in every form, from the tea-plant up to the prepared article ready for shipment. One has only to come here to see the many uses to which the Japanese put fibrous grasses in making mats, overcoats, and similar things; and there are like displays of the serviceability of bamboo. From the north of Japan there are otter and other skins, and from various points there are models of boats and nets

A GRASS OVERCOAT.

to illustrate the fishing business. The engineering department shows some fine models of bridges and dams, and has evidently made good progress since its organization."

CHAPTER X.

WALKS AND TALKS IN TOKIO.

WHILE the Doctor and his companions were at table in the restaurant at Uyeno, they were surprised by the presence of an old acquaintance. Mr. A., or "The Mystery," who had been their fellow-passenger from San Francisco, suddenly entered the room, accompanied by two Japanese officials, with whom he was evidently on very friendly terms. They were talking in English, and the two natives seemed to be quite fluent in it, but they evidently preferred to say little in the presence of the strangers. Mr. A. was equally disinclined to talk, or even to make himself known, as he simply nodded to Doctor Bronson and the boys, and then sat down in a distant corner. When the waiter came, he said something to him in a low tone, and in a few minutes the proprietor appeared, and led the way to a private room, where the American and his Japanese friends would be entirely by themselves.

As Frank expressed it, "something was up," but what that something was they did not see any prospect of ascertaining immediately. After a few moments devoted to wondering what could be the meaning of the movements of the mysterious stranger, they dropped the subject and resumed their conversation about Japan.

Fred had some questions of a religious character to propound to the Doctor. They had grown out of his observations during their visits to the temples.

"I noticed in some of the temples," said Fred, "that there were statues of Buddha and also other statues, but in other temples there were no statues of Buddha or any one else. What is the meaning of this?"

"It is because the temples belong to different forms of religion," the Doctor answered. "Those where you saw the statues of Buddha are Buddhist in their faith and form of worship, while the rest are of another kind which is called Shinto."

"And what is the difference between Buddhism and Shintoism?" Frank inquired.

"The difference," Doctor Bronson explained, "is about the same as that between the Roman Catholic faith and that of the Protestants. As I understand it—but I confess that I am not quite clear on the subject—Shintoism is the result of a reformation of the Buddhist religion, just as our Protestant belief is a reformation of Catholicism.

A HIGH-PRIEST IN FULL COSTUME.

"Now, if you want to study Buddhism," he continued, "I must refer you to a work on the religions of the world, or to an encyclopedia, as we have no time to go into a religious dissertation, and, besides, our lunch might be spoiled while we were talking. And another reason why we ought not to enter deeply into the subject is that I should find it impossible to make a clear exposition of the principles of the Buddhist faith or of Shintoism; and if you pressed me too closely, I might become confused. The religions of the East are very difficult to comprehend, and I have known men who had lived twenty years in China or India, and endeavored to study the forms and principles of the religions of those countries, who confessed their inability to understand them. For my own part, I must admit that when I have listened to explanations by Japanese, or other people of the East, of their religious faith, I have heard a great deal that I could not comprehend. I concede their sincerity; and when they say there is a great deal in our forms of worship that they do not understand, I believe they are telling the truth. Our ways of thought are not their ways, and what is clear to one is not at all so to another.

"I have already told you of the overthrow of the Shogoon, or Tycoon, and the return of the Mikado to power as the ruler of all the country. The Shogoon and his family were adherents of Buddhism, while the Mikado's followers were largely of the Shinto faith. When the Mikado's power was restored, there was a general demand on the part of the Shintoists that the Buddhist temples should be destroyed and the religion effaced. A good number of temples were demolished, and the government took

10

A JAPANESE TEMPLE.

away much of the revenue of those that remained. The temples are rapidly going to decay, as there is no money to expend on them for repairs, and it is quite possible that the beginning of the next century may
see them overthrown. Some of them are magnificent specimens of architecture, and it is a great pity that they should thus go to ruin. Adherents
of the old religion declare that the government had at one time deter-

mined to issue an order for the demolition of every Buddhist temple in the country, and only refrained from so doing through fear that it would lead to a revolution. The Shiba temple in Tokio, one of the finest in Japan, was burned under circumstances that led many persons to accuse the government of having had a hand in the conflagration, and I know there are foreigners in Tokio and Yokohama who openly denounce the authorities for the occurrence.

"As you have observed, the Buddhist temples contain the statue of Buddha, while the Shinto temples have nothing of the sort. For all practical purposes, you may compare a Buddhist temple- to a Catholic church, with its statues and pictures of the saints; and a Shinto temple to a Protestant church, with its bare walls, and its altar with no ornament of consequence. The Buddhists, like the Catholics, burn a great deal of incense in front of their altars and before their statues; but the Shintoists do not regard the burning of incense as at all necessary to salvation. Both religions have an excellent code of morals; and if all the adherents of either should do as they are told by their sacred teachers, there would not be much wickedness in the country. As for that matter, there is enough of moral precept in nearly every religion in the world to live by, but the trouble is that the whole world will not live as it should. Buddhism is more than five hundred years older than Christianity. The old forms of Shintoism existed before Buddhism was brought to Japan; but the modern is so much changed from the old that it is virtually, as I told you, a reformation of Buddhism. At all events, that was the form which it assumed at the time the Shogoon's government was overthrown.

"You have only to see the many shrines and temples in all parts of the country to know how thoroughly religious the whole population is, especially when you observe the crowds of devout worshippers that go to the temples daily. Every village, however small and poor, has its temple; and wherever you go, you see little shrines by the roadside with steps leading up to them. They are invariably in the most picturesque spots, and always in a situation that has a view as commanding as possible. You saw them near the railway as we came here from Yokohama, and you can hardly go a mile on a Japanese road without seeing one of them. The Japanese have remembered their love for the picturesque in arranging their temples and shrines, and thus have made them attractive to the great mass of the people.

"Since the opening of Japan to foreigners, the missionaries have devoted much attention to the country as a field of labor. Compared with the result of missionary labors in India, the cause has prospered, and a

A WAYSIDE SHRINE.

great deal of good has been accomplished. The Japanese are not an un-
thinking people, and their faculties of analysis are very keen. They show
more interest in the doctrines of Christianity than do the Chinese and
some other Oriental people, and are quite willing to discuss them whenever they are properly presented."

The discussion came to an end, and the party prepared to move on.
They were uncertain where to go, and, after a little time spent in debate,
the Doctor suggested that they might as well go once more to the Nihon
Bashi, or Central Bridge, and enjoy an afternoon view of the river. Off
they started, and in due time were at the famous bridge, and in the midst
of the active life that goes on in its vicinity.

The view up and down the river was an animated one. Many boats
were on the water, some of them lying at anchor, or tied up to the bank;
while others were slowly threading the stream in one way and another.
The banks of the river were lined with gay restaurants and other places
of public resort, and from some of them came the sounds of native music,
indicating that the patrons were enjoying themselves. The great mountain of Japan was in full view, and was a more welcome sight than the
crowds of beggars that lined the bridge and showed altogether too much
attention to the strangers. The bridge itself is not the magnificent structure that one might expect to find when he remembers its national impor-

tance. It is a rickety affair, built of wood, and showing signs of great antiquity; and its back rises as though somebody had attempted to lift it up by pressing his shoulders beneath and had nearly succeeded in his effort.

Near the southern end of the bridge the boys observed something like a great sign-board with a railing around it, and a roof above to keep the rain from injuring the placards which were painted beneath. The latter were in Japanese, and, of course, neither Frank nor Fred could make out their meaning. So they asked the Doctor what the structure was for and why it was in such a conspicuous place.

"That," answered the Doctor, "is the great kosatsu."

Frank said he was glad to know it, and he would be more glad when he knew what the kosatsu was.

"The kosatsu," continued Doctor Bronson, "is the sign-board where the official notices of the government are posted. You find these boards in all the cities, towns, and villages of Japan; there may be several in a city, but there is always one which has a higher character than the rest, and is known as the *great* kosatsu. The one you are now looking at is the most celebrated in the empire, as it stands near the Nihon Bashi, whence all roads are measured, as I have already explained to you."

"Please, Doctor," said Frank, "what is the nature of the notices they put on the sign-board?"

"Any public notice or law, any new order of the government, a regulation of the police, appointments of officials; in fact, anything that would be published as an official announcement in other countries. There was formerly an edict against Christians which was published all over the empire, and was on all the kosatsus. The edict appeared on the kosatsu of the Nihon Bashi down to the overthrow of the Shogoon's government, in 1868, when it was removed."

"And what was the edict?"

"It forbade Christianity in these words: 'The evil sect called Christians is strictly prohibited. Suspicious persons should be reported to the proper officers, and rewards will be given.' Directly under this edict was another, which said, 'Human beings must carefully practise the principles of the five social relations: Charity must be shown to widowers, widows, orphans, the childless, and sick. There must be no such crimes as murder, arson, or robbery.' Both these orders were dated in the month of April, 1868, and consequently are not matters of antiquity. The original edict against Christians was issued two hundred years ago, and was never revoked. St. Francis Xavier and his zealous comrades had introduced the religion of Europe into Japan, and their success was so great that the

THE GREAT KUSATSU, NEAR THE NIHON BASHI.

government became alarmed for its safety. They found proofs that the new religionists intended to subjugate the country and place it under the dominion of Spain; and in the latter part of the sixteenth and beginning of the seventeenth century there was an active persecution of the Christians. Many were expelled from the country, many more were executed, and the cause of Christianity received a blow from which it did not recover until our day. Now the missionaries are at liberty to preach the Gospel, and may make as many converts as they please."

As they walked away from the kosatsu they saw a group engaged in the childish amusement of blowing soap-bubbles. There were three persons in the group, a man and two boys, and the youngsters were as happy as American or English boys would have been under similar circumstances. While the man blew the bubbles, the boys danced around him and endeavored to catch the shining globes. Fred and Frank were much interested in the spectacle, and had it not been for their sense of dignity, and the manifest impropriety of interfering, they would have joined in the sport. The players were poorly clad, and evidently did not belong to the wealthier class; but they were as happy as though they had been princes; in fact, it is very doubtful if princes could have had a quarter as much enjoyment from the chase of soap-bubbles.

BLOWING BUBBLES.

Evening was approaching, and the party concluded to defer their sight-seeing until the morrow. They returned to the railway station, and were just in time to catch the last train of the day for Yokohama. There was a hotel at Tokio on the European system, and if they had missed the train, they would have patronized this establishment. The Doctor had spent a week there, and spoke favorably of the Sei-yo-ken, as the hotel is called.

It is kept by a Japanese, and all the servants are natives, but they manage to meet very fairly the wants of the strangers that go there. It was some time after the opening of Tokio to foreigners before there was any hotel there, and a visitor was put to great inconvenience. He was compelled to accept the hospitality of his country's representative. As he generally had no personal claims to such hospitality, he was virtually an intruder; and if at all sensitive about forcing himself where he had no business to go, his position could not be otherwise than embarrassing. The American ministers in the early days were often obliged to keep free boarding-houses, and even at the present time they are not entirely exempt from intrusions. Our diplomatic and consular representatives abroad are the victims of a vast amount of polite fraud, and some very impolite frauds in addition. It is a sad thing to say, but nevertheless true, that a disagreeably large proportion of travelling Americans in distant lands make pecuniary raids on the purses of our representatives in the shape of loans, which they never repay, and probably never intend to. Another class manages to sponge its living by quartering at the consular or diplomatic residence, and making itself as much at home as though it owned everything. There are many consuls in Europe and Asia who dread the entrance of a strange countryman into their offices, through the expectation, born of bitter experience, that the introduction is to be followed by an appeal for a loan, which is in reality a gift, and can be ill afforded by the poorly paid representative.

The next day the party returned to Tokio, but, unfortunately for their plans, a heavy rain set in and kept them indoors. Japanese life and manners are so much connected with the open air that a rainy day does not leave much opportunity for a sight-seer among the people. Finding the rain was likely to last an indefinite period, they returned to the hotel at Yokohama. The boys turned their attention to letter-writing, while the Doctor busied himself with preparations for an excursion to Hakone—a summer resort of foreigners in Japan—and possibly an ascent of Fusiyama. The boys greatly wished to climb the famous mountain; and as the Doctor had never made the journey, he was quite desirous of undertaking it, though, perhaps, he was less keen than his young companions, as he knew it could only be accomplished with a great deal of fatigue.

The letters were devoted to descriptions of what the party had seen in their visit to Tokio, and they had a goodly number of comments to make on the manners and customs of the Japanese. Frank declared that he had never seen a more polite people than the Japanese, and then he added that he had never seen any other people outside of his own country, and therefore his judgment might not be worth much. Fred had been greatly impressed with his discovery that the babies of Japan do not cry, and he suggested that the American babies would do well to follow the example of the barbarian children. Then, too, he was much pleased with the respect the children showed for their parents, and he thought the parents were very fond of their children, if he were to judge by the great number of games that were provided for the amusement of the little folks. He described what he had seen in the temple at Asakusa, and in other parts of Tokio, and enclosed a picture of a Japanese father seated with his children, the one in his arms, and the other clinging to his knee, and forming an interesting scene.

FATHER AND CHILDREN.

Frank had made a discovery about the cats of Japan, and carefully recorded it in his letter as follows:

"There are the funniest cats in this country that you ever saw. They have the shortest kind of tails, and a good many of them haven't any tails at all any more than a rabbit. You know we expect every kitten in America to play with her tail, and what can she do when she has no tail to play with? I think that must be the reason why the Japanese cats are

so solemn, and why they won't play as our cats do. I have tried to find
out how it all happens, but nobody can tell. Doctor Bronson says the kit-
tens are born without tails, and that is all he knows about it. I think they
must be a different kind of cat from ours ; but, apart from the absence of
tails, they don't look any way dissimilar. Somebody says that an American
once took one of these tailless cats to San Francisco as a curiosity, and
that it would never make friends with any long-tailed cat. It would spit
and scratch, and try to bite off the other cat's tail ; but one day, when they
put it with a cat whose tail had been cut off by a bad boy, it was friendly
at once."

Fred wanted ever so much to send home a goldfish with a very wide
and beautiful tail. The fish didn't seem to be much unlike a common
goldfish, except in the tail, which was triple, and looked like a piece of
lace. As it swam around in the water, especially when the sun was shining
on the globe, its tail seemed to have nearly as many colors as the rainbow,
and both the boys were of opinion that no more beautiful fish was ever
seen. But the proposal to send it to America was rather dampened by
the statement of the Doctor that the experiment had been tried several
times, and only succeeded in a very few instances. Almost all the fish
died on the voyage over the Pacific ; and even when they lived through
that part of the trip, the overland journey from San Francisco to the Atlantic coast generally proved too much for them. The Japanese name for
this fish is *kin-giyo*, and a pair of them may be bought for ten cents. It
is said that a thousand dollars were offered for the first one that ever
reached New York alive, which is a large advance on the price in Yokohama.

The Japanese dogs were also objects of interest to our young friends,
though less so than the cats and the goldfish. They have several varieties
of dogs in Japan, some of them being quite without hair, while others
have very thick coats. The latter are the most highly prized, and the
shorter their noses, the more valuable they are considered. Fred found a
dog, about the size of a King Charles spaniel, that had a nose only half an
inch long. He was boasting of his discovery, when Frank pointed out
one that had less than a third of an inch. Then the two kept on the hunt
for the latest improvement in dogs, as Frank expressed it, and they finally
found one that had no nose at all. The nostrils were set directly in the
end of the little fellow's head, and his under-jaw was so short that the
operations of barking and eating were not very easy to perform. In spite
of the difficulty of barking, he made a great deal of noise when the boys
attempted to examine him, and he gave Frank to understand in the most

practical way that a noseless dog can bite. As they walked away from the shop where they found him, he kept up a continual snarling, which led to the remark by Fred that a noseless dog was very far from noiseless.

As they had been kept in by the rain, Frank thought he could not do better than send to his sister a Japanese picture of a party caught in a rain-storm. He explained that the rain in Japan was quite as wet as in any other country, and that umbrellas were just as necessary as at home. He added that the Japanese umbrellas were made of paper, and kept the rain off very well, but they did not last a long time. You could buy one for half a dollar, and a very pretty one it was, and it spread out farther than the foreign umbrella did. The sticks were of bamboo, and they were covered with several thicknesses of oiled paper carefully dried in the sun. They were very much used, since nearly everybody carried an umbrella, in fair weather as well as in foul; if the umbrella was not needed against the rain, it was useful to keep off the heat of the sun, which was very severe in the middle of the day.

The letters were ready in season for the mail for America, and in due time they reached their destination and carried pleasure to several hearts. It was evident that the boys were enjoying themselves, and at the same time learning much about the strange country they had gone to see.

CAUGHT IN THE RAIN.

CHAPTER XI.

AN EXCURSION TO DAI-BOOTS AND ENOSHIMA.

A FAVORITE resort of the foreign residents of Yokohama during the summer months is the island of Enoshima. It is about twenty miles away, and is a noted place of pilgrimage for the Japanese, on account of certain shrines that are reputed to have a sacred character. Doctor Bronson arranged that his party should pay a visit to this island, as it was an interesting spot, and they could have a glimpse of Japanese life in the rural districts, and among the fishermen of the coast.

They went thither by jin-riki-shas, and arranged to stop on the way to see the famous bronze statue of Dai-Boots, or the Great Buddha. This statue is the most celebrated in all Japan, as it is the largest and finest in every way. Frank had heard and read about it; and when he learned from the Doctor that they were to see it on their way to Enoshima, he ran straightway to Fred to tell the good news.

"Just think of it, Fred," said he, "we are to see a statue sixty feet high, all of solid bronze, and a very old one it is, too."

"Sixty feet isn't so very much," Fred answered. "There are statues in Europe a great deal larger."

"But they were not made by the Japanese, as this one was," Frank responded, "and they are statues of figures standing erect, while this represents a sitting figure. A sitting figure sixty feet high is something you don't see every day."

Fred admitted that there might be some ground for Frank's enthusiasm, and, in fact, he was not long in sharing it, and thinking it was a very good thing that they were going to Enoshima, and intending to see Dai-Boots on the way.

At the appointed time they were off. They went through the foreign part of Yokohama, and through the native quarter, and then out upon the Tokaido. The boys were curious to see the Tokaido, and when they reached it they asked the Doctor to halt the jin-riki-shas, and let them press their feet upon the famous work of Japanese road-builders. The

A VILLAGE ON THE TOKAIDO.

halt was made, and gave a few minutes' rest to the men that were drawing them, and from whose faces the perspiration was running profusely.

The Tokaido, or eastern road, is the great highway that connects Kioto with Tokio—the eastern capital with the western one. There is some obscurity in its history, but there is no doubt of its antiquity. It has been in existence some hundreds of years, and has witnessed many and many a princely procession, and many a display of Oriental magnificence. It was the road by which the Daimios of the western part of the empire made their journeys to Tokio in the olden days, and it was equally the route by which the cortége of the Shogoon went to Kioto to render homage to the Mikado. It is a well-made road; but as it was built before the days of wheeled carriages, and when a track where two men could ride abreast was all that was considered requisite, it is narrower than most of us would expect to find it. In many places it is not easy for two carriages to pass without turning well out into the ditch, and there are places on the great route where the use of wheeled vehicles is impossible. But in spite of these drawbacks it is a fine road, and abounds in interesting sights.

Naturally the Tokaido is a place of activity, and in the ages that have elapsed since it was made many villages have sprung into existence along its sides. Between Yokohama and Tokio there is an almost continuous hedge of these villages, and there are places where you may ride for miles as along a densely filled street. From Tokio the road follows the shore of the bay until near Yokohama, when it turns inland; but it comes to or near the sea again in several places, and affords occasional glimpses of the great water. For several years after the admission of foreigners to Japan the Tokaido gave a great deal of trouble to the authorities, and figured repeatedly in the diplomatic history of the government. The most noted of these affairs was that in which an Englishman named Richardson was killed, and the government was forced to pay a heavy indemnity in consequence. A brief history of this affair may not be without interest, as it will illustrate the difficulties that arose in consequence of a difference of national customs.

Under the old laws of Japan it was the custom for the Daimios to have a very complete right of way whenever their trains were out upon the Tokaido or any other road. If any native should ride or walk into a Daimio's procession, or even attempt anything of the kind, he would be put to death immediately by the attendants of the prince. This was the invariable rule, and had been in force for hundreds of years. When the foreigners first came to Yokohama, the Daimios' processions were frequently on the road; and, as the strangers had the right to go into the

A PARTY ON THE TOKAIDO.

country, and consequently to ride on the Tokaido, there was a constant fear that some of them would ignorantly or wilfully violate the ancient usages and thus lead the Daimios' followers to use their swords.

Things were in this condition when one day (September 14th, 1862) the procession of Shimadzu Saburo, father of the last Daimio of Satsuma, was passing along the Tokaido on its way from the capital to the western part of the empire. Through fear of trouble in case of an encounter with the train of this prince, the authorities had previously requested foreigners not to go upon the Tokaido that day; but the request was refused, and a party of English people—three gentlemen and a lady—embraced the opportunity to go out that particular afternoon to meet the prince's train. Two American gentlemen were out that afternoon, and encountered the same train; they politely turned aside to allow the procession to pass, and were not disturbed.

When the English party met the train, the lady and one of the gentlemen suggested that they should stand at the side of the road, but Mr. Richardson urged his horse forward and said, "Come on; I have lived fourteen years in China, and know how to manage these people." He rode into the midst of the procession, and was followed by the other gentlemen, or partially so; the lady, in her terror, remained by the side of the road, as she had wished to do at the outset. The guards construed the movements of Mr. Richardson as a direct insult to their master, and fell upon him with their swords. The three men were severely wounded. Mr. Richardson died in less than half an hour, but the others recovered. The lady was not harmed in any way. On the one hand, the Japanese were a proud, haughty race who resented an insult to their prince, and punished it according to Japanese law and custom. On the other, the foreigners had the technical right, in accordance with the treaty, to go upon the Tokaido; but they offered a direct insult to the people in whose country they were, and openly showed their contempt for them. A little forbearance, and a willingness to avoid trouble by refraining from visiting the Tokaido, as requested by the Japanese authorities, would have prevented the sad occurrence.

As a result of this affair, the Japanese government was compelled to pay a hundred thousand pounds sterling to the family of Mr. Richardson, or submit to the alternative of a war with England. In addition to this, the city of Kagoshima, the residence of the Prince of Satsuma, was bombarded, the place reduced to ashes, forts, palaces, factories, thrown into ruins, and thousands of buildings set on fire by the shells from the British fleet. Three steamers belonging to the Prince of Satsuma were captured, and the prince was further compelled to pay an additional indemnity of twenty-five thousand pounds. The loss of life in the affair has never been made known by the Japanese, but it is certain to have been very great. It would not be surprising if the Japanese should entertain curious notions of the exact character of the Christian religion, when such acts are perpetrated by the nations that profess it. The blessings of civilization have been wafted to them in large proportion from the muzzles of cannon; and the light of Western diplomacy has been, all too frequently, from the torch of the incendiary.

But we must not forget our boys in our dissertation on the history of foreign intervention in Japan. In fact, they were not forgotten in it, as they heard the story from the Doctor's lips, and heard a great deal more besides. The Doctor summarized his opinion of the way the Japanese had been treated by foreigners somewhat as follows:

"The Japanese had been exclusive for a long time, and wished to continue so. They had had an experience of foreign relations two hundred years ago, and the result had well-nigh cost them their independence. It was unsatisfactory, and they chose to shut themselves up and live alone. If we wanted to shut up the United States, and admit no foreigners among us, we should consider it a matter of great rudeness if they forced themselves in, and threatened to bombard us when we refused them admittance. We were the first to poke our noses into Japan, when we sent Commodore Perry here with a fleet. The Japanese tried their best to induce us to go away and let them alone, but we wouldn't go. We stood there with the copy of the treaty in one hand, and had the other resting

BEGINNING OF RELATIONS BETWEEN ENGLAND AND JAPAN.

on a cannon charged to the muzzle and ready to fire. We said, 'Take the one or the other; sign a treaty of peace and good-will and accept the blessings of civilization, or we will blow you so high in the air that the pieces won't come down for a week.' Japan was convinced when she saw that resistance would be useless, and quite against her wishes she entered the family of nations. We opened the way and then England followed, and then came the other nations. We have done less robbing and bullying than England has, in our intercourse with Japan, and the Japanese like us better in consequence. But if it is a correct principle that no man should be disturbed so long as he does not disturb any one else, and does no harm, the outside nations had no right to interfere with Japan, and compel her to open her territory to them."

This conversation occurred while they were halted under some venerable shade-trees by the side of the Tokaido, and were looking at the people that passed. Every few minutes they saw groups varying from two to six or eight persons, very thinly clad, and having the appearance of wayfarers with a small stock of money, or none at all. The Doctor explained that these men were pilgrims on their way to holy places—some

PILGRIMS ON THE ROAD.

of them were doubtless bound for Enoshima, some for Hakone, and some for the great mountain which every now and then the turns in the road revealed to the eyes of the travellers. These pilgrimages have a religious character, and are made by thousands of persons every year. One member of a party usually carries a small bell, and as they walk along its faint tinkle gives notice of their religious character, and practically warns others that they are not commercially inclined, as they are without more money than is actually needed for the purposes of their journey. They wear broad hats to protect them from the sun, and their garments, usually of white material, are stamped with mystic characters to symbolize the particular divinity in whose honor the journey is made.

Village after village was passed by our young adventurers and their older companion, and many scenes of Japanese domestic life were un-folded to their eyes. At one place some men were engaged in removing the hulls from freshly gathered rice. The grain was in large tubs, made of a section of a tree hollowed out, and the labor was performed by beating the grain with huge mallets. The process was necessarily slow, and re-quired a great deal of patience. This mode of hulling rice has been in use in Japan for hundreds of years, and will probably continue for hun-dreds of years to come in spite of the improved machinery that is being introduced by foreigners. Rice is the principal article of food used in

THRESHING GRAIN.

Japan, and many people have hardly tasted anything else in the whole course of their lives. The opening of the foreign market has largely in-creased the cost of rice; and in this way the entrance of Japan into the family of nations has brought great hardships upon the laboring classes. It costs three times as much for a poor man to support his family as it did before the advent of the strangers, and there has not been a corresponding advance in wages. Life for the coolie was bad enough under the old form of government, and he had much to complain of. His condition has not been bettered by the new order of things, according to the observation of impartial foreigners who reside in Yokohama and other of the open ports.

About ten miles out from Yokohama the party turned from the To-kaido, and took a route through the fields. They found the track rather narrow in places; and on one occasion, when they met a party in jin-riki-shas, it became necessary to step to the ground to allow the vehicles to be lifted around. Then, too, there had been a heavy rain—the storm that cut short their visit to Tokio; and in some places the road had been washed out so that they were obliged to walk around the breaks. Their journey was consequently somewhat retarded; but they did not mind the detention, and had taken such an early start that they had plenty of time to reach Enoshima before dark. They met groups of Japanese peasants returning home from their work; and in every instance the latter made way for the strangers, and stood politely by the roadside as the manpower carriages went rolling by. Frank wanted to make sketches of some of the groups, and was particularly attracted by a woman who was carrying a teapot in one hand and a small roll or bundle under her other arm.

By her side walked a man carrying a couple of buckets slung from a pole, after the fashion so prevalent in Japan and China. He steadied the pole with his hands, and seemed quite indifferent to the presence of the foreigners. Both were dressed in loosely fitting garments, and their feet were shod with sandals of straw. The Japanese sandal is held in place by two thongs that start from near the heel on each side and come together in front. The wearer inserts the thong between the great toe and its neighbor. When he is barefooted this operation is easily performed; and, in order to accommodate his stockinged feet to the sandal, the Japanese stocking has a separate place for the "thumb-toe," as one of them called the largest of his "foot-fingers." The foot of the Japanese stocking closely resembles the mitten of America, which young women in certain localities are said to present to discarded admirers.

PEASANT AND HIS WIFE RETURNING FROM THE FIELD.

The road wound among the fields where the rice was growing luxuriantly, and where now and then they found beans and millet, and other products of Japanese agriculture. The cultivation was evidently of the most careful character, as the fields were cut here and there with little channels for irrigation; and there were frequent deposits of fertilizing materials, whose character was apparent to the nose before it was to the eye. In some places, where

A JAPANESE SANDAL.

the laborers were stooping to weed the plants, there was little more of them visible than their broad sun-hats; and it did not require a great stretch of the imagination to believe they were a new kind of mushroom from Brobdingnagian gardens. Hills like sharply rounded cones rose from each side of the narrow valley they were descending; and the dense growth of wood with which the most of them were covered made a marked contrast to the thoroughly cleared fields. The boys saw over, and over, and over again the pictures they had often seen on Japanese fans and boxes and wondered if they were realities. They had already learned that the apparently impossible pictures we find in Japanese art are not only possible, but actual; but they had not yet seen so thorough a confirmation of it as on this day's ride.

Several times they came suddenly upon villages, and very often these discoveries were quite unexpected. As they rode along the valley narrowed, and the hills became larger and more densely covered with trees. By-and-by they halted at a wayside tea-house, and were told to leave the little carriages and rest awhile. Frank protested that he was not in need of any rest; but he changed his mind when the Doctor told him that they had reached one of the objects of their journey, and that he would miss an interesting sight if he kept on. They were at the shrine of Dai-Boots.

They went up an avenue between two rows of trees, and right before them was the famous statue. It was indeed a grand work of art.

Frank made a careful note of the figures indicating the height of the statue. He found that the whole structure, including the pedestal, measured sixty feet from the ground to the top of the head, and that the figure alone was forty-three feet high. It was in a sitting, or rather a squatting, posture, with the hands partly folded and turned upwards, with the knuckles touching each other. The eyes were closed, and there was an expression of calm repose on the features such as one rarely sees in statuary. There was something very grand and impressive in this towering statue, and the boys gazed upon it with unfeigned admiration.

THE GREAT DAI-BOOTS.

Fred asked if the statue was cast in a single piece. But after asking the question, he looked up and saw that the work was evidently done in sections, as the lines where the plates or sections were joined were plainly visible. But the plates were large, and the operation of making the statue was one that required the handling of some very heavy pieces. In many places the statue was covered with inscriptions, which are said to be of a religious character.

The figure was hollow, and there was a sort of chapel inside where devout pilgrims were permitted to worship. On the platform in front there were several shrines, and the general surroundings of the place were well calculated to remind one of a sanctuary of Roman Catholicism. Thousands and thousands of pilgrims have come from all parts of Japan to worship at the feet of the great Buddha; and while our friends stood in front of the shrine, a group of devotees arrived and reverently said their prayers.

A little way off from Dai-Boots are the temples of Kamakura, which are celebrated for their sanctity, and are the objects of much veneration. They are not unlike the other temples of Japan in general appearance; but the carvings and bronze ornamentations are unusually rich, and must have cost a great deal of money. There was once a large city at Kamakura, and traces of it are distinctly visible. The approach to the temples is over some stone bridges, crossing a moat that must have been a formidable defence in the days before gunpowder was introduced into warfare.

After their sight-seeing in the grove of Dai-Boots was over, the party proceeded to Enoshima. When they arrived at the sea-shore opposite the island, they found, to their dismay, that the tide was up; and they were obliged to hire a boat to take them to their destination. At low tide one can walk upon a sand-bar the entire distance; but when the sea is at its highest, the bar is covered, and walking is not practicable. The beach slopes very gradually, and consequently the boats were at some distance out, and the travellers were compelled to wade to them or be carried on men's shoulders. The boys tried the wading, and were successful; the Doctor, more dignified, was carried on the shoulders of a stout Japanese, who was very glad of the opportunity to earn a few pennies. But he came near having a misadventure, as his bearer stumbled when close to the edge of the boat, and pitched the Doctor headlong into the craft. He was landed among a lot of baskets and other baggage, and his hat came in unpleasant contact with a bucket containing some freshly caught fish. Luckily he suffered no injury, and was able to join the others in laughing over the incident.

On their arrival at the island, it was again necessary to wade to the shore. Frank found the slippery rocks such insecure footing that he went down into the water, but was not completely immersed. The others got ashore safely, and it was unanimously voted that the next time they came to Enoshima they would endeavor to arrive when the tide was out. An involuntary bath, before one is properly dressed, or undressed, for it, is no more to be desired in Japan than in any other country.

A street leads up from the water towards the centre of the island, and along this street are the principal houses of the town. The most of these houses are hotels for the accommodation of the numerous pilgrims that come to the sacred shrines of Enoshima; and, as our party approached,

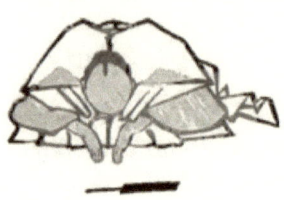

there was a movement among the attendants of the nearest hostelry to invite the strangers to enter. They halted at the door of a large building on the left. The proprietor was just inside the entrance, and bowed to them in true Japanese style, with his head touching the floor. He not only bowed to the party

SALUTATION OF THE LANDLORD.

in general, but to each one of them separately, and it took two or three minutes to go through with the preliminaries of politeness and begin negotiations for the desired accommodations.

In a little while all was arranged to the satisfaction of everybody concerned, and our friends were installed in a Japanese inn. What they did there, and what they saw, will be made known in the next chapter.

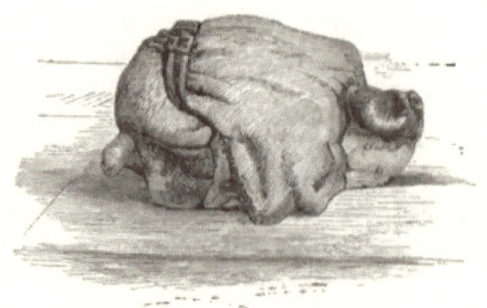

THE HEAD WAITER RECEIVING ORDERS.

CHAPTER XII.

SIGHTS AT ENOSHIMA.

THE party was shown to a large room at the rear of the house. Frank suggested that a front room would be preferable; but the Doctor told him that in a Japanese hotel the rear of the establishment was the place of honor, and that in a hundred hotels of the true national type he would probably not be located half a dozen times in a front apartment. The room where they were was very speedily divided into three smaller ones by means of paper screens, such as we find in every Japanese house, and which are known to most Americans in consequence of the large number that have been imported in the last few years. They can be shifted with the rapidity of scenes in a theatre, and the promptness with which the whole appearance of a house can be changed in a few minutes is an approach to the marvellous.

There is very little of what we call privacy in a Japanese house, as the paper screens are no obstructors of sound, and a conversation in an ordinary tone can be heard throughout the entire establishment. It is said that this form of building was adopted at a time when the government was very fearful of conspiracies, and wished to keep everybody under its supervision. Down to quite recent times there was a very complete system of espionage all over the country; and it used to be said that when three persons were together, one of them was certain to be a spy, and the other two were pretty sure to be spies as well. At the time Commodore Perry went to Japan, it was the custom to set a spy over every official to observe what he did and report accordingly. The system has been gradually dropped, but it is said to exist yet in some quarters.

It was rather late, and our party were hungry. Consequently the Doctor ordered dinner to be served as soon as possible, and they sat down to wait for it. The kitchen was near the entrance of the hotel, and in full view of the strangers as they came in. Fred could not help contrasting this arrangement with that of an American hotel, where the kitchen is quite out of sight, and not one visitor in a thousand ever gets the faintest glimpse of it. He thought the plan was well calculated to insure cleanliness in the management of the house, since the kitchen, being so prominently placed, would ruin the prosperity of the house if it were not properly kept. As there seemed to be no objection to their doing so, the boys went there and watched the preparation of the meal for which their appetites were waiting.

They found a large and well-lighted room in the centre of the house; and, as before stated, near the entrance. In the middle of this room there was a raised platform, with some little furnaces set in the floor. On this floor the cooking of some fish was going on under the supervision of a woman, who was watching to see that everything progressed satisfactorily. A few pots and pans were visible, but not a tenth of the number

A JAPANESE KITCHEN.

that would be found in the kitchen of a hotel of similar capacity in America. The Japanese cookery is not elaborate, and therefore only a few articles are required for it. A small fire in a brazier that could be carried in the hand is all that is needed to offset the enormous ranges with which we are familiar. From the roof two or three safes are hung for the preservation of such things as the dogs and cats might take a fancy to. At first glance they are frequently taken for bird-cages, and this mistake was made by Fred, who innocently remarked that he wondered what kind of birds they kept there.

At one side of the kitchen there was a long table, where the food was prepared previous to its introduction to the cooking-pot, and near this table there was a series of shelves where the plates, cups, saucers, and other articles of the dinner-service were kept. The kitchen could be shut off at night, like the other rooms, by means of paper screens, and it was here that the cook and her assistants slept when the labors of the day were over. The bedding, what little there was of it, was brought from a cupboard in one side of the room, and was altogether out of sight in the day. When not wanted, it was speedily put away, and a few minutes sufficed to convert the kitchen into a sleeping-room, or the sleeping-room into a kitchen.

BOILING THE POT.

In due time the dinner or supper, whichever it was called, was brought to our travellers, and they lost no time in sitting down to eat it; or, rather, they squatted to it, as the hotel contained no chairs, or any substitute for them. The floor was covered with clean mats—in fact, it is very difficult to find dirty mats in Japan—and our travellers had followed the universal custom of removing their boots as they entered the front door. One of the complaints that the Japanese make against foreigners is that the latter often enter their houses without removing their boots, no matter if those boots are covered with mud and bring ruin to the neat mattings. It is always polite to offer to remove your foot-covering on going inside a Japanese dwelling, and a rudeness to neglect the offer. If the weather is dry and your shoes are clean, the host will tell you to remain as you are, and then you will be quite right to do so.

There was a laugh all around at the oddity of the situation in which the boys found themselves. They tried various positions in front of the little table that had been spread for them, but no attitude they could assume was thoroughly comfortable. They squatted, they knelt, and then they sat flat on the floor, but all to no purpose. They were uncomfortable, and no mistake. But they had a merry time of it, and both Fred and Frank declared they would not have missed this dinner in Japan for a great deal. It was a novelty, and they thought their schoolmates would envy them if they knew where they were.

The dinner consisted of stewed fish for the first course, and it was so thoroughly stewed that it resembled a thick soup. Then they had cold fish with grated radishes, and, finally, a composite dish of hard-boiled eggs, cut in two, and mixed with shrimps and seaweed. The table was cleared after each course before the next was brought, and the food was served in shallow bowls, which were covered to retain the heat. At the side of each person at table there were two cups. One of these contained *soy*, a sort of vinegar flavored with spices of different kinds, and in which each mouthful of food was dipped before it was swallowed. It is said that our word "sauce" comes from the Japanese (or Chinese) word which has just been quoted. The other cup was for

FRANK'S INVENTORY.

sa-kee, a beverage which has been already mentioned in the pages of this book. They were not inclined to sa-kee; but the soy was to their taste, and Frank was especially warm in its praise.

Not liking sa-kee, they called for tea, and in a moment the servant appeared with a steaming teapot. The flavor of the herb was delicious, and the boys partook liberally of the preparation. While they were engaged in tea-drinking, Frank made an inventory of the furniture of the room for the benefit of his sister and Miss Effie, in case they should wish to fit up a room in Japanese style to welcome him home. Here is what he found:

No chairs, no sofas, no benches—nothing but the rush matting to sit upon.

No clocks, no pictures on the walls, no mirrors; in fact, the room was quite bare of ornament.

Two small tables, about twelve inches high and fifteen inches square.

These tables held the dinner and tea service, and were removed when the meal was over.

A little low stool, on which was a broad and very flat pot for holding hot water to put in the tea.

Another stool for holding anything that was not wanted at the moment.

A lamp-stand with three lamps. One was octagonal, and on the top of an upright stick; the others were oval, and hung at the ends of a horizontal bar of metal. Each lantern bore an inscription in Japanese. It was painted on the paper of which all the lanterns were composed; and as the light shone through, the letters were plainly to be seen. They were more visible than readable to our friends, as may be readily inferred.

This completed the furniture of the room. When it was removed after dinner, Frank remarked that the only furniture remaining was Doctor Bronson, Fred, and himself. And, as they were quite weary after their ride, they were disposed to be as quiet as well-regulated furniture usually is.

When it was time to go to sleep, the servant was called and the beds were made up. A thickly wadded quilt was spread on the floor for each person, and another was used for the covering. The quilt was not quite thick enough to take away all suggestion of hardness from the floor, and the covering was not the most convenient one in the world. Frank said that when the quilt was over him, he was altogether too warm, and when it was off he was too cold. Fred declared

HOW THE JAPANESE SLEEP.

that his experience was exactly like that of Frank, except that it was more so. He had been bitten by fleas during the night, and, as he couldn't speak Japanese, he could not tell them to go away—at least, not in any language they would understand. Then the walls of the room were thin, or, rather, there were no walls at all. They had heard all the noises that the house afforded; and, as pilgrims were coming and going all night, and some of those in the building were engaged in a noisy game of an unknown character, sleep was not easy. The boys were more weary after their night's rest than before they took it, and they agreed that they could not recommend a Japanese inn as the most quiet spot in the world. They rose very early, and would have been up much sooner if there had been any way of getting up.

They went down to the water-side to try the effects of a bath in the surf as it rolled in from the Pacific Ocean. They found it refreshing, and were tempted to linger long in the foam-crested waves. Near by there was a fishing-place, where several Japanese were amusing themselves with rod and line, just as American boys and men take pleasure in the same way. Fish seemed to be abundant, as they were biting freely, and it took but a short time to fill a basket. In the little harbor formed between the island and the shore several junks and boats were at anchor, and in the foreground some smaller boats were moving about. There was not an American feature to the scene, and the boys were thoroughly delighted at this perfect picture of Japanese life. It was sea-life, too; and they had island and main, water and mountain, boats and houses, all in a single glance.

The Japanese are great lovers of fish, and, fortunately for them, the coasts and bays which indent the country are well provided with finny life. The markets of Yokohama, Tokio, Osaka, and all the other great cities of Japan are well supplied with fish, and the business of catching them gives occupation to thousands of men. Many of the Japanese are fond of raw fish which has been killed at the table, and is to be eaten immediately. The fish is brought alive to the table; its eyes are then gouged out, and strong vinegar is poured into the sockets. The epicures say that this process gives a delicate flavor that can be obtained in no other way; and they argue that the fish does not suffer any more in this form of death than by the ordinary process of taking him out of the water. But since the advent of foreigners in Japan, the custom has somewhat fallen off, as the Japanese are quite sensitive to the comments that have been made concerning their cruelty.

In the interior of Japan a traveller on the great roads, and on the smaller ones too, will sometimes see a runner carrying a couple of open pans, slung at the ends of a pole over his shoulder. He will observe that these pans contain water, and that there is a single fish in each pan. The man goes at a rapid pace, and keeps his eyes on his burden, to make sure that the water is not spilled.

A JAPANESE FISHING SCENE.

These runners are in the employ of the men who supply live fish for the tables of those who live at a distance from the sea or from the lakes, and are willing to pay for the luxury. A runner stands waiting, and the instant the fish is in his charge he is off. If the distance is great, there are relays of men stationed along the route; and so the precious merchandise goes forward from one to the other without a moment's delay. Only the wealthy can afford this mode of transporting fish, as the cost is often very heavy. Some of the princes, in the olden time, were in the habit of eating fresh fish at their tables every day that had been brought in this way for a hundred and fifty miles. Great quantities of fish are still carried in this primitive manner, but not for such long distances as formerly. Many fish are transported on horseback, in barrels of water; but the most delicate and valuable are borne only on the shoulders of men, as the jolting of a horse will soon kill them.

After their bath, the boys returned with the Doctor to their breakfast in the hotel. The breakfast was almost identical with the dinner of the

"BREAKFAST IS READY."

previous evening; and as their appetites were not set so sharply, the consumption of food was not so great. After breakfast they went on a stroll through the streets of the town and up the sharp hill where it is built. The shops along the streets were filled with curiosities, made principally from shells and other marine products; and the Doctor said he was forcibly reminded of Naples, Genoa, and other seaport places along the Mediterranean. There were numerous conch-shells; and Fred was desirous of blowing them, until told by the Doctor that they had probably been blown by many of the Japanese pilgrims, and he would run the risk of contracting some troublesome disease which had been left from the sores on their lips. So the boys were cautious, and politely rejected the invitation of the dealers to make a trial of the sonorous qualities of their wares. They bought a few small shells and some pieces of shell jewelry, which would be sure to please the girls at home.

There are several small temples and shrines on the island, and the most of them are in picturesque spots in the forest, or on crags that overlook the sea. As they walked about they met parties of pilgrims on their way to these shrines; and on the summit they found a shaded resting-place, where some chairs had been set out on a cliff overlooking the broad waters of the Pacific. Two or three servants were in attendance, and our party thought they could not do better than stop awhile and sip some of the fragrant tea of Japan. So they sat down, and in a few moments the tea was before them. The tea-house was not a large one, and, as Frank expressed it, the most of the house was out of doors and under the shade of the trees.

As every one knows who has read about the country, Japan contains a great many tea-houses, or places of rest and refreshment. They are to Japan what the beer-hall is to Germany, the wine-shop to France, or the whiskey-saloon to America, with the difference in their favor that they are much more numerous, and patronized by all classes of people. The first visitors to Japan came away with erroneous notions about the character of the tea-house, and these errors have found their way into books on the country and been repeated many times, to the great scandal of the people of the empire of the Mikado. The truth is that the tea-house is a perfectly reputable and correct place in nineteen cases out of twenty. It may have a bad character in the twentieth instance, just as there is now and then a hotel in New York or other city that is the resort of thieves and various bad persons. Nearly all classes of people in Japan, who can afford to do so, resort to the tea-houses, either in the hot hours of the day or in the evening. One can purchase, in addition to tea, a variety of light refreshments, and the building is almost invariably well ventilated and prettily situated. A person may sit in public if he wishes, or he may have one of the rooms partitioned off for himself and be quite secluded. The rooms are made, as in the hotels and other houses, by means of paper partitions, and can be formed with great rapidity.

At Tokio, Osaka, Kioto, and other large and wealthy cities many of the tea-houses are so extensive that they take the name of gardens, and cover large areas of ground. The attendants are invariably girls, and the number is by no means niggardly. They are selected for their intelligence and good-looks, as the business of the house depends considerably upon the attractiveness of the servants. Their movements are graceful, and a Japanese tea-house, with its bevy of attendants, is no unpleasant

12

INTERIOR OF A TEA-GARDEN.

sight.   Foreigners in Japan are liberal patrons of the tea-houses, and many a stranger has found a cordial welcome within the walls of one of these popular establishments.

From the tea-house at the top of the hill, Doctor Bronson led the way down a steep path to the sea.   At the end of the path, and opening upon

THE PATH IN ENOSHIMA.

the sea, there is a cavern which the Japanese consider sacred.   Formerly they would not allow a stranger to enter the cavern for fear of polluting it; but at present they make no opposition, for the double reason that they have found the cave remains as if nothing had happened, and, moreover, the stranger is so willing to pay for the privilege of exploration that a considerable sum is annually obtained from him.   When the tide is in, the cave can only be entered by means of a boat; but at low-water one can creep along a narrow ledge of rock where a pathway has been cut, which he can follow to the terminus.   Our party engaged a guide with torches, and were taken to the end of the cave, where they found a hideous-looking idol that was the presiding divinity of the place.   A shrine had been erected here, and when it was lighted up the appearance was fairly imposing.   The pilgrims consider it a pious duty to visit this shrine whenever they come to the island, and it has become quite famous throughout Japan.

The boys were not inclined to stay long in the cave, as the sound of the waters beating in at the entrance was almost deafening.   They very soon sought the open air, where a new entertainment awaited them. There was a group of men and boys on the rocks at the entrance of the cavern, and they called to the strangers to throw coins into the water and see how soon they could be recovered by diving. Frank threw a small piece of silver into the clear water of the Pacific, and in an instant half a dozen boys sprang for it. One of them caught it before it reached the bottom, and came up with the piece in his mouth. Several coins were thrown, with a similar result; and finally it was proposed to let the money reach the bottom before the divers started. This was done, and, as the depth was about twelve feet, the work of finding the bit of silver was not very easy. But it was found and brought to the surface; and after the divers had been complimented on their skill, our friends moved on. It is hardly necessary to add that the money thrown into the water became the property of the youth who secured it; though it was rumored that the divers were associated, and everything obtained went into a common purse. The Oriental people are famous for their guilds, or labor and trade associations, and nearly every occupation in life is under the control of a guild, which has very arbitrary rules. It is not at all impossible that the boys who dive for small coins at Enoshima are under the control of an association, and that its rules and regulations may have been in force for hundreds of years.

As the walk through the woods would have been fatiguing, and it was near the middle of the day, when the sun was high and the heat severe, Doctor Bronson engaged a boat to take the party back to the hotel. They returned safely, and, after resting awhile, went on another walk, in a a direction slightly different from the first.

They soon found themselves among the huts of the fishermen, and the quantity of fish that lay around in various stages of preparation told that the business was not without prosperity. In a secluded part of the island they came upon a pretty summer-house, where a wealthy citizen of Tokio spent the hot months of the year. Through the gateway of the garden they had a glimpse of a group of three ladies that were evidently out for an airing. Frank thought he had never seen a prettier group in all his life, and while he looked at them he whispered his opinion to Fred.

Fred agreed with him, and then added, "I tell you what, Frank, we'll get three dresses just like those, if they don't cost too much; and when we get home, we'll have Miss Effie and your sister and my sister put them on. Then we'll arrange the garden to look like that one as much as possible, with a little furnace and teapot in front of the girls, and the pedestal of a statue near them. Won't that be nice?"

Frank agreed that it would, and, lest he should forget the arrangement of the group, he made a rough sketch of the scene, and said they could

A GROUP OF JAPANESE LADIES.

rely upon photographs for the costumes and their colors.   If they got the dresses, the girls could easily arrange them with the aid of the pictures.

When the sketch was finished, they returned to the hotel.   The tide was now out, and so the Doctor settled their account and they started for Yokohama, following the most direct route, and making no halts for sight-seeing.   They arrived late in the evening, well pleased with their excursion to Dai-Boots and Enoshima, and determined to give their friends at home a full and faithful account of what they had seen and learned.

SPECIMEN OF GROTESQUE DRAWING BY A JAPANESE ARTIST.

CHAPTER XIII.

ON THE ROAD TO FUSIYAMA.

THE morning after their return from Enoshima was mostly spent at the hotel, as all three of the excursionists were somewhat fatigued with their journey. The boys embraced the opportunity to ask the Doctor the meaning of certain things they had observed in Japan, and which had not been brought up in conversation.

"For one thing," said Frank, "why is it that so many of the people, the coolies especially, have large scars on their skins, as if they had been burned. There is hardly a coolie I have seen that is without them, and one of the men that drew my jin-riki-sha to Enoshima had his legs covered with scars, and also a fresh sore on each leg."

"Those scars," the Doctor answered, "are from the moxa, which is used to some extent in medical practice in Europe and America. Don't you remember that when your uncle Charles had a disease of the spine the doctors applied a hot iron to his back, along each side of the backbone?"

"Certainly, I remember that," Frank replied; "and it cured him, too."

"Well, that was the moxa. It is not very often used in our country, nor in Europe, but it is very common in Japan."

"I should think it would be a very painful remedy," Fred remarked, "and that a man would be quite unwilling to have it applied."

"That is the case," answered the Doctor, "with us, but it is not so here. The Japanese take the moxa as calmly as we would swallow a pill, and with far less opposition than some of us make to a common blister.

"They take the moxa for nearly everything, real or imaginary. Sometimes they have the advice of a doctor, but oftener they go to a priest, who makes a mark on them where the burn is to be applied; then they go to a man who sells the burning material, and he puts it on as a druggist with us would fill up a prescription."

"What do they use for the burning?"

"They have a little cone the size of the intended blister. It is made of the pith of a certain tree, and burns exactly like the punk with which all boys in the country are familiar. It is placed over the spot to be cauterized, and is then lighted from a red-hot coal. It burns slowly and steadily down, and in a few minutes the patient begins to squirm, and perhaps wish he had tried some milder mode of cure. Sometimes he has half a dozen of these things burning at once, and I have seen them fully an inch in diameter.

"Nearly every native has himself canterized as often as once a year by way of precaution; and if he does not feel well some morning, he is very likely to go to the temple and have an application of the moxa. It is even applied to very young children. I have seen an infant not a month old lying across its mother's knee while another woman was amusing herself by burning a couple of these pith cones on the abdomen of the child. He objected to the operation by screaming and kicking with all his might, but it was of no use. The moxa was considered good for him, and he was obliged to submit."

"Another thing," said Fred—"why is it that the grooms are covered with tattoo-marks, and wear so little clothing?"

"I cannot say exactly why it is," the Doctor replied, "further than that such is the custom. If you ask a Japanese for the reason, he will answer that it is the old custom, and I can hardly say more than he would.

"But the grooms, or 'bettos,' as the Japanese call them, are not the only ones who indulge in tattooing. You will see many of the 'sendos,' or boat-coolies, thus marked, but in a less degree than the bettos. Perhaps it is because the grooms are obliged to run so much, and consequently wish to lay aside all garments. As they must wear something, they have their skins decorated in this way, and thus have a suit of clothing always about them.

"And, speaking of these grooms, it is astonishing at what a pace they can run, and how long they will keep it up. You may go out with your carriage or on horseback, and, no matter how rapidly you go, the groom will be always at your side, and ready to take the bridle of your horse the moment you halt. They are powerful fellows, but their reputation for honesty is not first-class."

Conversation ran on various topics for an hour or more, and then Doctor Bronson announced that he would go out for a while, and hoped to give them some interesting information on his return. The boys busied themselves with their journals, and in this way a couple of hours slipped along without their suspecting how rapidly the time was flying. They were still occupied when the Doctor returned.

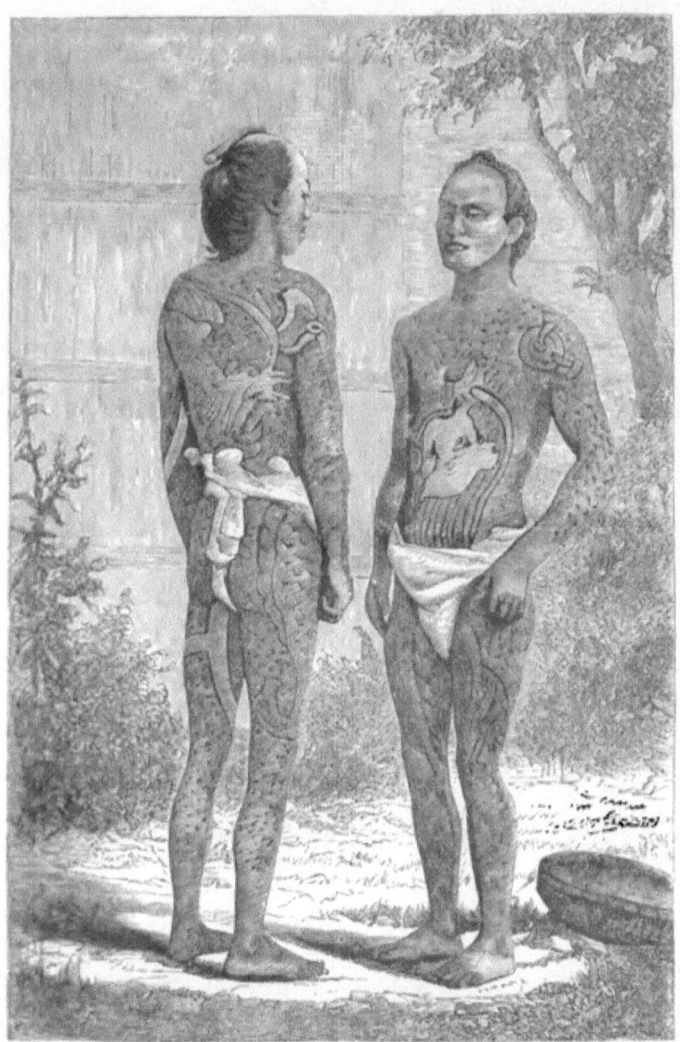

BETTOS, OR GROOMS, IN FULL DRESS.

"Well, my boys," he said, "you must be ready for another journey to-morrow. And it will be much longer and more fatiguing than the one we have just made."

"Where are we going, please?" said Frank.

"I have arranged to go to Hakone and Fusiyama," the Doctor replied; "and if we get favorable weather, and are not too tired when we arrive, we will go to the summit of the mountain."

Frank and Fred clapped their hands with delight, and thought of nothing else for some minutes than the journey to Fusiyama. It was an excursion they had wanted very much to make, and which very few visitors to Japan think of attempting. And now Doctor Bronson had arranged it for them, and they were to be off the next morning. Could anything be more fortunate?

The arrangement for the journey was somewhat more serious than the one for Enoshima. It would take several days, and for a considerable part of the way the accommodations were entirely Japanese. This might do for a trip of a day or two where no unusual fatigue was to be expected; but in a tour of considerable length, where there was likely to be much hard work, and consequently much exhaustion, it was necessary to make the most complete preparations. The Doctor foresaw this, and arranged his plans accordingly.

A Japanese who had been with parties to the holy mountain, and understood the ways and wants of the foreigners, had made a contract to accompany our friends to Fusiyama. He was to supply them with the necessary means of conveyance, servants, provisions, and whatever else they wanted. The contract was carefully drawn, and it was agreed that any points in dispute should be decided by a gentleman in Yokohama on their return.

They were off at an early hour, and, as before, their route was along the Tokaido. The provisions and other things had been sent on ahead during the night, and they did not see them until they came to the place where they were to sleep. They took a light meal before starting from Yokohama, and found a substantial breakfast waiting for them at Totsooka. Their host was a famous character in the East—an English actor who had drifted through China and Japan, and finally settled down here as a hotel-keeper.

"I met George Pauncefort in China years ago," said the Doctor, as they entered the hotel; "I wonder if he will recognize me."

George greeted the travellers with all the dignity of an emperor saluting an embassy from a brother emperor, and wished them welcome to his roof and all beneath it. Then he straightened up to the very highest line of erectness, and rested his gaze upon Doctor Bronson.

For fully a minute he stood without moving a muscle, and then struck an attitude of astonishment.

"Can it be? Yes! No! Impossible!" he exclaimed. "Do my eyes deceive me? No, they do not; it is; it must be he! it must! it must!"

Then he shook hands with the Doctor, struck another attitude of astonishment, and with the same Macbethian air turned to a servant and told him to put the steaks and the chicken on the table.

It is said by the residents of Yokohama, with whom the hotel at Totsooka is a favorite resort, that George Panneefort stirs an omelette as though he were playing Hamlet, and his conception of Sir Peter Teazle is manifested when he prepares a glass of stimulating fluid for a thirsty patron.

Various industrial processes were visible as our party rode along. Some women were weaving cotton at a native loom, and they halted the jin-riki-shas a few moments to look at the process. The loom was a very primitive affair, and the operator sat on the floor in front of it. A man who appeared to be the chief of the establishment was calmly smoking a pipe close by, and on the other side of the weaver a woman was winding some cotton thread on a spool by means of a simple reel. After looking a few moments at the loom, and the mode of weaving in Japan, the party moved on. The boys had learned to say "Sayonara" on bidding farewell to the Japanese, and they pronounced it on this occasion in the most approved style. The Japanese salutation on meeting is "Ohio," and it is pronounced exactly like the name of our Western state of which Columbus is the capital. Everywhere the Japanese greet you with "Ohio," and a stranger does not need to be long in the country to know how exceedingly polite are the people we were accustomed only a few years ago to consider as barbarians.

There is a story current in Japan of a gentleman from Cincinnati who arrived one evening in Yokohama, and the following morning went into the country for a stroll. Everywhere the men, women, and children greeted him with the customary salutation, "Ohio, ohio," and the word rang in his ears till he returned to his hotel.

He immediately sought the landlord and said, "I wish to ask if there is anything in my personal appearance that indicates what part of the States I am from."

The landlord assured him that there was no peculiarity of his costume that he could point out as any such indication.

"And yet," answered the stranger, "all the Japanese have discovered it. They knew me at a glance as a native of Ohio, as every one of them invariably said 'Ohio' when I met them. And I must give them the credit to say that they always did it very politely."

A JAPANESE LOOM.

He was somewhat astonished, and also a trifle disappointed, when he learned the exact state of affairs.

They passed a house where some artists were at work with the tools of their trade on the floor before them, forming a neat and curious collection. There were little saucers filled with paints of various colors, and the ever-present teapot with its refreshing contents. There were three persons in the group, and they kept steadily at their occupation without regarding the visitors who were looking at them. They were engaged upon pictures on thin paper, intended for the ornamentation of boxes for packing small articles of merchandise. Larger pictures are placed on an easel, as with us, but the small ones are invariably held in the hand.

ARTISTS AT WORK.

In front of a house by the roadside some coopers were hooping a vat, and Frank instantly recognized the fidelity of a picture he had seen by a native artist showing how the Japanese coopers performed their work. They make excellent articles in their line, and sell them for an astonishingly low price, when we compare them with similar things from an American maker. The fidelity of the work is to be commended, and the pails and tubs from their hands will last a long time without the least necessity of repairs.

Near the end of the first day's journey the party stopped at a Japanese inn that had been previously selected by their conductor, and there they found their baggage, and, what was quite as welcome, a substantial dinner from the hands of the cook that had been sent on ahead of them. They had sharp appetites, and the dinner was very much to their liking. It was

COOPERS HOOPING A VAT.

more foreign than Japanese, as it consisted largely of articles from America; but there was a liberal supply of boiled rice, and the savory stew of fish was not wanting.

The boys were rather surprised when they sat down to a dinner at which stewed oysters, green corn, and other things with which they were familiar at home were smoking before them; and Fred remarked that the Japanese cooking was not so unlike that of America, after all. Doctor Bronson smiled and said the cooking was done in America, and all that the Japanese cook had to do with the articles was to warm them up after opening the cans.

"And so these things come here in cans, do they?" Frank inquired.

"Certainly," the Doctor responded, "these things come here in cans, and a great many other things as well. They serve to make life endurable to an American in a distant land like Japan, and they also serve to keep him patriotic by constantly reminding him of home.

"No one," he continued, "who has not been in foreign lands, or has no direct connection with the business of canning our fruits, meats, and vegetables, can have an idea of the extent of our trade in these things. The invention of the process of preserving in a fresh state these products which are ordinarily considered perishable has enabled us to sell of our abundance, and supply the whole world with what the whole world could not otherwise obtain. You may sit down to a dinner in Tokio or Cairo, Calcutta or Melbourne, Singapore or Rome, and the entire meal may consist of canned fish, canned meats, canned fruits, or canned vegetables from the United States. A year or two ago the American consul at Bangkok, Siam, gave a Christmas dinner at which everything on the table was of home production, and a very substantial dinner it was."

"I wonder what they had for dinner that day," said Fred, with a laugh.

"As near as I can remember," the Doctor replied, "they began with oyster and clam soup. Then they had boiled codfish and fresh salmon, and, as if there were not fish enough, they had stewed eels. For meats they had turkey, chicken, ham, a goose that had been put up whole, stewed beef, roast beef, tongue, sausages, prairie chickens, ducks, and a few other things ; and as for vegetables and fruits, you can hardly name any product of our gardens and orchards that they did not have before them. For drinks they had American wines, American beer, American cider, and, besides, they had honey just out of the comb that astonished everybody with its freshness. All who were present pronounced the dinner as good as any they had ever eaten, and it made them feel very patriotic to think that everything came from home.

"You can hardly go anywhere in the world where there is an approach to civilization without finding our canned goods, as the merchants call them. They are widely known and appreciated, and well deserve the reputation they bear."

This conversation went on while the party were engaged in the consumption of the dinner, and the presence of many of the things named gave it an additional point. When they were through dinner, they took a short period of lounging on the veranda, and soon retired to rest. We can be sure they slept well, for they had had a long and weary ride.

They were off again early in the morning, and in a little while came to the banks of a river which they were to cross. Frank looked for a bridge, and saw none ; then he looked for a ferry-boat, but none was visible.

"Well," he said, half to himself, "I wonder how we are to get over to the other bank."

"There are the boatmen, but no boats," said Fred, as he pointed to some stalwart men who were sitting on the bank, and evidently waiting for something to turn up.

The mystery was soon solved. The river was neither wide nor deep, and the men they saw waiting by the bank were porters who carried people across, and also carried merchandise. The stream was said to rise very rapidly, and owing to the nature of the bottom it was difficult to maintain a bridge there for any length of time. The porters took the party across very speedily : they carried the servants by what the boys called " pick-a-back," while Doctor Bronson and the boys were borne on chairs resting on poles, with six men to each chair. Some horses belonging to another party were led through the river at the same time, and evidently were not pleased with the bath they were receiving.

Frank wondered if accidents did not happen sometimes, and asked their conductor about it. The latter told him that the Japanese law protected the traveller by requiring the head of the porter in case a person should

CROSSING THE RIVER.

be drowned in his charge. He said the law allowed no excuse, and the porter must pay with his life for any accident.

Frank thought it would be a good thing to have the same system in the management of railways in America; but then he remembered that Miss Effie's uncle, who lived in New York, was a director in a railway, and perhaps it would be just as well to say nothing about his new discovery. It might bring trouble into the family and lead to unpleasant remarks.

Since the party made their excursion to Fusiyama a bridge has been built over the river, and the occupation of the porters is gone. Some of them cling to the hope that the river will one day rise in its might, and protest against this invasion of its rights by sweeping away the structure that spans it, thus compelling travellers to return to the methods of the olden time.

From the river they proceeded to Odiwara, where they had a rest of several hours, as the town contained certain things that they wished to see. They found that foreigners were not very numerous at Odiwara, and there was considerable curiosity to see them. Whenever they halted in front of a shop, or to look at anything of interest, a crowd was speedily collected; and the longer they stood, the greater it became. But there was no impertinence, and not the least insult was offered to them; there was a manifestation of good-natured curiosity, and nothing more. Men, women, and children were equally respectful; and whenever they pressed too closely it was only necessary for the guide to say that the strangers were being inconvenienced, when the crowd immediately fell back. Every day and hour of their stay in Japan confirmed our friends more and more in the belief that there are no more polite people in the world than the Japanese.

MOTHER AND SON.

Fred tried to open a conversation with a boy who was evidently out for a walk with his mother. The little fellow was somewhat shy at first, but very soon he became entirely confident that the stranger would not harm him, and he did his best to talk. They did not succeed very well in their interchange of ideas, as neither could speak the language of the other, and so they attempted an exchange of presents. Fred gave the young native an American lead-pencil that opened and closed with a screw, and received in return the fan which the youth carried in his hand. Both appeared well pleased with the transaction, and after several bows and "sayonaras" they separated.

Frank had several fish-hooks in his pockets, and was determined not to be behind Fred in making a trade. His eye rested on a family group that was evidently returning from a fishing excursion; the man was carrying some fishing-tackle and a small bag, while the woman bore a basket of

A FISHING PARTY.

fish on her head and held a child to her breast. A boy six or eight years old was dragging a live tortoise by a string, and it occurred to Frank to free the tortoise from captivity.

So he produced one of his fish-hooks, and intimated that he would give it for the captive. There was a brief conversation between father and son, which resulted in the desired exchange. Frank handed the tortoise over to the guide, with instructions to set it free at a favorable time and place. The latter complied by delivering the prize to the cook as an agreeable addition to the bill of fare for the next meal. So the freedom of the tortoise was not exactly the kind that his liberator had intended.

But there was an unforeseen result to this transaction, for it was soon noised about among the small boys that the foreigners were giving fish-hooks for tortoises; and as there was a good supply of the latter, and not a good one of the former, there was a public anxiety to benefit by the newly opened commerce. In less than half an hour there was a movement in the market that assumed serious importance, and Frank found himself in the character of a merchant in a foreign land. He became the owner of nearly a dozen of the kindred of his first purchase, and would have kept on longer had not his stock-in-trade given out. The guide took the purchases in charge, and they followed the fate of the pioneer in the business in finding their way to the cooking-pot. When the traffic was ended, and the Japanese urchins found that the market was closed, they pronounced their "sayonaras" and withdrew as quietly as they had come.

From Odiwara the roads were worse than they had found them thus far. They had come by jin-riki-shas from Yokohama, and had had no trouble; but from this place onward they were told that the roads were not everywhere practicable for wheeled carriages. The Japanese are improving their roads every year, and therefore a description for one season does not exactly indicate the character of another. Anybody who reads this story and then goes to Japan may find good routes where formerly there were only impassable gorges, and hotels and comfortable lodging-houses where, only a year before, there was nothing of the kind. In no country in the world at the present time, with the possible exception of the Western States of North America, are the changes so rapid as in the land of the Mikado. Wheeled carriages were practically unknown before Commodore Perry landed on Japanese soil, and the railway was an innovation undreamed of in the Japanese philosophy. Now wheeled vehicles are common, and the railway is a popular institution, that bids fair to extend its benefits in many directions. Progress, progress, progress, is the motto of the Japan of to-day.

Besides the natural desire to see Odiwara, the party had another reason for their delay, which was to give the conductor time to engage cangos for their transport in such localities as would not admit of the jin-riki-sha. We will see by-and-by what the cango is.

The boys had been much amused at the appearance of a Japanese they met on the road just before reaching Odiwara, and wondered if they would be obliged to adopt that mode of riding before they finished their journey. The man in question was seated on a horse, not in the way in which we are accustomed to sit, but literally on the back of the animal. His baggage was fastened around him behind and on each side, and he was rather uncomfortably crouched (at least, so it seemed to Fred) on a flat pad like the one used by a circus-rider. A servant led the horse, and the pace was a walking one. Altogether, the appearance of the man was decidedly ludicrous, and the boys were somewhat surprised to learn that this was the ordinary way of travelling on horseback in the olden time.

THE MAN THEY MET.

Before the arrival of foreigners in Japan it was not the fashion for a traveller to be in a hurry, and, even at the present time, it is not always easy to make a native understand the value of a day or an hour. A man setting out on a journey did not concern himself about the time he would consume on the road; if the weather was unfavorable, he was perfectly willing to rest for an indefinite period, and it mattered little if he occupied three weeks in making a journey that could be covered in one. In matters of business the Japanese have not yet learned the importance of time, and the foreign merchants complain greatly of the native dilatoriness. A Japanese will make a contract to deliver goods at a certain date; on the day appointed, or perhaps a week or two later, he will inform the other party to the agreement that he will not be ready for a month or two, and he is quite unable to comprehend the indignation of the disappointed merchant. He demurely says, "I can't have the goods ready," and does not realize that he has given any cause for anger. Time is of no consequence to him, and he cannot understand that anybody else should have any regard for it. The Japanese are every year becoming more and more familiarized with the foreign ways of business, and will doubtless learn, after a while, the advantages of punctuality.

CHAPTER XIV.

THE ASCENT OF FUSIYAMA.

THEY did not get far from Odiwara before it was necessary to leave the jin-riki-shas and take to the cangos. These were found waiting for them where the road ended and the footpath began, and the boys were delighted at the change from the one mode of conveyance to the other. Doctor Bronson did not seem to share their enthusiasm, as he had been in a cango before and did not care for additional experience. He said that cango travelling was very much like eating crow—a man might do it if he tried, but he was not very likely to "hanker after it."

It required some time for them to get properly stowed in their new conveyances, as they needed considerable instruction to know how to double their legs beneath them. And even when they knew how, it was not easy to make their limbs curl into the proper positions and feel at home. Frank thought it would be very nice if he could unscrew his legs and put them on the top of the cango, where he was expected to place his boots; and Fred declared that if he could not do that, the next best thing would be to have legs of India-rubber. The cango is a box of light bamboo, with curtains that can be kept up or down, according to one's pleasure. The seat is so small that you must curl up in a way very uncomfortable for an American, but not at all inconvenient for a Japanese. It has a cushion, on which the traveller sits, and the top is so low that it is impossible to maintain an erect position. It has been in use for hundreds of years in Japan, and is not a great remove from the palanquin of India, though less comfortable. The body of the machine is slung from a pole, and this pole is upheld by a couple of coolies. The men move at a walk, and every few hundred feet they stop, rest the pole on their staffs, and shift from one shoulder to the other. This resting is a ticklish thing for the traveller, as the cango sways from side to side, and gives an intimation that it is liable to fall to the ground. It does fall sometimes, and the principal consolation in such an event is that it does not have far to go.

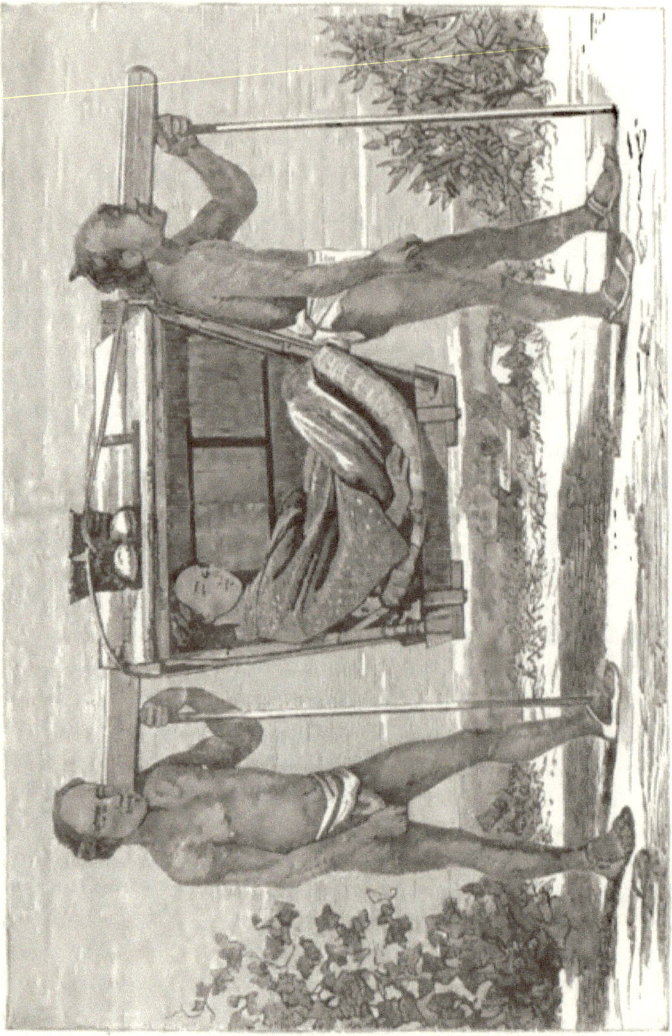

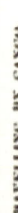

TRAVELLING BY CANGO.

A more aristocratic vehicle of this kind is the norimon. The norimon is larger than the cango, and is completely closed in at the sides, so that it may be taken as a faint imitation of our covered carriages. The princes of Japan used to travel in norimons; and they are still employed in some parts of the empire, though becoming less and less common every year. The norimon has four bearers, instead of two, and, consequently, there is much more dignity attached to its use. The rate of progress is about the same as with the cango, and after several hours in one of them a foreigner feels very much as if he were a sardine and had been packed away in a can. It was always considered a high honor to be the bearer of a princely personage; and when the great man came out in state, with his army of retainers to keep the road properly cleared, the procession was an imposing one. The style and decorations of the norimon were made to correspond with the rank of the owner, and his coat-of-arms was painted on the outside, just as one may see the coats-of-arms on private carriages in London or Paris. When a prince or other great man expected a distinguished visitor, he used to send his private norimon out a short distance on the road to meet him.

JAPANESE NORIMON.

The boys tried all possible positions in the cangos, in the hope of finding some way that was comfortable. Frank finally settled down into what he pronounced the least uncomfortable mode of riding, and Fred soon followed his example. They had taken open cangos, so as to see as much of the country as possible and have the advantage of whatever air was in circulation; and but for the inconvenience to their lower limbs, they would have found it capital fun. Frank doubled himself so that his feet were as high as his head; he gave his hat into the care of the con-

FRANK'S POSITION.

ductor, and replaced it with a cloth covering, so that he looked not much unlike a native. His bearers found him rather unwieldy, as he frequently moved about, and thus disturbed the equilibrium of the load. To ride properly in a cango or a norimon, one should not move a muscle from the time he enters till he leaves the vehicle. This may do for the phlegmatic Oriental, but is torture for a foreigner, and especially for an American.

Doctor Bronson was a tall man, and could not fold himself with as much facility as could the more supple youths. He rode a mile or so and then got out and walked; and he continued thus to alternate as long as they were travelling in this way. He was emphatic in declaring that the way to ride in a cango and enjoy it thoroughly was to walk behind it, and let somebody else take the inside of the vehicle.

Their journey brought them to Hakone, which has long been a favorite summer resort of the Japanese, and of late years is much patronized by foreigners. Those who can afford the time go there from Yokohama, Tokio, and other open ports of Japan; and during July and August there is quite a collection of English and Americans, and of other foreign nationalities. The missionaries, who have been worn down and broken in health by their exhaustive labors in the seaports during the winter, find relief and recuperation at Hakone as the summer comes on. There they gather new strength for their toils by breathing the pure air of the mountains and climbing the rugged paths, and they have abundant opportunities for doing good among the natives that reside there.

Before reaching Hakone it was necessary to traverse a mountain pass, by ascending a very steep road to the summit and then descending another. In the wildest part of the mountains they came to a little village, which has a considerable fame for its hot springs. The boys had a fancy to bathe in these springs, and, as the coolies needed a little rest after their toilsome walk, it was agreed to halt awhile. There were several of the

HOT BATH IN THE MOUNTAINS.

springs, and the water was gathered in pools, which had a very inviting appearance and increased the desire of our friends to try them. They went into one of the small rooms provided for the purpose, removed their clothing, and then plunged in simultaneously. They came out instantly, and without any request to do so by the Doctor, who stood laughing at the edge of the pool. For their skins the water was almost scalding-hot, though it was far otherwise to the Japanese. The Japanese are very fond of hot baths, and will bathe in water of a temperature so high that a foreigner cannot endure it except after long practice. The baths here in the mountains were just suited to the native taste; and Frank said they would be suited to his taste as well if they could have a few blocks of ice thrown into them.

A JAPANESE BATH.

Public and private baths are probably more numerous in Japan than in any other country. The qualities of most of the natural sources are well known, and thousands flock to them every year to be cured of real or imaginary maladies. The country contains a great number of these springs; and, since the arrival of foreigners, and a careful analysis of the waters, certain properties have been discovered that were not known before. In some cases the curative powers of the Japanese springs are remarkable, and it has been predicted that patients will one day come to Japan from distant lands to be healed.

The Lake of Hakone is a beautiful sheet of water, not unlike Lake

THE LAKE OF HAKONE.

Tahoe in California—an aquatic gem in a setting of rugged mountains.
These are not lofty, like the mountains of the Golden State, so far as their
elevation above the lake is concerned; but they rise directly from the
water, and present nearly everywhere a bold frontage. The surface of
the lake is said to be more than six thousand feet above the level of the
sea; and the water is clear and cold. Our young friends tried a bath in
the lake, and found it as inconveniently cold as the springs had been inconveniently warm. "Some people are never satisfied," said Fred, when
Frank was complaining about the temperature of the water in the lake.
"You wouldn't be contented with the springs because they boiled you,
and now you say the lake freezes you. Perhaps we'll find something by-
and-by that will come to the point."

The boys had observed that the farther they penetrated from Yokohama and Tokio, the less did they find the people affected in their dress
and manners by the presence of the foreigners. Particularly was this the
case with the women. They had seen in the open ports a good many
women with blackened teeth; and the farther they went inland, the
greater did they find the proportion of the fair sex who had thus dis-
figured themselves. So at the first opportunity they asked the Doctor
about the custom.

"I know," said Frank, "that it is the married women that blacken
their teeth; but how does it happen that there are so many more married
ones here than on the shores of Yeddo Bay?"

"You are wrong there," answered the Doctor; "there is probably as
large a proportion of married women in the one region as in the other.
The difference is that the custom is rapidly falling off."

"Is there any law about it?" Fred inquired.

"Not in the least," Doctor Bronson explained. "It is an old custom
for married women to blacken their teeth, and formerly it was most rigidly observed; but of late years, since the foreigners came to Japan, it has
not been adhered to. The Japanese see that a married woman can get
along without having her teeth discolored, and as they are inclined to fall
into the customs of Europe, the most progressive of them not only permit,
but require, their wives to keep their teeth white."

"That is one point," said Frank, "in which I think the Japanese have
gained by adopting the European custom. I don't think it improves their
appearance to put on European clothes instead of their own; but when it
comes to this habit of blackening the teeth, it is absolutely hideous."

From this assertion there was no dissent. Then the question naturally
arose, "How is the operation performed?"

Doctor Bronson explained that it was done by means of a black paint or varnish, peculiar to Japan. The paint was rubbed on the teeth with a rag or stiff brush, and made the gums very sore at first. It remained quite bright and distinct for the first few days, but in the course of a week it faded, and by the end of ten or twelve days a renewal was necessary. If left to itself, the coloring would disappear altogether within a month from the time of its application.

Frank wished to know if the women were desirous of having the custom abolished, but on this point it was not easy for him to obtain precise information. The Doctor thought it was a matter of individual rather than of general preference, and that the views of the women were largely influenced by those of their husbands. "The Japanese wives," said he, "are like the wives of most other countries, and generally wish to do according to the tastes and desires of their husbands. As you grow older you will find that the women of all lands endeavor to suit their modes of dressing and adornment to the wishes of the men with whom they come mostly in contact; of course, there are individual exceptions, but they do not weaken the force of the general rule. In America as in England, in China as in Japan, in India as in Peru, it is the fancy of the men that governs the dress and personal decoration of the other half of the race. As long as it was the fashion to blacken the teeth in this country, the women did it without a murmur; but as soon as the men showed a willingness for them to discontinue the practice, and especially when that willingness became a desire, they began to discontinue it. Twenty years from this time, I imagine, the women with blackened teeth will be less numerous than those at present with white ones.

"The abandonment of the custom began in the open ports, and is spreading through the country. It will spread in exactly the same ratio as Japan adopts other customs and ways of the rest of the world; and as fast as she takes on our Western civilization, just so fast will she drop such of her forms as are antagonistic to it."

The party rested a portion of a day at Hakone, and then went on their way. Travelling by cango had become so wearisome that they engaged a horse-train for a part of the way, and had themselves and their baggage carried on the backs of Japanese steeds. They found this an improvement on the old plan, though the horses were rather more unruly than the cango coolies, and frequently made a serious disturbance. Occasionally, when the train was ready to start, the beasts would indulge in a general kicking-match all around, to the great detriment of their burdens, whether animate or otherwise. The best and gentlest horses had been selected for

ANTICS OF THE HORSES.

riding, and consequently the greatest amount of circus performances was
with the baggage animals. The grooms had all they wished to attend to
to keep the beasts under subjection, and not infrequently they came out
of the contest with gashes and other blemishes on their variegated skins.
But they showed great courage in contending with the vicious brutes, and
it is said of a Japanese betto that he will fearlessly attack the most ill-tem-
pered horse in the country, and not be satisfied till he has conquered him.

There are several populous towns between Hakone and the base of
Fusiyama. Among them may be mentioned Missimi, Noomads, and
Harra, none of them containing any features of special importance after
the other places our friends had seen. Consequently our party did not
halt there any longer than was necessary for the ordinary demands of the
journey, but pushed on to the foot of the Holy Peak. As they approached it they met many pilgrims returning from the ascent, and their
general appearance of fatigue did not hold out a cheering prospect to the
excursionists. But they had come with the determination to make the
journey to the summit of the mountain, and were not to be frightened at
trifles. They were full of enthusiasm, for the great mountain showed
more distinctly every hour as they approached it, and its enormous and
symmetrical cone was pushed far up into the sky, and literally pierced the
clouds. At times the clouds blew away; the sunlight streamed full upon
the lofty mass of ever-during stone, and seemed to warm it into a tropical
heat. But the snow lying unmelted in the ravines dispelled the illusion,
and they knew that they must encounter chilling winds, and perhaps
biting frosts, as they ascended to the higher altitudes.

There lay the great Fusiyama, the holy mountain of Japan, which

A NEAR VIEW OF FUSIYAMA.

they had come so many thousand miles to see. In the afternoon the clouds rolled at its base, but the cone, barren as a hill in the great desert, was uncovered, and all the huge furrows of its sloping sides were distinctly to be seen. Close at hand were forests of the beautiful cedar of Japan, fields of waving corn, and other products of agriculture. Not far off were the waters of the bay that sweeps in from the ocean to near the base of the famous landmark for the mariners who approach this part of the coast. Now and then the wind brought to their ears the roar of the breakers, as they crashed upon the rocks, or rolled along the open stretches of sandy beach.

Hitherto they had been favored by the weather, but now a rain came on that threatened to detain them for an indefinite period. It blew in sharp gusts that sometimes seemed ready to lift the roof from the house where

IN A STORM NEAR FUSIYAMA.

they were lodged. The conductor explained that these storms were frequent at the base of the mountain, and were supposed by the ignorant and superstitious inhabitants of the region to be the exhibition of the displeasure of the deities of Fusiyama in consequence of something that had been done by those who professed to worship them. "When the gods are angry," said he, "we have storms, and when they are in good-humor we have fair weather. If it is very fine, we know they are happy; and when the clouds begin to gather, we know something is wrong, and it depends upon the amount of sacrifices and prayers that we offer whether the clouds clear away without a storm or not."

Near the foot of the mountain there are several monasteries, where the pilgrims are lodged and cared for when making their religious visits to the God of Fusiyama. Some of these are of considerable importance, and are far from uncomfortable as places of residence. Our party spent the night at one of these monastic settlements, which was called Muriyama, and was the last inhabited spot on the road. And as they were considerably fatigued by the ride, and a day more or less in their journey would not make any material difference, they wisely concluded to halt until the second morning, so as to have all their forces fully restored. Frank said, "This day doesn't count, as we are to do nothing but rest; and if we want to rest, we must not see anything." So they did not try to see anything; but the Doctor was careful to make sure that their conductor made all the necessary preparations for the ascent.

Early on the second morning after their arrival, they started for the final effort. They rode their horses as far as the way was practicable, and then proceeded on foot. Their baggage was mostly left in charge of the grooms to await their return, and such provisions and articles as they needed were carried by "yamabooshees," or "men of the mountain," whose special business it is to accompany travellers to the summit, and to aid them where the way is bad, or in case they become weary. If a person chooses, he may be carried all the way to the top of the mountain and back again; but such an arrangement was not to the taste of our robust adventurers. They were determined to walk, and walk they did, in spite of the entreaties of the coolies who wanted to earn something by transporting them. In addition to the yamabooshees, they had an escort of two "yoboos," or priests, from one of the temples. These men were not expected to carry burdens, but simply to serve as guides, as they were thoroughly familiar with the road and knew all its peculiarities.

The first part of their way was through a forest, but, as they ascended, the trees became smaller and fewer, and their character changed. At the base there were pines and oaks, but they gradually made way for beeches and birches, the latter being the last because the hardiest. From the forest they emerged upon the region of barren rock and earth and the fragments left by the eruptions of the volcano. The last eruption took place in 1707, and there have been few signs of any intention of returning activity since that date. But all around there are abundant traces of what the mountain was when it poured out its floods of lava and covered large areas with desolation. In some places the heaps of scoriæ appear as though the eruption, whence they came, had been but a week ago, as they are above the line of vegetation, and their character is such that

14

they undergo hardly any change from the elements from one century to another.

This part of Japan, and, in fact, the whole of Japan, has a good deal of volcanic fire pent up beneath it. Earthquakes are of frequent occurrence, and sometimes they are very destructive; whole towns have been destroyed by them, and as for the little ones that do no material damage, but simply give things a general shaking-up, they are so frequent as to be hardly noticeable. That there is an underground relation between the disturbances in different parts of the country is evident, and the tradition is that at the time of the last eruption of Fusiyama the ground rose considerably in the vicinity of the mountain, while there was a corresponding depression of the earth near Kioto, on the other side of the island. Occasionally there are slight rumblings in the interior of Fusiyama, but none of them are serious enough to excite any alarm.

From the place where our friends left their horses to the summit the distance is said to be not far from twenty miles, but it is not exactly the equivalent of twenty miles on a level turnpike or a paved street. Frank said it reminded him of a very muddy road somewhere in California, which a traveller described as nine miles long, ten feet wide, and three feet deep; and he thought a fair description of the way up the mountain would include the height and roughness as well as the length.

The path wound among the rocks and scoriæ, and through the beds of lava. Altogether they found the ascent a most trying one, and sometimes half wished that they had left the visit to Fusiyama out of their calculations when they were planning how to use their time in Japan. But it was too late to turn back now, and they kept on and on, encouraging each other with cheering words, stopping frequently to take breath and to look at the wonderful panorama that was unfolded to their gaze. The air grew light and lighter as they went on, and by-and-by the periods when they halted, panting and half suffocated, became as long as those devoted to climbing. They experienced the same difficulty that all travellers encounter at high elevations, and Fred remembered what he had read of Humboldt's ascent of the high peaks of the Andes, where the lungs seemed ready to burst and the blood spurted from the faces of himself and his companions in consequence of the rarity of the atmosphere.

About every two miles along the way they found little huts or caves, partly dug in the mass of volcanic rubbish, and partly built up, with roofs to protect the interior from the rain. These were intended as refuges for the pilgrims for passing the night or resting during storms, and had no doubt been of great service to those who preceded them. At one of these

ASCENT OF FUSIYAMA.

they halted for luncheon, which they took from the pack of one of their bearers, and later on they halted at another to pass the night. It is considered too great a journey to be made in a single day, except by persons of unusual vigor and long accustomed to mountain-climbing. The customary plan is to pass a night on the mountain when little more than half way up, and then to finish the ascent, and make the whole of the descent on the second day.

It was cold that night in the upper air, and there was a strong wind blowing that chilled our young friends to the bone. The sleeping accommodations were not of the best, as there were no beds, and they had nothing but the rugs and shawls they had brought along from the foot of the mountain. Fred asked if there was any danger of their being disturbed by tigers or snakes, and was speedily reassured by Frank, who thought that any well-educated beast or serpent would never undertake a pilgrimage to the top of Fusiyama; and if one should have strayed as far as their resting-place, he would be too much played out to attend to any business. But though large game did not abound, there was plenty of a smaller kind, as they found before they had been ten minutes in the huts. Previous visitors had left a large and well-selected assortment of fleas, for which they had no further use, and their activity indicated that they had been for some time without food. They made things lively for the strangers, and what with chilling winds, hard beds, cramped quarters, and the voracity of the permanent inhabitants of the place, there was little sleep in that hut during the time of their stay.

They were up before daylight, and, while the coffee was boiling, the boys watched the approach of morning. They looked far out over the waters of the Pacific, to where a thin line of light was curving around the rim of the horizon. At first it was so faint that it took a sharp eye to discover it, but as they watched and as the day advanced it grew more and more distinct, till it rounded out like a segment of the great circle engirdling the globe. The gleam of light became a glow that seemed to warm the waters of the shimmering ocean and flash a message of friendship from their home in another land; the heavens became purple, then scarlet, then golden, and gradually changed to the whiteness of silver. Far beneath them floated the fleecy clouds, and far beneath these were the hills of Hakone and the surrounding plain. Land and sea were spread as in a picture, and the world seemed to be lying at their feet. The boys stood spellbound and silent as they watched the opening day from the heights of Fusiyama, and finally exclaimed in a breath that they were doubly paid for all the fatigue they had passed through in their journey thus far.

The light breakfast was taken, and the adventurers moved on. At each step the way grew more and more difficult. Every mile was steeper than its predecessor, and in many instances it was rougher. The rarefaction of the air increased, and rendered the work of breathing more and more severe. The travellers panted like frightened deer, and their lungs seemed to gain little relief from the rest that the Doctor and his young friends were compelled to take at frequent intervals. The last of the huts of refuge was passed, and it seemed only a short distance to the summit. But it required more than an hour's effort to accomplish this final stage. The boys refused all offers of assistance, and struggled manfully on; but Doctor Bronson was less confident of his powers, and was glad of the aid of the strong-limbed and strong-handed yamabooshees. All were glad enough to stand on the summit and gaze into the deep gulf of the crater, while their brows were cooled by the clear breezes from the Pacific. They were at the top of Fusiyama, 14,000 feet above the level of the ocean that lay so far below them, eighty miles from their starting-point at Yokohama, and their vision swept an area of the surface of the earth nearly two hundred miles in diameter. East and south lay the broad ocean. West and north was the wondrous land of Japan, a carpet of billowy green, roughened here and there with wooded hills and small mountains, indented with bays and with silver threads of rivers meandering through it. It was a picture of marvellous beauty which no pen can describe.

They remained an hour or more on the mountain, and then began the descent. It was far easier than the upward journey, but was by no means a pleasurable affair. The boys slipped and fell several times, but, luckily, received no severe hurts; and in little more than three hours from the top they were at the spot where the horses were waiting for them. Altogether, they had been through about twelve hours of the hardest climbing they had ever known in their lives. Frank said he didn't want to climb any more mountains for at least a year, and Fred quite agreed with him. As they descended from their saddles at Muriyama, they were stiff and sore, and could hardly stand. They threw their arms around each other, and Frank said:

"The proudest day of my life—I've been to the top of Fusiyama."

"And it's my proudest day, too," Fred responded; "for I've been there with you."

As they rested that evening, Frank thought of some lines that he had seen somewhere, which were appropriate to the journey they had made, and he wound up the day's experiences by repeating them. They were as follows:

"As we climb from the vale to the high mountain's peak,
    We leave the green fields far below;
We go on through the forest, beyond it we seek
    The line of perpetual snow.
Cold and thin grows the air, the light dazzles our eyes,
    We struggle through storm-cloud and sleet;
With courage undaunted we mount toward the skies,
    Till the world spreads out at our feet.

"We are journeying now up the mountain of life,
    The green fields of youth we have passed;
We've toiled through the forest with unceasing strife,
    And gained the bright snow-line at last.
We are whitened by frost, we are chilled by the breeze—
    With weariness hardly can move;
But, faithful to duty, in our work we'll ne'er cease
    Till we look on the world from above."

CHAPTER XV.

EXECUTIONS AND HARI-KARI.

THE return to Yokohama was accomplished without any incident of consequence. Fred was a little disappointed to think that their lives had not been in peril. "Just a little danger for the fun of the thing," he remarked to Frank; and at one time on the way he was almost inclined to gloominess when he reflected on the situation. "There hasn't been any attack upon us," he said to himself, "when there might have been something of the kind just as well as not. Not that I wanted any real killing, or anything of the sort, but just a little risk of it to make things lively. It's really too bad."

He was roused from his revery by the Doctor, who told him they were approaching the spot where some Englishmen were set upon by a party of two-sworded Samurai, in the early times of the foreign occupation. The attack was entirely unprovoked, and quite without warning. One of the Englishmen was killed and another seriously wounded, while the natives escaped unharmed. Fred wanted to know the exact character of the Samurai, and why they were nearly always concerned in the attacks upon foreigners.

"It is a long story," said Doctor Bronson, "and I am not sure that you will find it altogether interesting; but it is a part of Japanese history that you ought to know, especially in view of the fact that the Samurai exist no longer. With the revolution of 1868 and the consequent overthrow of the old customs, the Samurai class was extinguished, and the wearing of two swords is forbidden.

"The population of Japan was formerly divided into four great classes. The first was the military and official class, and these are what were called Samurai; the second was the farmer class that rented the lands from the government, and engaged in agriculture; the third was the artisan class, and included all the trades and occupations of an industrial character; and the fourth was the merchant class, including all kinds of traders from the wholesale merchant to the petty peddler. Of course there were subdivi-

THE FOUR CLASSES OF SOCIETY.

sions of these classes, and sometimes several of them in a single class, but the general outline of the system is as I have stated it. Below these classes, and outside the ordinary scale of humanity, were the *Eta* and *Hinin* castes, who comprised beggars, tanners, grave-diggers, and, in fact, all persons who had anything to do with the handling of a dead body, whether human or of the lower animals. It was pollution to associate with a person of the Eta caste, and these people were compelled to dwell in villages by themselves. As they were not respected by others, they had no great respect for themselves, and lived in the most filthy condition. They could not enter a house where other people lived, and were not permitted to sit, eat, or drink with others, and they could not cook their food at the same fire.

"This was the way society in Japan was made up till the revolution of 1868, when the whole fabric was swept away, and the principles of our Declaration of Independence were adopted. The Japanese have virtually declared that all men were created equal, by putting the classes on the same level and abolishing the distinctions of caste. The Eta and Hinin castes were made citizens, the Samurai (or gentry) were deprived of their hereditary rights, and the feudal princes were compelled to turn their possessions into the hands of the general government. The change was very great for all, but for none more so than the Samurai.

"These fellows had been for centuries a class with extraordinary privileges. Their ideas in regard to work of any kind were like those of their kindred in Europe and some other parts of the world; it would degrade them to do anything, and consequently they were generally addicted to a life of idleness. There were studious and enterprising men among them, but they were the exceptions rather than the rule. The ordinary Samurai was, more or less, and usually more, a worthless fellow, whose sole idea of occupation was to follow the lord of his province and be present at ceremonials, and, for the rest, to spend his time in drinking-shops and other improper places, and indulge in occasional fights with the men of other clans. They were the only persons allowed to wear two swords; and it was the constant wearing of these swords, coupled with the drinking of sa-kee, that brought on most of the difficulties between the natives and the foreigners. A group of these men would be drinking in a tavern, and, while they were all heated with the spirits they had swallowed, one of them would propose to kill a foreigner. They would make a vow to go out and kill the first one they met, and in this mood they would leave the tavern and walk along the principal street. They would fall upon the first foreigner they met, and, as they were three or four to one, and were all well armed, the foreigner was generally slaughtered. Mr Heusken, the interpreter of the American Legation, was thus murdered at Yeddo in 1861, and the German consul at Hakodadi met his death in the same way. The Samurai were the class most opposed to the entrance of foreigners into Japan, and, so long as they were allowed to wear swords and inflame themselves with sa-kee, the life of a stranger was never safe."

"If they did no work," said Frank, "how did they manage to live?"

"They were supported by the government," the Doctor answered, "in accordance with the ancient custom. Every Samurai received an allowance, which was paid to him in rice, the staple article of food, and what he did not eat he could convert into money. His pay was in proportion to his rank, and the great number of Samurai made their support a heavy burden upon the laboring class. It is said that nine tenths of the product of the soil went, in one way and another, for taxes; that is, for every hundred bushels of rice that a farmer raised, ninety bushels went to the local and general governments, and only ten bushels remained to the farmer. It was by being thus saddled on the country that the Samurai were able to live without work, and, as the right had been conceded to them for generations, they naturally looked with contempt upon all kinds of industry. Their dissipated way of living was very likely to lead them into debt, just as it leads similar men into debt everywhere else. The merchants and tradesmen of all kinds were their victims, as the law allowed no redress for the wrongs they committed. They would sometimes enter a shop, select what goods they wanted, hand them over to a servant, and then leave without paying. If the merchant intimated that he would like to be paid for his property, they became very insolent and threatened to report him to the police as a swindler. They would enter a

TWO-SWORDED NOBLES.

tavern or tea-house with a crowd of their followers, and, after eating and drinking what they wished, walk coolly away. If the landlord asked for payment, he was not very likely to get it; and if he repeated the request, he not infrequently had his head slashed off by the sword of one of the offended gentlemen. The head of a landlord was not of much consequence; but he was generally quite unwilling to lose it, as, when once taken off, it was difficult to restore it to its place.

"If the Samurai had been on the most friendly terms with each other, they would have rendered Japan too hot for anybody else to live in. But, fortunately for the rest of the population, there were many feuds among the different clans, and there was rarely an occasion when one clan was not in open warfare with some other. In this way they devoted their energies to cutting each other's throats, to the great delight of the merchants and tradesmen. Where two clans were in hostility to each other, and two opposing groups met in the streets, they used to fall to fighting without ceremony and furnish occupation for the coroner before the interview was over. They were a terror to all the rest of the populace; and it is safe to say that there was general rejoicing among the other classes when the Samurai ceased to exist."

A SAMURAI IN WINTER DRESS.

Fred asked if the government took away the pensions of these men and gave them nothing in return.

"Not by any means," the Doctor answered. "The government gave to each man a money allowance, or gift, to take the place of his pension, and let him do with it whatever he pleased. Some of them spent it in dissipation, and found themselves eventually without a penny, and with no means of obtaining anything. They were then obliged to go to work like other people, and some of them had a very hard time to exist. I was told in Yokohama that some of the former Samurai were working as coolies in various ways, not only in that city, but all through the empire. A good many of them have found employment among the foreign merchants as clerks and salesmen, and there are many in government employ in the offices at Tokio and in other cities. The officers you saw at the custom-house were probably ex-Samurai, and ten years ago they would have been wearing two swords apiece. The Japanese book-keeper you saw in the office of the American merchant on whom we called the day of our arrival was once a Samurai of high degree. He spent his government allowance in a short time after receiving it, and was then compelled to find employment or starve. He tried the starvation system a short time, and concluded he did not like it. He turned his education to account by undertaking to keep the Japanese accounts of a foreign merchant, and his employer is well pleased with him.

"As the Samurai were the military class before the revolution, they retain the same character, to a large degree, under the present system. They are the officers of the army and navy, and, to a great extent, they fill the ranks of the soldiery. Those who accepted the change and remained loyal to the government have received appointments where there were vacancies to be filled, and the strength of Japan to-day is largely in the hands of the old Samurai. But, as might be expected, there was much discontent at the change, and some of the Samurai went into open rebellion against the government. This was the cause of the revolt in 1877, and for a time it was so formidable that many people believed it would succeed. Not a few among the foreigners predicted that the Mikado would be dethroned, and the power of the Tycoon restored; but the government triumphed in the end, and those of the leaders of the insurrection who did not perish in battle were beheaded."

Frank asked how the Japanese performed the ceremony of beheading, and whether it was very frequent.

"As to that," said Doctor Bronson, "much depends upon what you would call frequent. In former times a man might lose his head for a very slight reason, or, perhaps, no reason at all. Crimes that we would consider of small degree were punished with death, and there was very little time wasted between the sentence and its execution. As the Japanese have become more and more familiar with the customs of Western nations, they have learned that we do not remove the heads of our people for trifles, and they show their good sense by following our example. Of late years, executions by decapitation are much less frequent than formerly, but even now there are more of them than there need be.

"As to the manner of performing it, a few words will describe it. The ceremonies that precede it are somewhat elaborate, but the affair itself is performed in the twinkling of an eye, or, rather, in the twinkling of a sword. It is a single flash, and all is over.

"When I was in Japan the first time, I was invited to be present at an execution, and, as I had a scientific reason for being there, I accepted the invitation. As a friend and myself approached the prison we met a large crowd, and were told that the prisoner was being paraded through the streets, so that the public could see him. There was quite a procession to escort the poor fellow, and the people seemed to have very little sympathy for him, as they were doubtless hardened by the frequency of these occurrences. In front of the procession there were two men bearing large placards, like banners. One of the placards announced the name and residence of the victim, and the other the crime of which he had been convicted, together with his sentence. Close behind these men was the prisoner, tied to the horse on which he rode, and guarded by a couple of soldiers. Following him were more soldiers, and then came a couple of officers, with their attendants; for at that time every officer had a certain number of retainers, who followed him everywhere. We joined the party and went to the prison-yard, where we found the ground ready prepared for the execution. But first, according to the usual custom,

BEHEADING A CRIMINAL.

the prisoner was provided with a hearty breakfast; and it was rather an astonishing circumstance that he ate it with an excellent appetite, though he complained of one dish as being unhealthy. In half an hour or so he had finished, and was led to the spot where he was to lose his head. He was required to kneel behind a small hole that had been dug to receive his head; a bandage was tied around his eyes, and as it was fastened he said 'Sayonara' to his friends and everybody present. When all was ready, the officer in command gave the signal, and the executioner, with a single blow, severed the head from the body. It fell into the hole prepared for it, and was immediately picked up and washed. Then the procession was formed again, and the head was taken to a mound by the side of the road, where it was placed on a post. According to law, it was to remain there six days, as a terror to all who were disposed to do wrong. It was the first Japanese execution I ever witnessed, and my last."

Frank asked the Doctor if this execution was anything like the "hari-kari" of which he had read, where a Japanese was said to commit suicide by cutting open his stomach.

"Not by any means," was the answer; "hari-kari is quite another thing."

"Please tell us how it is performed," said Fred.

"It is not altogether a pleasant subject," remarked the Doctor, with a slight shudder; "but as we want to learn all we can of the manners and customs of the people we are among, and as we are now among the Japanese, I suppose we must give some attention to hari-kari.

"To understand the question thoroughly, it will be necessary to bear in mind that the Oriental way of thinking is very often the exact reverse of our way. We have one idea of honor and the Japanese have another; who is right or who is wrong we will not pretend to say, as each party has its own particular views and will not readily yield to the other. Writers on Japan differ considerably in their views of Japanese points of honor, and there are disagreements on the subject among the Japanese themselves; therefore I cannot speak with absolute exactness about it. According to the old code, all persons holding office under the government were required to kill themselves in the way mentioned whenever they had committed any crime, though not till they had received an order to do so from the court. If they disobeyed the order, their families would be disinherited, and none of their descendants would be allowed to hold office ever after; consequently a regard for one's family required a cheerful submission to the custom. There was no disgrace attached to a death by hari-kari, and in former times its occurrence was almost an every-day affair. One writer says, 'The sons of all persons of quality exercise themselves in their youth, for five or six years, with a view to performing the operation, in case of need, with gracefulness and dexterity; and they take as much pains to acquire this accomplishment as youth among us to become elegant dancers or skilful horsemen; hence the profound contempt of death which they imbibe in early years.' Curious custom, isn't it, according to our notions?"

Both the boys thought it was, and said they were glad that they were not born in a country where such ideas of honor prevailed.

The Doctor told them that an old story, which he had no doubt was true, since it accorded with the Japanese ideas of honor, would be a very good illustration of the subject. It was concerning two high officers of the court who met one day on a staircase, and accidentally jostled each other. One was a very quick-tempered man, and demanded satisfaction; the other was of a more peaceable disposition, and said the circumstance was accidental, and could be amply covered by an apology, which he was ready to make. The other tried to provoke him to a conflict, and when he found he could not do so he drew his short-sword and slashed himself open according to the prescribed mode. The other was compelled, as a point of honor, to follow his example. It often happened that where one man had offended another the court required that they should both perform hari-kari, and they always did so without the least hesitation. And when a man went to another's house, sat down and disembowelled himself, the owner of the house was obliged by law to do the same thing. There was no escaping it, and it is but fair to the Japanese to say that they did not try to escape it.

"If you are deeply interested in the subject of hari-kari," said the Doctor, "I advise you to read Mitford's book entitled 'Tales of Old Japan.' Mr. Mitford lived some time in Japan in an official capacity, and on one occasion he was called upon to be present at the hari-kari of an officer who had given orders for firing on some foreigners. He gives an account of this affair, including a list of the ceremonies to be observed on such an occasion, which he translated from a Japanese work on the subject. Nothing could be more precise than the regulations, and some of them are exceedingly curious, particularly the one that requires the nearest friend of the victim to act as his second. The duty of the second is to cut off the principal's head at the moment he plunges the knife into his body. It is a post of honor, and a gentleman who should refuse thus to act for his friend would be considered no friend at all. Again I say it is a curious custom all through.

"The term hari-kari means 'happy despatch,' and for the Japanese it was a happy form of going out of the world. It is still in use, the custom as well as the expression, but not so much so as formerly. The Japanese ideas of honor have not changed, but they have found that some of their ways of illustrating them are not in accordance with the customs of Europe. There are cases of hari-kari now and then at the present time, but they are very private, and generally the result of the sentence of a court. At the termination of the rebellion of 1877, several of the officers concerned in it committed hari-kari voluntarily just before the surrender, and others in consequence of their capture and sentence.

"In the administration of justice," Doctor Bronson continued, "Japan has made great progress in the past few years. Formerly nearly all trials were conducted with torture, and sometimes the witnesses were tortured as well as the accused. The instruments in use were the refinement of cruelty: heavy weights were piled on the body of a prisoner; he was placed in a caldron of water, and a fire was lighted beneath which slowly brought the water to the boiling-point; he was cut with knives in a variety of ways that indicated great ingenuity on the part of the torturers; in fact, he was put to a great deal of pain such as we know nothing about. Under the old system the only persons at a trial were the prisoner, the torturer, the secretary, and the judge; at present the trials are generally open, and the accused has the benefit of counsel to defend him, as in our own courts.

JAPANESE COURT IN THE OLD STYLE.

Torture has been formally abolished, though it is asserted that it is sometimes employed in cases of treason or other high crimes. Law-schools have been established, reform codes of law have been made, and certainly there is a manifest disposition on the part of the government to give the best system of justice to the people that can be found. Japan is endeavoring to take a place among the nations of the world, and show that she is no longer a barbarian land. The United States have been the foremost to acknowledge her right to such a place, but their action has not been seconded by England and other European countries. It will doubtless come in time, and every year sees some additional step gained in the proper direction.

"As I have before stated," the Doctor continued, "the Japanese have made great progress in military and naval matters. They have ship-yards at several places, and have built ships of their own after the European models; in addition to these, they have ships that they bought from foreigners, but they are entirely commanded and managed by their own officers, and equipped with crews entirely Japanese. The old war-junks of the country have been discarded for the modern ships, and the young Japanese are trained in the Western mode of warfare; their schools for naval instruction have made

JAPANESE NAVAL OFFICER.

remarkable advancement, and the teachers who were brought from other countries repeatedly declared that they never had seen anywhere a more intelligent assemblage of pupils than they found here. The Japanese naval officer of to-day is uniformed very much like

JAPANESE STEAM CORVETTE.

his fellow-officer in Europe or America, and his manners are as polished as the most fastidious among us could wish. The Japanese ships have made long cruises, and visited the principal ports of Europe and America, and their commanders have shown that they understand the theory and practice of navigation, and are able to take their ships wherever they may be ordered to go. The picture of a Japanese war-junk of the olden time, and that of the war-steamer of to-day do not show many points of resemblance. They illustrate the difference between the old and the new, very much as do the cango and the railway car when placed side by side."

The Doctor thought he had given the boys quite as much information as they would be likely to remember in his dissertation, and suggested that they should endeavor to recapitulate what he had said. Frank thought the discussion had taken a wide range, as it had included the status of the four classes of Japanese society, had embraced the Samurai and their peculiarities, some of the changes that were wrought by the revolu-

15

tion, and had told them how executions were conducted in former times. Then they had learned something about hari-kari and what it was for; and they had learned, at the same time, the difference between the old courts of justice and the new ones. What with these things and the naval progress of the empire of the Mikado, he thought they had quite enough to go around, and would be lucky if they remembered the whole of it.

Fred thought so too, and therefore the discussion was suspended, with the understanding that it should be renewed on the first convenient occasion.

A JAPANESE WAR-JUNK OF THE OLDEN TIME.

CHAPTER XVI.

AMUSEMENTS.—WRESTLERS AND THEATRICAL ENTERTAINMENTS.

AFTER the party had recovered from the fatigues of the journey to Fusiyama, the boys were on the lookout for something new. Various suggestions were made, and finally Frank proposed that they should go to a theatre. This was quite to Fred's liking, and so it did not take a long time to come to a determination on the subject. The Doctor agreed that the theatre was an interesting study, and so the matter was settled.

"What time in the evening must we go," said Fred, "so as to be there in season for the beginning of the performance?"

"If you want to be there in season for the beginning," the Doctor answered, "you should go in the morning, or, at all events, very early in the day."

"Wouldn't it be well to go the day before?" Frank ventured to ask.

"Certainly you could do so," Fred responded, "or you might go next week or last summer."

"The Japanese performances," Doctor Bronson continued, "do not all begin in the morning, but the most of them do, and they last the entire day. In China they have historic plays that require a week or more for their complete representation ; but in Japan they are briefer in their ways, and a performance is not continued from one day to the next. They have greater variety here than in China, and the plays are less tedious both to one who understands the language and to one who does not. The Japanese are a gayer people than the Chinese, and consequently their plays are less serious in character."

It was agreed that a day should be given to amusements, and these should include anything that the boys and their tutor could find. Frank went in pursuit of the landlord of the hotel, and soon returned with the information that there was a theatrical performance that very day in the native theatre, and also a wrestling match which was sure to be interesting, as the Japanese wrestlers are different from those of any other country. After a little discussion it was determined that they would first go to the wrestling match, and Frank should write a description of the wrestlers and what they did. After the wrestling match was disposed of, they would take up the theatre, and of this Fred should be the historian.

Here is Frank's account of the wrestling as it appeared in the next letter he sent home:

A JAPANESE WRESTLER.

"I thought we were going to a hall, but it was nothing of the sort, as we understand a hall. We went into a large tent, which was made by stretching matting over a space enclosed by a high fence; the fence formed the walls of the building, and the matting made the roof. We had the ground to sit on or stand on, but soon after we went in a man brought us some chairs, and we sat down. In the centre of the tent there was a circular mound something like a circus ring; it was perhaps two feet high and ten feet across, and there was a flat place outside of it where the master of ceremonies was to stand and see that everything was fair. We paid twenty-five cents to go in, and then we paid about five cents more for each chair; of course we were in the best places, and only a few others were in that part. I don't know how much the Japanese paid in the poor places, but I don't believe it was more than five cents.

"In a little while after we went in, the performance began. A boy came into the ring from a room at one side of the tent, and he walked as if he were playing the king, or some other great personage. When he got to the middle of the ring, he opened a fan he carried in his right hand. He opened it with a quick jerk, as though he were going to shake it to pieces; and after he had opened it he announced the names of the wrestlers who were to come into the first act. If I hadn't been told what he was doing, I should have thought he was playing something from Shakspeare, he made such a fuss about it. Then he went out and the wrestlers came in, with a big fellow that Fred said must be the boss wrestler. He looked like an elephant, he was so big.

"The wrestlers were the largest men I have seen in Japan; and the fact is I didn't suppose the country contained any men so large. As near as I could see, they had more fat than muscle on them; but there must have been a good deal of muscle, too, for they were strong as oxen. Doctor Bronson says he has seen some of these wrestlers carry two sacks of rice weighing a hundred and twenty-five pounds each, and that one man carried a sack with his teeth, while another took one under his arm and turned somersets with it, and did not once lose his hold. The Doctor says these men are a particular race of Japanese, and it used to be the custom for each prince to have a dozen or more of these wrestlers in his suite to furnish amusement for himself and his friends. Sometimes two princes would get up a match with their wrestlers, just as men in New York get up matches between dogs and chickens. Then there were troupes of wrestlers, who went around giving exhibitions, just as they sometimes do in America. But you never saw such fat men in all your life as they were; not fat in one place, like the man that keeps the grocery on

A PAIR OF WRESTLERS AND THEIR MANAGER.

the corner of the public square in our town, but fat all over. I felt the back and arms of one of them, and his muscles were as hard as iron. The flesh on his breast was soft, and seemed like a thick cushion of fat. I think you might have hit him there with a mallet without hurting him much.

"Some of them could hardly see out of their eyes on account of the fat around them; and when their arms were doubled up, they looked like the hams of a hog. I was told that the Japanese idea of a wrestler is to have a man as fat as possible, which is just the reverse of what we think is right. They train their men all their lives to have them get up all the fat they can; and if a man doesn't get it fast enough, they put him to work, and tell him he can never be a wrestler. It is odd that a people so thin as the Japanese should think so much about having men fat; but I suppose it is because we all like the things that are our opposites. But this isn't telling about the wrestling match.

"After the herald had given the names of the wrestlers who were to make the first round, the fellows came in. They were dressed without any clothes to speak of, or rather they were quite undressed, with the exception of a cloth around their loins. They came in on opposite sides of the ring, and stood there about five feet apart, each man resting his hands on his knees, and glaring at the other like a wild beast. They looked more like a pair of tigers than human beings, and for a moment I thought it was not at all unlike what a bull-fight in Spain might be.

"There they stood glaring, as I told you, and making a noise like animals about to fight. They stamped on the ground and made two or three rushes at each other, and then fell back to watch for a better chance. They kept this up a minute or so, and then darted in and clinched; and then you could see their great muscles swell, and realize that they were as strong as they were fat.

"They did not try to throw each other, as we do when we wrestle, but they tried to push from one side of the ring to the other. I couldn't understand this until the Doctor told me that it is not necessary for one of the men to be thrown. All that is to be done is for one of them to push

THE CLINCH.

the other outside the ring; and even if he only gets one foot out, the game is up. Only once during all we saw of the match did anybody get thrown down, as we should expect to see him in a wrestling match in America. And when he did get fairly on the ground, it was not very easy for him to rise, which is probably the reason why the rules of the Japanese ring are so different from ours.

"They had several matches of this kind with the two men standing up facing each other before they clinched; and then they tried another plan. One man took his place in the ring, and braced himself as though he were trying to stop a locomotive. When he was ready a signal was given, and another man came out full tilt against him. They butted their heads together like two rams, and tried to hit each other in the breast. In a short time they were covered with blood, and looked very badly; but the Doctor says they were not hurt so much as they seemed to be. They kept this up for nearly a quarter of an hour, and took turns at the business—one of them being bull for the other to play railway train against. It was as bad for one as for the other; and if I had my choice which character to play, I wouldn't play either.

"After the wrestling was over they had some fencing, which I liked much better, as there was more skill to it and less brutality. The fencers were announced in the same way as the other performers had been. They wore large masks that protected their heads, and their fencing was with wooden swords or sticks, so that no harm was done. The game was for each to hit his adversary's head, and when this was done a point was scored for the man who made the hit. They did a good deal of shouting and snarling at each other, and sometimes their noise sounded more as if made by cats than by human beings. In other respects their fencing was very much like ours, and was very creditable to the parties engaged in it. One of the best fencers in the lot was a young girl. She wasn't more than sixteen years old, and she had arms strong enough for a man of thirty. The performance ended with the fencing, and then we went back to the hotel.

It was determined that the evening would be quite early enough to go to the theatre, and so the party did not start until after seven o'clock. They secured a box at one side of the auditorium, where they could see the stage and the audience at the same time. When you go to the play in a strange land, the audience is frequently quite as interesting a study as the performance, and sometimes more so. In no country is this more truly the case than in Japan. But it was agreed that Fred should give the account of the play, and so we will listen to him. Here is his story:

"The theatre was a small one, according to our notions, but it was well ventilated, which is not always the case in America. The man that sold the tickets was very polite, and so was the one who took them at the door. The latter called an usher, who showed us to our box, and brought the chairs for us; and then he brought a programme, but we couldn't read a word of it, as it was all in Japanese. We cared more about looking at the people than trying to read something that we couldn't read at all; and so I folded up the programme and put it into my pocket.

"The house had a floor and galleries like one of our theatres, but there were only two galleries, and one of them was on a level with the parquet. The parquet, or floor, was divided into boxes, and they were literally boxes, and no mistake. They were square, and the partitions between them were little more than a foot high, with a flat board on the top for a rail. This was about five inches wide, and I soon saw what it was used for, as the people walked on it in going to and from their boxes. The boxes had no chairs in them, but they were carpeted with clean matting; and anybody could get cushions from the ushers by asking for them. Each box was intended to hold four persons; but it required that the four should not be very large, and that each should stick to his own corner. One box in front of us had six women in it, and there were two or three boxes crowded with children. They had tea and sweetmeats in many of

JAPANESE ACTOR DRESSED AS A DOCTOR.

the boxes, and I noticed that men and boys were going around selling these things. I asked if we had come to the right place, as it occurred to me that it was only at the Bowery and that kind of theatre in New York that they sold peanuts and such things; but the Doctor said it was all right, and they did this in all the best theatres in Japan.

"Of course, if they come and stay all day, they must have something to eat, and so I saw the reason of their having tea and other refreshments peddled about the house. Then there were men who sold books which gave an account of the play, and had portraits of some of the principal players. I suppose these books were really the bills of the play; and if we could have read them, we should have known something about the performance more than we do now.

"While we were looking at the audience there came half a dozen raps behind the curtain, as if two pieces of wood had been knocked together; and a moment after the rapping had stopped, the curtain was drawn aside. It was a common sort of curtain, and did not open in the middle like some of ours, or roll up like others; it was pulled aside as if it ran on a wire, and when it was out of sight we saw the stage set to represent a garden with lots of flower-pots and bushes. The stage was very small compared with an American one, and not more than ten or twelve feet deep; but it was set quite well, though not so elaborately as we would arrange it. The orchestra was in a couple of little boxes over the stage, one on each side, and each box contained six persons, three singers and three guitar-players. This is the regulation orchestra and chorus, so they say, in all the Japanese theatres, but it is sometimes differently made up. If a theatre is small and poor, it may have only two performers in each box, and sometimes one box may be empty, but this is not often.

"The orchestra furnishes music by means of the guitar, or 'samisen.' It is played something like our guitar, except that a piece of ivory is used for striking the strings, and is always used in a concert that has any pretence to being properly arranged. There are two or three other instruments, one of them a small drum, which they play upon with the fingers; but it is not so common as the samisen, and I don't think it is so well liked. Then they have flutes, and some of them are very sweet, and harmonize well with the samisen; but the singers do not like them for an accompaniment

THE SAMISEN.

unless they have powerful voices. The samisen-players generally sing, and in the theatres the musicians form a part of the chorus. A good deal of the play is explained by the chorus; and if there are any obscure points, the audience is told what they are. I remember seeing the same thing almost exactly, or, at any rate, the same thing in principle, in the performance of "Henry V." at a theatre in New York several years ago, so that this idea of having the play explained by the chorus cannot be claimed as a Japanese invention.

PLAYING THE SAMISEN.

"In the theatre the singing goes on sometimes while the actors are on the stage, and we got tired of it in a little while. I don't suppose the Japanese get so tired of it, or they would stop having it. Some of them admit that it would be better to have the orchestra in front of the stage, as we do; but others say that so long as the chorus must do so much towards explaining the play, they had better remain where they are. The Japanese seem to like their theatre as it is, and therefore they will not be apt to change in a hurry.

"Just after the curtain was pulled away, they opened a door in the middle of the garden, and the actors who were to be in the play came in. They sat down on the stage and began a song, which they kept up for ten or fifteen minutes, each of them singing a part that was evidently prepared for himself alone. The music in the little boxes joined them, and it made me think of the negro minstrels in a concert hall at home, where they all come on together. After they finished this part of the performance, there was a pantomime by a woman, or rather by a man disguised as a woman, as all the acting is done by men. They get themselves up perfectly, as they have very little beards, and they can imitate the voice and movements of a woman, so that nobody can tell the difference. I couldn't tell what the pantomime was all about, and it was so long that I got tired of it before they were through, and wondered when they would come on with something else.

SCENE FROM A JAPANESE COMEDY.—WRITING A LETTER OF DIVORCE.

"Then the real acting of the piece began, and I wished ever so much that it had been in English, so that I could understand it. The story was a supernatural one, and there were badgers and foxes in it, and they had a woman changed to a badger, and the badger to a woman again. Gentlemen who are familiar with Japanese theatres say there are many of these stories, like our Little Red Riding-hood, and other fairy tales, acted on the stage, and that the play we saw is one of the most popular, and is called 'Bumbuku Chagama,' or 'The Bubbling Teapot.' One gentleman has shown me a translation of it, and I will put it in here, just to show you what a Japanese fairy story is like.

"'Once upon a time, it is said, there lived a very old badger in the temple known as Morin-je, where there was also an iron teapot called Bumbuku Chagama, which was a precious thing in that sacred place. One day when the chief priest, who was fond of tea and kept the pot always hanging in his sitting-room, was about taking it, as usual, to make tea for drinking, a tail came out of it. He was startled, and called together all the little *bourges*, his pupils, that they might behold the apparition. Supposing it to be the mischievous work of a fox or badger, and being resolved to ascertain its real character, they made due preparations. Some of them tied handkerchiefs about their heads, and some stripped the coats from their shoulders, and armed themselves with sticks and bits of firewood. But when they were about to beat the vessel down, wings came out of it; and as it flew about from one side to another, like a dragon-fly, while they pursued it, they could neither strike nor secure it. Finally, however, hav-

SCENE FROM A JAPANESE COMEDY.—LOVE-LETTER DISCOVERED.

ing closed all the windows and sliding-doors, after hunting it vigorously from one corner to another, they succeeded in confining it in a small space, and presently in capturing it.

"'While they were consulting what to do with it, a man entered whose business it was to collect and sell waste paper, and they showed him the teapot with a view of disposing of it to him if possible. He observed their eagerness, and offered a much lower price than it was worth; but as it was now considered a disagreeable thing to have in the temple, they let him have it at his own price. He took it and hastily carried it away. He reached his home greatly pleased with his bargain, and looking forward to a handsome profit the next day, when he would sell it for what it was worth.

"'Night came on, and he lay down to rest. Covering himself with his blankets, he slept soundly.

"'But near the middle of the night the teapot changed itself into the form of a badger, and came out of the waste paper, where it had been placed. The merchant was aroused by the noise, and caught the teapot while it was in flight. By treating it kindly he soon gained its confidence and affection. In the course of time it became so docile that he was able to teach it rope-dancing and other accomplishments.

"'The report soon spread that Bumbuku Chagama had learned to dance, and the merchant was invited to go to all the great and small provinces, where he was summoned to exhibit the teapot before the great daimios, who loaded him down with gifts of gold and silver. In course of time he

TELLING THE STORY OF BUMBUKU CHAGAMA.

reflected that it was only through the teapot, which he had bought so cheap, that he became so prosperous, and felt it his duty to return it again, with some compensation, to the temple. He therefore carried it to the temple, and, telling the chief priest of his good fortune, offered to restore it, together with half the money he had gained.

"'The priest was well pleased with his gratitude and generosity, and consented to receive the gifts. The badger was made the tutelary spirit of the temple, and the name of Bumbuku Chagama has remained famous in Morin-je to this day, and will be held in remembrance to the latest ages as a legend of ancient time.'

"This is the fairy story," Fred continued, "which we saw on the stage; but it was varied somewhat in the acting, as the badger at times took the form of a woman, and afterwards that of a badger again, as I have already told you. A good deal of the acting was in pantomime, and in the scene where they are all trying to catch the teapot as it flies around the room they had quite a lively dance. We enjoyed the play very much, but I don't care to go again till I know something about the Japanese language. And a well-cushioned chair would add to the comfort of the place."

CHAPTER XVII.

A STUDY OF JAPANESE ART.

FRANK thought it was pretty nearly time to be thinking about the purchases he was to make for Mary. So he looked up the paper she gave him before his departure, and sat down to examine it. The list was not by any means a short one, and on consulting with the Doctor he learned that it would make a heavy inroad upon his stock of cash if he bought everything that was mentioned. He was rather disconcerted at the situation, but the good Doctor came to his relief.

"It is nothing unusual," said he, "for persons going abroad to be loaded down with commissions that they are unable to execute. A great many people, with the best intentions in the world, ask their friends who are going to Europe to bring back a quantity of things, without stopping to think that the purchase of those things will involve a heavy outlay that cannot be easily borne by the traveller. The majority of people who go abroad have only a certain amount of money to expend on their journeys, and they cannot afford to lock up a considerable part of that money in purchases that will only be paid for on their return, or quite as often are never paid for at all. There is a good little story on this subject, and it may be of use to you to hear it.

"A gentleman was once leaving New York for a trip to Europe, and many of his friends gave him commissions to execute for them. Some were thoughtful enough to give him the money for the articles they wanted; but the majority only said, 'I'll pay you when you get back, and I know how much it comes to.' When he returned, he told them that a singular circumstance had happened in regard to the commissions. 'The day after I sailed,' said he, 'I was in my room arranging the lists of things I was to get for my friends, and I placed the papers in two piles; those that had the money with them I put in one pile, and the money on top; and those that had no money with them I put in another pile. The wind came in and set things flying all around the room. The papers that had the money on them were held down by it, but those that had no money to keep them in place were carried out of the window and lost in the sea. And so you see how it is that the commissions that my friends gave me the money for are the only ones I have been able to execute.'

"But in the present case," said Doctor Bronson, "it is all right, as your father privately gave me the money to buy the articles your sister wants. So you can go ahead and get them without any fear that you will trench on the amount you have for your personal expenses."

The boys went on a round of shopping, and kept it up, at irregular intervals, during their stay in Japan. And in their shopping excursions they learned much about the country and people that they would not have been likely to know of in any other way.

One of the first things on the list was a silk wrapper with nice em-

FRANK'S PURCHASE.

broidery. This gave rather a wide latitude in the way of selection, and Frank was somewhat puzzled what to get. He went to the store of one of the greatest silk-merchants of Yokohama and stated his wants. He was bewildered by the variety of things placed before him, and by their great beauty in color and workmanship. There were so many pretty things for sale there that he did not know when to stop buying; and he privately admitted to Fred that it was fortunate he was restricted in the amount he was to expend, or he would be in danger of buying out the whole of the establishment. He found the goods were admirably adapted to the foreign taste, and, at the same time, they preserved the national characteristics that gave them value as the products of Japan.

He selected a robe of a delicate blue, and finely embroidered with silk of various colors. The embroideries represented flowers and leaves in curious combinations; and when the robe was placed on a frame where the light could fall full upon it, Frank thought he had never seen anything

half so pretty. And it is proper to add
that he bought two of these robes. Why
he should buy two, when he had only one
sister—and she would not be likely to want
two wrappers of the same kind—I leave
the reader to guess.

JAPANESE PATTERN-DESIGNER.

Then there were fans on the list, and
he went in pursuit of fans. He found
them, and he thus had the opportunity of
seeing the fan-makers at work. He found that there is a great variety in
the fans which the Japanese make, and that the articles vary from prices
which are astonishingly low to some which are dear in proportion. There
is such a large trade in fans that he expected to find an extensive factory,
employing hundreds of hands. He found, instead, that the fan-makers
work on a very small scale, and that one person generally does only a

FAN-MAKERS AT WORK.

small portion of the work,
then turns it over to an-
other, who does a little
more, and so on. Cer-
tain low - priced fans are
all finished in one shop;
but with the high grades
this is not the case, and,
from first to last, a fan
must pass through a good
many hands. The fan-
makers include women as
well as men in their guild;
and Frank thought it was
by no means an unpleas-
ant sight to see the wom-
en seated on the floor in
front of low benches and gracefully handling the parts of the fan that
was approaching completion in consequence of their manipulations.

Mary had been seized with the prevailing mania for Japanese porcelain, and among the things in her list she had noted especially and under-
scored the words "some good things in Japanese *cloisonné*." Frank had
seen a good many nice things in this kind of work, and he set about se-
lecting, with the help of the Doctor and Fred, the articles he was to send
home. He bought some in Yokohama, some in Tokio, and later on he

made some purchases in Kobe and Kioto. We will look at what he bought and see if his sister had reason to be pleased when the consignment reached her and was unpacked from its carefully arranged wrappings.

For hundreds of years Japan has been famous for its productions of porcelain of various kinds, from the tiny cup no larger than a lady's thimble to the elaborately decorated vase with a capacity of many gallons. Each province of Japan has its peculiar product, and sometimes one is in fashion, and sometimes another. For the last few years the favor has turned in the direction of Satsuma ware, which has commanded enormous figures, especially for the antique pieces. So great was the demand for old Satsuma that a good many manufacturers turned their attention to its production. They offer to make it to any amount, just as the wine-dealers in New York can accommodate a customer with wine of any vintage

CHINESE CLOISONNÉ ON METAL.

he requires, if he will only give them time enough to put on the proper labels. It is proper to say, on behalf of the Japanese, that they learned this trick from the foreigners; and their natural shrewdness has taught them to improve upon the lesson, so that in some instances they have actually sold to their instructors new ware for old, and convinced the purchasers of its genuineness.

We have not space enough to go into a full account of art in Japan, as a whole volume could be written on the subject without exhausting it. Frank followed the directions in Mary's note to find some good things in cloisonné; and, as he did not pay much attention to other matters, we will, for the present at least, follow his example and take a look at this branch of art in Japan.

JAPANESE CLOISONNÉ ON METAL.

Frank thought it would be proper to have his sister understand the process by which the articles she desired were prepared, and, with the assistance of Doctor Bronson, he was able to write her an account of it that she could study, and, if she chose, could read or tell to her friends. Here is what he produced on the subject:

"The term *cloisonné* comes from the French word *cloison*, which means a *field* or *enclosure*, and you will see as you go on how appropriate it is to this kind of work. If you examine the bowl which you will find in the box, you

JAPANESE BOWL.

will see that it has a groundwork of light blue, and that
on this groundwork there
are fine threads of brass
enclosing little squares and
other figures in colors quite
different from the body
of the bowl. If you look
at the cover, you will find
that these squares and figures are repeated, and also
that there are three cir-
cles, like plates with serrated edges, that seem to
be lying on the top of the
cover. These plates, or cir-
cles, have pictures of flowers

COVER OF JAPANESE BOWL.

on them, and the designs of the flowers on each one are different from
those of the other two. Every leaf and petal is distinct from the others
by means of the brass wires, and the colors do not at any time run
together.

"In the first place, the bowl of plain porcelain is ground, so that the
enamel will stick closely, which it would not do if the surface were glazed.
Then the artist makes a design, on paper, of the pattern he intends putting on the bowl. When his design is finished, he lays it on a flat surface,
and takes little pieces of brass wire which has been passed between rollers
so that it becomes flattened; these he bends with pincers, so that they take
the shape of the figure he wants to represent. Thus he goes over his
whole design until every part of the outline, every leaf, flower, and stem—
in fact, every line of his drawing—is represented by a piece of wire bent to
the exact shape. The wire then forms a series of partitions; each frag-
ment of it is a cell, or *cloison*, intended to retain the enamel in place and
keep the colors from spreading or mingling. That is the first step in the
work.

"The second step is to attach these flattened threads of wire by their
edges to the bowl. This is done by means of a fusible glass, which is
spread over the surface of the bowl in the form of paste; the bits of wire
are carefully laid in their places in the paste, and the bowl is then baked
just enough to harden the surface and make it retain the threads where
they belong. Now comes the third step.

"This consists of filling the little cells or enclosures with the proper enamel, and, to do this correctly, the original design must be carefully followed. The design is drawn in colors, and as the artist proceeds with his work he has the colors ready mixed in little cups that are ranged before him. These colors are like thick pastes of powdered glass mixed with the proper pigments, and one by one the cells of the surface are filled up. Then the groundwork is filled in the same way; and when all this is done, the bowl is put into the oven and submitted to a strong heat.

"The baking serves to fix the colors firmly in their cells, as the fire is hot enough to melt the glass slightly and fuse it to a perfect union with the body of the bowl. For common work, a single coating of enamel and a single baking are sufficient, but for the finer grades this will not answer. Another coating of colors is laid on, and perhaps a third or a fourth, and after each application the bowl is baked again. When this process is finished, the surface is rough, and the bowl is not anything like what we see it now. It must be polished smooth, and, with this object, it is ground and rubbed, first with coarse stones, then with finer ones, then with emery, and finally with powdered charcoal. In this way the bowl was brought to the condition in which you will find it, if it comes all right and uninjured from the box. A good many pieces of this ware are broken in the handling, and consequently they add to the price of those that come out unharmed.

"The fine threads of brass that run through the surface give a very pretty appearance to the work, as they look like gold, and are perfectly even with the rest of what has been laid on to the original bowl. In some of the most expensive of the enamel-work the threads are of fine gold instead of brass; but there is no particular advantage in having them of gold, as the brass answers all purposes and the gold serves as a temptation to robbers. There is an endless variety of designs in *cloisonné* work, and you see so many pretty things in porcelain that you are at a loss what to choose.

"But the artists do not confine themselves to porcelain; they do a great deal of enamelling on metal, and some of their productions in this way are quite as interesting as their enamelling on porcelain. They did not invent the art, so it is said, but borrowed it from the Chinese, who had in their turn borrowed it from Persia or some other of the Central Asiatic countries. Some of the Japanese artists claim that the art was borrowed from their country, but the most of those who have studied the subject say that this claim is incorrect. But no matter who invented the process, it is very beautiful and is of great antiquity; it is capable of a great many variations, and, although it has been in use for centuries, hardly a year passes without some improvements in it. In making the metal enamels the strips of brass are soldered to the surface and the cavities are filled up with the liquid coloring. The whole is then baked as in the porcelain process, and the surface of the work is carefully polished until all the lines are fully developed and the completed article shines like glass.

"I shall send you," Frank added, "several specimens of this kind of work, and I am sure that all of you will be delighted with them. In addition to the Japanese enamel, I have been able to pick up a few from

CHINESE METAL VASE.

China by the help of a gentleman who has been a long time in the country, and knows where to get the best things. And as I can't get all I want, I shall send you some pictures of very rare specimens, and you can judge by them of the quality of what you have. It is very difficult to find some of the varieties, as there have been a good many men out here making purchases for the New York and London markets, and they gather up everything that is curious. The demand is so great that the Japanese makers have all they can do to supply it; but I suppose that in a few years the taste of the public will change, and then you can buy all you want. But you can't get tired all at once of the pretty things that I have found; and I think that the more you look at the pictures on the bowls and plates, the more you will admire them. You are fond of birds and flowers, and you will find them on the porcelain; and there is one piece that has a river and some mountains on it, as well defined as if it were a painting on a sheet of paper. Look at the bridge over the river,

and the trees on the side of the mountain, and then say if you ever saw anything nicer. I am in love with the Japanese art work, and sorry I can't buy more of it. And I think that is the case with most people who come to Japan, and take the trouble to look at the nice things it contains."

Mary's list included some carvings in ivory and some lacquered boxes to keep her gloves in. These were not at all difficult to find, as they were everywhere in the shops, and it would have been much harder to avoid them if he had wanted to do so. There were chessmen of ivory, and representations of the divinities of the country; and then there were little statues of the kings and high dignitaries from ancient times down to the present. As it was a matter of some perplexity, Frank sought the advice of Doctor Bronson; the latter told him it would be just as well to restrain himself in the purchase of ivory carvings, as there was better work of the kind in China, and a few samples of the products of Japan would

JAPANESE METAL CLOISONNÉ.

be sufficient. Frank acted upon this hint, and did not make any extensive investments in Japanese ivory. He found a great variety of what the Japanese call "nitschkis," which are small pieces of ivory carved in various shapes more or less fanciful. They were pretty, and had the merit

CHINESE PORCELAIN CLOISONNÉ.

of not being at all dear; and as they would make nice little souvenirs of Japan, he bought a good many of them. They are intended as ornaments to be worn at a gentleman's girdle, and in the olden times no gentleman considered his dress complete without one or more of these at his waist, just as most of the fashionable youths of America think that a scarf-pin is necessary to make life endurable. A large number of carvers made a living by working in ivory, and they displayed a wonderful amount of patience in completing their designs. One of these little carvings with which Frank was fascinated was a representation of a man mounting a horse with the assistance of a groom, who was holding the animal. The piece was less than two inches in length, and yet the carver had managed to put in this contracted space the figures of two men and a horse, with the dress of the men and the trappings of the horse as carefully shown as in a painting. There was a hole in the pedestal on which the group stood, and Frank found, on inquiry, that this hole was intended for the passage of a cord to attach the ornament to the waist of the wearer. And then he observed that all the carvings had a similar provision for rendering them useful.

Frank also ascertained that another ornament of the Japanese waist-belt was a pipe and a tobacco-pouch, the two being so inseparable that they formed a single article. The pipe was a tiny affair which only held a pinch of tobacco the size of a pea, and he learned that the smoker, in using it, took but a single whiff and then found the bowl exhausted. When not

GROUP CARVED IN IVORY.

in use, the pipe was carried in a little case, which was made, like the pouch, of leather, and was generally embroidered with considerable care. Many of the pipe-cases were made of shark-skin, which has the double merit of being very durable and also quite pretty. It is polished to a condition of perfect smoothness, and the natural spots of the skin appear to be as regular as though drawn by an artist. Frank tried a few whiffs of the tobacco and found it very weak. He was thus informed of the reason why a Japanese can smoke so much as he does without being seriously affected by it. He can get through with a hundred of these little pipes in a day without the least trouble, and more if the time allows.

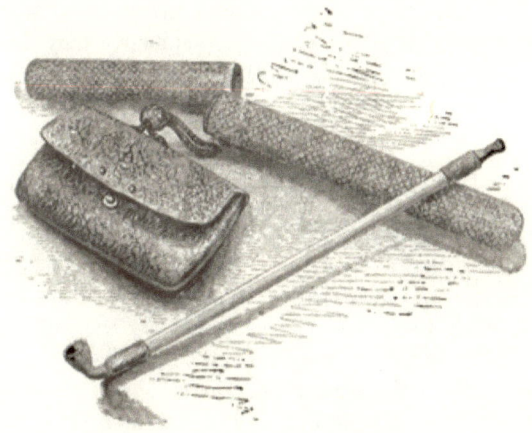

JAPANESE PIPE, CASE, AND POUCH.

Of lacquer-ware, of all kinds and prices, there was literally no end. There were trays and little boxes which could be had for a shilling or two, and there were cabinets and work-stands with numerous drawers and sliding panels curiously contrived, that a hundred dollars, or even five hundred, would not buy. Between these two figures there was a wide range, so that the most modest purse could be gratified as well as the most plethoric one. Frank found that the dealers did not put their best goods where they could be most readily seen. The front of a shop contained only the most ordinary things; and if you wanted to look at the better articles, it was necessary to say so. When the merchant knew what his customer wanted, he led the way to the rear store, or perhaps to an upper floor, where the best goods were kept. It was necessary to walk very carefully in these shops, as they were very densely crowded with goods, and the least incaution might result in overthrowing some of the brittle articles. A clumsy visitor in one of these establishments a few days before Frank called there had broken a vase valued at fifty dollars, and while stooping to pick up the fragments he knocked down another worth nearly half that amount. He paid for the damage, and in future declined to go around loosely in a Japanese store.

The Japanese lacquer of the present time is not so highly prized as that of the last or the previous century. It is not so well made, partly for the reason that the workmen have lost their skill in the art, and partly because labor is much more expensive now than formerly. The prices obtained for some of the specimens of this kind of work have been very high, but they are not enough to meet the advance that has been made in wages in the past few years. The manufacturers are anxious to turn their money as rapidly as possible, and consequently they do not allow their productions to dry thoroughly. To be properly prepared, a piece of lacquer should dry very slowly; and it used to be said that the best lacquer was dried under water, so that the process should not be too rapid. The article, whatever it may be, is first shaped from wood or papier-maché, and then covered with successive coatings of varnish or lacquer this is made from the gum of a tree, or, rather, from the juice, and it is said to have the peculiar property of turning black from exposure to the air, though it is of a milky whiteness when it exudes from the tree. It can be made to assume various colors by the addition of pigments; and while it is in a fresh condition coatings of gold-leaf are laid on in such a way as to form the figures that the artist has designed. Every coating must be dried before the next is laid on; and the more elaborate and costly the work, the more numerous are the coatings. Sometimes there may be a dozen or more of them, and pieces are in existence that are said to have received no less than fifty applications of lacquer. A box may thus require several years for its completion, as the drying process should never be hastened, lest the lacquer crack and peel when exposed to the air, and especially to heat. Good lacquer can be put into hot water without the least injury; but this is not the case with the ordinary article.

In 1874 a steamer was lost on the coast of Japan. She had as a part of her cargo the Japanese goods from the Vienna Exhibition, and none of them were recovered for nearly a year. There they lay under the salt-water, and it was supposed that nearly everything would be ruined. But it was found that the lacquered ware had suffered very little, and some of these very articles were shown at Philadelphia in 1876.

JAPANESE ARTIST CHASING ON COPPER.

A few of the pieces required to be freshly polished, but there were many of them that did not need even this slight attention.

The boys were greatly interested in their shopping excursions, and learned a good deal about Japanese art and industry before they had ended their purchases. By the time they were through they had an excellent collection of porcelain and other ware, of ivory carvings, lacquered boxes, and similar things; silk robes, wrappers, and handkerchiefs; and quite enough fans to set up a small museum. They tried at first to get a sample of each kind of fan that they could find, but the variety proved so great that they were forced to give up the attempt. They bought some curious articles of bamboo, and were surprised to find to how many uses this vegetable production is put. Frank thought it was a pity the bamboo did not grow in America, as it could be turned to even more advantage by the enterprising Yankee than by the plodding Oriental, and Fred was inclined to agree with him. They changed their minds, how-

A JAPANESE VILLAGE.—BAMBOO POLES READY FOR MARKET.

ever, when the Doctor told them how far the bamboo entered into the life of the people of the East, and on the whole they concluded that the American couldn't improve upon it.

"The bamboo," said the Doctor, "is of use from a very early age. The young shoots are boiled and eaten, or soaked in sugar, and preserved as confectionery. The roots of the plant are carved so as to resemble animals or men, and in this shape are used as ornaments; and when the bamboo is matured, and of full size, it is turned to purposes almost without number. The hollow stalks are used as water-pipes; rafts are made of them; the walls and roofs of houses are constructed from them; and they serve for the masts of smaller boats and the yards of larger ones. The light and strong poles which the coolies place over their shoulders for bearing burdens are almost invariably of bamboo; and where it grows abundantly it is used for making fences and sheds, and for the construction of nearly every implement of agriculture. Its fibres are twisted into rope, or softened into pulp for paper; every article of furniture is made of bamboo, and so are hats, umbrellas, fans, cups, and a thousand other things. In fact, it would be easier to say what is not made of it in these Eastern countries than to say what is; and an attempt at a mere enumeration of its uses and the articles made from it would be tedious. Take away the bamboo from the people of Japan and China, and you would deprive them of their principal means of support, or, at any rate, would make life a much greater burden than it now is."

CHAPTER XVIII.

SOMETHING ABOUT JAPANESE WOMEN.

FRANK thought it was no more than proper that he should devote a letter to Miss Effie. He wanted to make it instructive and interesting, and, at the same time, he thought it should appeal to her personally in some way. He debated the matter in his own mind without coming to a conclusion, and finally determined to submit the question to Doctor Bronson, from whom he hoped to receive a suggestion that would be useful.

The Doctor listened to him, and was not long in arriving at a conclusion.

"You have just written to Mary on the subject of Japanese art," said he, "and she will be pretty certain to show the letter to her intimate friend."

"Nothing more likely," Frank answered.

"In that case," the Doctor continued, "you want to take up a subject that will be interesting to both, and that has not been touched in your letters thus far."

"I suppose so."

"Well, then, as they are both women, or girls, as you may choose to call them, why don't you take up the subject of women in Japan? They would naturally be interested in what relates to their own sex, and you can give them much information on that topic."

The proposal struck Frank as an excellent one, and he at once set about obtaining the necessary information for

A JAPANESE LADY'S-MAID.

the preparation of his letter. He
had already seen and heard a great
deal concerning the women of Japan,
and it was not long before he had
all the material he wanted for his
purpose. His letter was a long one,
and we will make some extracts from
it, with the permission of Miss Effie,
and also that of Mary, who claimed
to have an interest in the missive.

"From what I can learn," Frank
wrote, "the women of Japan are better off than those of most other Eastern countries. They are not shut up
in harems and never allowed to go
about among people, as in Turkey;
and they are not compelled to stay
indoors and see nobody, as in many

BRIDE AND BRIDESMAID.

other parts of the world. They have their share of the work to do; but
they are not compelled to do all of it, while their husbands are idle,
as in some parts of Europe, and among the American Indians. The
system of harems is not known here; or, at all events, if it is known, it is

MERCHANT'S FAMILY.

practised so little that we never hear
anything about it. The Japanese
women do not veil their faces, as the
women of all Mohammedan countries are compelled to do; and they
are free to go about among their
friends, just as they would be if they
were Americans. They blacken their
teeth when they get married; but
this custom is fast dying out since
the foreigners came here, and probably in twenty years or so we shall not
hear much about it. The married
women dress their hair differently
from the single ones; and when you
know the ways of arranging it, you
can know at once whether a woman
is married or not. I suppose they

MYSTERIES OF THE DRESSING-ROOM.

do this for the same reason that the women of America wear rings on their fingers, and let folks know if they are engaged or married or single. They remind me of what I have read about the Russian women, who wear their hair uncovered until they are married, and then tie it up in a net, or in a handkerchief. It is much better to have a sign of this sort than to have it in a ring, as the hair can be seen without any trouble, while you have to be a little impertinent sometimes to look at a lady's hand, and find out how her rings are.

"In China the women pinch their feet, so that they look like doubled fists, but nothing of the kind is done in Japan. Every woman here has her feet of the natural shape and size; and as to the size, I can say that there are women in Japan that have very pretty feet, almost as pretty as those of two young ladies I know of in America. They do not have shoes like those you wear, but instead they have sandals for staying in the house, and high clogs for going out of doors. The clogs are funny-look-

ing things, as they are four or five inches high, and make you think of pieces of board with a couple of narrow pieces nailed to the upper edges. They can't walk fast in them, but they can keep their feet out of the mud, unless it is very deep, and in that case they ought not to go out at all. I wish you could see a Japanese woman walking in her clogs. I know you would laugh, at least the first time you saw one; but you would soon get used to it, as it is a very common sight.

"In China and some other countries it is not considered necessary to give the girls any education; but in Japan it is not so. The girls are educated here, though not so much

LADY IN WINTER WALKING-DRESS.

as the boys; and of late years they have established schools where they receive what we call the higher branches of instruction. Every year new schools for girls are opened; and a great many of the Japanese who formerly would not be seen in public with their wives have adopted the Western idea, and bring their wives into society. The marriage laws have been arranged so as to allow the different classes to marry among

17

each other, and the government is doing all it can to improve the condition of the women. They were better off before than the women of any other Eastern country; and if things go on as they are now going, they will be still better in a few years. The world moves.

"A gentleman who has given much attention to this subject says that of the one hundred and twenty rulers of Japan, nine have been women; and that the chief divinity in their mythology is a woman—the goddess Kuanon. A large part of the literature of Japan is devoted to the praise of woman; her fidelity, love, piety, and devotion form the groundwork of many a romance which has become famous throughout the country, and popular with all classes of readers. The history of Japan abounds in stories of the heroism of women in the various characters of patriot, rebel, and martyr; and I am told that a comparison of the standing of women in all the countries of the East, both in the past and in the present, would unquestionably place Japan at the head.

"I suppose you will want to know something about the way the Japanese women dress. I'll try to tell you; but if I make any mistakes, you must remember that I have not had much practice in describing ladies' apparel.

"They don't wear any crinoline, such as the ladies do in America; and their clothes fit very tight around them when compared to what we see in New York—that is, I mean, they are tight in the skirts, though loose enough above the waist. They fasten them with strings and bands, and without hooks or buttons or pins. You remember the pocket pin-cushion you made for me? of course you do. Well, one day while we were taking tea in a Japanese tea-house, the attendants stood around looking at us, and examining our watch-chains and the buttons on our coats. I showed them that pin-cushion, and they passed it from one to the other, and wondered what it was; and so I took out a pin, and showed it was for carrying pins. Evidently they did not know what a pin was for, as they looked at it very curiously, and then made signs for me to show them its use. I did so by pinning up the wide sleeve of one of the black-eyed girls. She took the pin out a moment after to return it to me; and when I motioned that she might keep it, she smiled and said 'Arinyato,' which means 'Thank you,' as sweetly and earnestly as though I had given her a diamond ring. Then I gave each one of them a pin, and they all thanked me as though they really thought they had received something of value. Just think of it! half a dozen young women, not one of whom had ever seen a common dressing-pin!

"Their dresses are folded around them, and then held in place by an *obi*, which is nothing more nor less than a wide belt. It is of the most

A GIRL WHO HAD NEVER SEEN A DRESSING-PIN.

expensive material that the wearer can afford; and sometimes it costs a
great deal of money. Generally it is of silk, and they have it of all colors,
and occasionally it is heavily embroidered. It is several yards long, and the

work of winding it into place is no
small affair. I shall enclose some pictures of Japanese women in this letter, and you can see from them what
the dress of the women looks like,
and understand much better than you
will by what I write. I think the
women look very pretty in their dresses—much better, in fact, than when
they put on European garments.
Their hair is always black, and they
dress it with more grease than I wish
they would. It fairly makes the hair
shine, it is laid on so thick. But they
have some very pretty ornaments for
their hair, which they stick in with
large pins, something like the hair-
pins you use at home. I am told that
you can distinguish the social position
by the number and style of the hair-
ornaments worn on a woman's head;

LADIES' HAIR-DRESSER.

but I have not yet learned how to do it. I suppose I shall find out if I
stay long enough in Japan.

"Of course, you will want to know if the Japanese women are pretty.
Now, you mustn't be jealous when I say they are. Fred thinks so too, and
you know it won't do for me to have a quarrel with Fred when we are
travelling together, and especially when I think he's right. They are all
brunettes, and have sharp, bright eyes, full of smiles, and their skins are
clear and healthy. They look very pleasant and happy; and they have
such sweet, soft voices that nobody could help liking them even if he didn't
want to. They have such nice manners, too, that you feel quite at your
ease in their company. They may be wishing you ten thousand miles away,
and saying to themselves that they hate the sight of a foreigner; but if
they do, they manage to conceal their thoughts so completely that you can
never know them. You may say this is all deception, and perhaps it is;
but it is more agreeable than to have them treat you rudely, and tell you
to get out of the way.

"There are women here who are not pretty, just as there are some in America; but when you are among them, it isn't polite to tell them of it. Some of them paint their faces to make them look pretty. I suppose nobody ever does anything of the kind in America or any other country but Japan, and therefore it is very wicked for the Japanese ladies to do so. And when they do paint, they lay it on very thick. Dr. Bronson calls

LADIES AT THEIR TOILET.

it kalsomining, and Fred says it reminds him of the veneering that is sometimes put on furniture to make pine appear like mahogany, and have an expensive look, when it isn't expensive at all. The 'geishas,' or dancing and singing girls, get themselves up in this way; and when they have their faces properly arranged, they must not laugh, for fear that the effort of smiling would break the coating of paint. And I have heard it said that the covering of paint is so thick that they couldn't smile any more than a mask could; and, in fact, the paint really takes the place of a mask, and makes it impossible to recognize anybody through it.

"It is the rule in Japan for a man to have only one wife at a time, but he does not always stick to it. If he has children, a man is generally contented; but if he has none, he gets another wife, and either divorces the first one or not, as he chooses. Divorce is very easy for a man to obtain, but not so for the woman; and when she is divorced, she has hardly any means of obtaining justice. But, in justice to the Japanese, it should be said that the men do not often abuse their opportunities for divorce, and that the married life of the people is about as good as that of most countries. Among the reasons for divorce, in addition to what I have mentioned, there are the usual ones that prevail in America. Furthermore, divorce is allowed if a wife is disobedient to her husband's parents, and also if she talks too much. The last reason is the one most frequently given; but a woman cannot complain of her husband and become divorced from him for the same cause. I wonder if Japan is the only country in the world where women have ever been accused of talking too much.

"Nearly every amusement that is open to men is also open to women. They can go to the theatres, to picnics, parties, and anything of the sort, as often as they please, which is not the case with women in Moslem countries, and in some others that are not Moslem. They are very fond of boat excursions, and on pleasant days a goodly number of boating parties may be seen on the waters around Tokio and the other large cities. On the whole, they seem to have a great capacity for enjoyment, and it is pretty certain that they enjoy themselves.

JAPANESE LADIES ON A PICNIC.

"The houses in Japan are so open that you can see a great deal more of the life of the people than you would be likely to see in other countries. You can see the women playing with the children, and there are lots of the little ones everywhere about. I don't believe there is a country in the world where there is more attention to the wants of the children than in Japan, and I don't believe it is possible for a greater love to exist between parents and children than one finds here. There are so many things done for the amusement of children, and the children seem to enjoy them so much, that it is very pleasing to study the habits of the people in this respect. I have already told you about the amusements at the temple of Asakusa, and the sports and games that they have there for the children. They are not only at that temple, but all over Japan, and the man must

LADIES AND CHILDREN AT PLAY.

be very poor to feel that he cannot afford something to make his children
happy. In return, the children are not spoiled, but become very dutiful to
their parents, and are ready to undergo any privations and sacrifices for
their support and comfort. Respect for parents and devotion to them in
every possible way are taught by the religion of the country; and, whatever we may think of the heathenism of Japan, we cannot fail to admire
this feature of the religious creed.

"It would amuse you if you could see the interest that the Japanese
take in flying kites. And the funny part of it is that it is the men who
do the most of the kite-flying, while the children look on, which is the exact reverse of what we do in our country. They have the funniest kinds
of kites, and show a great deal of ingenuity in getting them up. Everybody has them, and they are so cheap that even the beggars can have kites
to fly. They are of all sizes and shapes; you can buy a plain kite a few
inches square, or you can get one as large as the side of a house, and covered all over with dragons and other things that sometimes cost a neat little
sum for the painting alone. The Japanese understand the trick of flying
a kite without a tail, and they do it by the arrangement of the strings,
which is quite different from ours. On the other hand, some of their
kites will have a whole line of strings hanging down as ornaments, and
sometimes it looks as if the kite were anchored by means of these extra
cords. They make their kites so large that three or four men are needed
to hold some of them; and there is a story that a man who one day tied the
cord of a kite to his waist was taken up in the air and never heard of

FLYING KITES.

again. And there is another story of a man in the country who had a
kite that he harnessed to a plough, and when the wind was good he used
to plough his fields by means of it. But the story does not explain how
he turned the furrow when he reached the end of the field. Perhaps he
had an accommodating wind that shifted at the right time.

"The first kite I saw in the air in Japan was so much like a large bird that I mistook it for one, and the delusion was kept up by a smaller one that seemed to be getting away from the other. The large one imitated the movements of a hawk to perfection, and it was some minutes before I could understand that it was nothing but a combination of sticks and paper and cords, instead of a real live bird. It rose and fell, and every few moments it swept down and seemed to be trying to swallow the little one out of sight. I never should have supposed such an imitation possible, and was thoroughly convinced that the Japanese must be very fond of kite-flying if they give it the study necessary to bring it to such a state of perfection.

"The more I see of the Japanese, the more I like them, and think them a kind-hearted and happy people. And, from all I can see, they deserve to be happy, as they do all they can for the pleasure of each other, or, at any rate, all that anybody ever does."

CHAPTER XIX.

FROM YOKOHAMA TO KOBE AND OSAKA.

TIME was going on, and it became necessary that our travellers should follow its example. The Doctor engaged places for them by the steamer for Kobe, the port for the western capital of Japan, and at the appointed time they went on board. Before their departure, they had an opportunity to visit one of the tea-packing establishments for which Yokohama is famous, and the process they witnessed there was of special in-

A VILLAGE IN THE TEA DISTRICT.

terest to the boys. Here is the account that Frank gave of it in his next letter home:

"The Japanese tea is brought from the country to the seaports in large boxes. It is partially dried when it is picked, but not enough to preserve it for a long sea-voyage. When it gets here, it is delivered to the large establishments that make a business of shipping teas to America; and let me say, by the way, that nearly all the tea of Japan that is exported goes to America, and hardly any of it to any other country. When we went into the warehouse — they call it a 'go-down,' from a Hindostanee word— they showed us a room where there were probably a hundred bushels of tea in a great pile on the floor. Men were at work mixing it up with shovels, and the clerk who showed us around said that they spread all the tea out in layers, one over the other, and then mixed them up. He said it was a very difficult job to have the teas properly mixed, so that the samples should be perfectly even.

TEA-MERCHANTS IN THE INTERIOR.

"We saw lots of tea in another room where the same kind of work was going on; and then they took us to the firing-room, and it was a firing-room, you may believe.

"It was like a great shed, and it had the solid ground for a floor. On this floor there were kettles, or pans, set in brickwork, and each one of them had a little furnace under it, in which there was a charcoal fire. There must have been two hundred of these pans, and the heat from them was so great that it almost took away my breath. I don't believe I could exist there a day, and yet there were people who had to spend the entire day in the firing-room, and go there day after day besides. Many of them were women, and some of them had little children strapped to their backs, and there was a whole lot of children in a little room at one side of the shed, where a couple of women were looking after them. How I did pity

the poor things! Fred and I just emptied our pockets of all the small change we could find in them for the benefit of the babies, and I wish we could have given them more. But there was hardly a cry from any of them, and they seemed as happy and contented as though their mothers were queens, instead of toiling over the firing-pan in that hot room for ten or fifteen cents a day.

"They put a pound and a half of tea into each pan, and with it they put a teaspoonful of some coloring substance that they keep a secret. People say that this coloring matter is Prussian blue, and others say it is indigo, and that a little gypsum is put with it, so as to give the tea a bright appearance. The clerk told us it was indigo and gypsum that his house used, and declared that it was all false that any poisonous material was ever put in. He said they only

THE TEA-PLANT.

used a teaspoonful of their mixture to a charge of tea, and the most of that little quantity was left in the pan in the shape of dust. When I asked him why they put anything in, he said it was to make the tea sell better in the American market. It looked so much better when it had been 'doctored' that their customers in New York and other cities would pay more for it, though they knew perfectly well what had been done. Then he showed me some of the tea that had been fired and put side by side with some that had not. I must say that the fired tea had a polished appearance that the other had not, and I could readily understand why it sells better.

"As I have said, they put a charge of a pound and a half of tea into the pan with a teaspoonful of the mixture, and they have a fire of charcoal beneath it. The man or woman that does the firing stands in front of the pan and keeps the tea in constant motion. It must be kept moving all the time, so that it will not be scorched, and it must be gently rubbed between the fingers in order to polish it. It is kept in the pan eighty minutes, and then is considered dry enough for the packing-cases.

FIRING TEA.

"You know how a tea-chest looks, so I need not describe it any more than to say that the chest is lined with tin, and that the tin is carefully soldered, so that not a single particle of dampness can get in while the tea is on the ocean. If it should, the tea would be spoiled, as the least dampness will injure it, and a great deal will make it quite useless. They always try to hurry the new crop of tea as rapidly as they can, since it is the best, and has more and better flavor than the crop of the previous year. When a ship sails with new tea, she races for home as hard as she can go, and the quickest voyages ever made from this part of the world to Europe and America have been made by ships with cargoes of new tea."

When the party sailed from Yokohama, they found themselves on board a steamer which was, and was not, Japanese. She was built in New York, and formerly ran between that city and Aspinwall. Subsequently she was sent to Japan in the service of the Pacific Mail Steamship Company, and was sold, along with several other American steamers, to a Japanese company. This company was formed with Japanese capital, and its management was Japanese; but the ships were foreign, and the officers and engineers were mostly English or American.

The Doctor told the boys that the Mitsu Bishi Company, as this Japanese organization was called, was increasing every year the number of its ships. It received assistance from the government in the form of a mail contract, and was evidently doing very well. The steamers ran once a week each way between Yokohama and Shanghai, touching at Kobe and Nagasaki, and there were lines to other ports of Japan. The Japanese were studying naval architecture and making good progress, and they hoped before many years to construct their own ships. Every year they reduced the number of foreigners in their service, and some of their establishments were entirely under native management.

The second morning after leaving Yokohama, they were at Kobe, and the steamer anchored off the town. Kobe and Hiogo are practically one

HIOGO (KOBE).

and the same place. The Japanese city that stands there was formerly known as Hiogo, and still retains that name, while the name of Kobe was applied to that portion where the foreigners reside. The view from the water is quite pretty, as there is a line of mountains just back of the city; and as the boys looked intently they could see that the mountains were inhabited. There are several neat little houses on the side of the hills, some of them the residences of the foreigners who go there to get the cool air, while the rest are the homes of the Japanese. There is a liberal allowance of tea-houses where the public can go to be refreshed, and there is a waterfall where a mountain stream comes rattling down from the rocks to a deep pool, where groups of bathers are sure to congregate in fine weather. The town stands on a level plain, where a point juts into the water, and there is nothing remarkable about it. If they had not seen Yokohama and Tokio, they might have found it interesting; but after those cities the boys were not long in agreeing that a short time in Kobe would be all they would wish.

But they were at the port of Osaka and Kioto, and their thoughts were turned towards those important cities. There was no difficulty in going there, as the railway was in operation to Osaka, twenty miles, and to Kioto, thirty miles farther on. But Frank was seized with an idea, which he lost no time in communicating to his friends. It was this:

"We can travel by rail almost anywhere," said he, "and needn't come away from America to do so. Now, instead of going to Osaka by rail, which wouldn't be anything remarkable, suppose we go by a Japanese junk. I have been asking the hotel-keeper about it, and he says it is perfectly easy to do so, and that we can sail there with a fair wind in a few hours."

Fred was in favor of the junk voyage on account of its novelty. Of course, the Doctor was not likely to oppose any reasonable scheme that would give his young companions an opportunity to learn something, provided it did not consume too much time. Inquiry showed that the voyage could be made there with a fair wind, as Frank had suggested; and, as the wind happened to be all right and promised to continue, it was agreed to go by junk on the following morning, provided there were no change.

A Japanese servant, who spoke English, was engaged from the hotel to accompany the party during their journey. He was sent to find a junk that was about to leave for Osaka, and in half an hour he returned with the captain of one. It was soon settled that he was to bring his craft to the anchorage near the hotel during the afternoon, and be ready to receive his passengers and their luggage at daylight if the wind held good. The

THE JUNK AT ANCHOR.

servant, who said he was named "John" by the first European that ever employed him, and had stuck to it ever since, was kept busy during the afternoon in making preparations for the journey, as it was necessary to take a stock of provisions very much as the party had equipped themselves when they went to ascend Fusiyama. Everything was arranged in time, and the trio went to bed early, as it would be necessary to rise before the sun, and they wanted to lay in a good supply of sleep.

The junk was all ready in the morning; and as soon as the passengers were on board, her sail was lifted, and she slowly worked her way through the water. The wind was all right for the voyage to the mouth of the river where Osaka lay; and if they had been on a sail-boat such as all New-Yorkers are familiar with, the journey would have been over in three or four hours. But the junk was not built for racing purposes, and the most that could be hoped for from her was a speed of about three miles an hour. This was no detriment, as they could thus make the mouth of the river by noon; and if the bar could be easily crossed, they would be at the city long before sunset. Life on a junk was a novelty, and therefore

THE HELMSMAN AT HIS POST.

they were not annoyed to think that their craft was not a swift one.

Fred thought that the stern of the junk was about the funniest thing in the way of a steering-place he had ever seen; and to make sure of remembering it, he made a sketch of the helmsman at his post. Frank insisted that he was not there at all, as his post was evidently the rudder-post, and it was at least ten feet off, owing to the length of the tiller. The deck where the man stood had a slope like that of a house-roof, and it was a mystery to the boys how the sailors could stand there when the planks were wet by the spray, or the sea was at all rough. But there was no denying that they did stay there, and so the boys concluded that the men must have claws on their feet like those with which a tiger is equipped. Fred remarked that the steep incline reminded him of a conundrum he had somewhere heard, which was as follows:

"Why is a dog with a broken leg like the space between the eaves and the ridge of a house?"

Frank could not answer, and the question was propounded to Dr. Bronson; the latter shook his head, and then Fred responded, in triumph, "Because he is a slow pup." It was three seconds at least before Frank could see the point of the joke.

The boys had too much to do in the way of sight-seeing to spend more time over conundrums. They proceeded to explore the interior of the junk, and to look about the decks in the hope of finding something new in the way of navigation. They discovered that there was considerable space for the stowage of cargo, in consequence of the great width of the craft in proportion to her length. The accommodations of the crew were not extensive; but as they did not expect much, they were not likely to complain. As the boys were near the bow of the junk, they came upon two of the sailors at dinner; the meal consisting of rice and fish, which they ate

JAPANESE SAILORS AT DINNER.

18

with the aid of chopsticks. The men were squatted on the deck in front of their food, or rather they had the food in front of themselves, and they evidently were the possessors of good appetites, to judge by the eagerness with which they attended to business and paid no heed to the strangers.

The Japanese are excellent sailors, both on their junks and on the foreign ships that have been introduced to their service since the opening of the country to other nations. But the Japanese landsman has a horror of the water, and cannot be induced to venture upon it. In this respect the Japanese are not unlike the Italians, who are naturally a maritime nation, and have covered themselves with marine glory in times that are past. But the Italian landsman is ready to suffer any inconvenience rather than risk himself on the ocean, and not a more woe-begone being can be found in the world than a sea-sick Italian unless it be a sea-sick Japanese.

The sailors on the junk were very prompt in obeying orders, but they went about everything with an air of coolness which one does not always see on an American vessel. Ordinarily they pulled at ropes

as though they would not hurt either the ropes or themselves; but it was observed that when the captain gave an order for anything, there was no attempt at shirking. One of the sailors stood at the sheet of the mainsail, and while he held on and waited for directions his mate was quietly smoking and seated on the deck. When the order came for changing the position of the sail, the pipe was instantly dropped and the work was attended to; when the work was over, the pipe was resumed as if nothing had happened. Evi-

JUNK SAILORS ON DUTY.

dently the sailors were not much affected by the fashions that the foreigners had introduced, for they were all dressed in the costume that prevailed previous to the treaty of Commodore Perry, and before a single innovation had been made in the way of navigation. The captain of the junk looked with disdain upon a steamer that was at anchor not far from where his craft was obliged to pass, and evidently he had no very high opinion of the barbarian invention. He was content with things as they were, and the ship that had borne his ancestors in safety was quite good enough for him and his comrades.

About six hours after the departure from Kobe, the junk reached the bar of the river on which Osaka is situated. The bar was passed, and then the unwieldy concern came to anchor to wait for a stronger breeze; at the advice of John a row-boat was engaged to finish the journey as far as the hotel where they were to stop. The row-boat was rapidly propelled by the strong arms of half a dozen men; and in less than two hours from the time they said "Sayonara" to the captain of their transport, the Doctor and his young friends were safely lodged in the house where their rooms had been previously engaged by letter. In a short time dinner was ready, and they had it served on a little balcony which overlooked the water, and gave them an opportunity to study the river life of the city while they devoured the stewed chicken and juicy steaks that the host had provided for them. Boats passed and repassed, and there was a good deal of animation on the stream. Just beyond the hotel there was a bridge which curved like a quarter of a circle, as Fred thought, and beyond it was another of similar construction. Crowds of people were coming and going over these bridges, and Frank ventured to ask the Doctor if there were any more bridges and any more people in Osaka.

"Certainly, my boy," the Doctor answered, "there are thirteen rivers and canals in Osaka, so that the city has an abundance of water communication. The streets are generally at right angles, and there are more than a hundred bridges over the water-ways. From this circumstance Osaka has received the name of the Venice of Japan, and she certainly deserves it. Formerly her commerce by water was very great, and you would see a large fleet of junks in the river below the town. The opening of the railway to Kobe has somewhat diminished the traffic by water; but it is still quite extensive, and employs a goodly amount of capital.

"Osaka is one of the most important cities of Japan," Dr. Bronson continued, "and has long been celebrated for its commercial greatness. If you look at its position on the map, you will see that it is admirably situated to command trade both by land and by water; and when I tell

VIEW FROM THE HOTEL.

you that it contains half a million of inhabitants, you will understand that it must have had prosperity to make it so great. The streets are of good width, and they are kept cleaner than those of most other cities in Japan. The people are very proud of Osaka, and are as tender of its reputation as the inhabitants of any Western city in America are tender of theirs. There are not so many temples as in Tokio, and not so many palaces, but there is a fair number of both; and, what is better in a practical way, there are many establishments where cotton, iron, copper, bronze, and other goods are manufactured. As a commercial and manufacturing centre, Osaka is at the head, and without a rival so far as Japan is concerned."

Towards sunset the party took a stroll through the city, stopping in front of several shops, and entering one or two of the larger. The boys were of opinion that the shops of Osaka were larger than those of Tokio, and there was one silk-store that was twice the size of any they had seen in the eastern capital. The goods that were displayed were not materially different from what they had already seen, and consequently they were not disposed to linger long on the way. They extended their walk to the upper part of the city, where several temples are situated, and they finally reached the famous Castle of Osaka, whence there is a fine view from the walls. There was some difficulty in entering the castle, but through the explanations of John the matter was arranged and they went inside.

One of the wonders of Japan is the wall of the Castle of Osaka, or

THE CASTLE OF OSAKA.

rather of a portion of it. During the sixteenth century Osaka was the capital of the empire, and remained so for many years; while it was the capital the emperor commanded the tributary princes to assist in building the walls of the imperial residence, and each was to send a stone for that purpose. The stones are there, and it would be no small matter to remove them. Our friends had no means of measurement at hand, but they estimated that some of the stones were twenty feet long by half that width, and six feet in depth. They were as large as an ordinary street-car, and some of them were larger; and how they could have been transported over the roads of Japan and hoisted into their places was a mystery no one could explain.

The view from the top of the castle walls is magnificent, and well repays the trouble of making the ascent. In front is the city like a broad map, and there is no difficulty in tracing the lines of the streets and the sinuosities of the rivers and canals. Beyond the city, on the right, is the water of the bay, which opens into the Pacific, while on the left is the plain that stretches away to Kobe and Hiogo. Beyond the plain is the range of sharp hills and mountains; and as one turns slowly to the west and north he can sweep the landscape almost to the gates of Kioto and the shores of Lake Biwa. To the east, again, there are mountains rising sharply from the fertile plain, so that one seems to be standing in a basin of low land with a curving rim of mountains. The sun was about setting as our party reached the top of the high wall, and they remained there in full enjoyment of the scene until the shadows began to fall and the light to fade out from the sky. It was the most delightful landscape view that had fallen to the lot of the youths since their ascent of Fusiyama.

They regretted the necessity of departing from the castle, but regrets were of no use, and they descended to the streets just as the lamps were getting into full blaze.

CHAPTER XX.

THE MINT AT OSAKA.—FROM OSAKA TO NARA AND KIOTO.

THROUGH the assistance of a gentleman to whom Doctor Bronson had a letter of introduction, our friends were enabled to pay a visit to the imperial mint at Osaka.

They found a large establishment, like a foundry, on the bank of the river, and just outside the thickly settled portion of the city. A tall chimney was smoking vigorously, and gave signs of activity; and there was an air of neatness about the surroundings quite in keeping with what they had observed thus far in their journey through Japan. They were met at the entrance by the director of the mint, a Japanese gentleman who had spent a considerable time in Europe and America, and spoke English with fluency and precision. They were invited to seats in the office, and, after a brief delay, were escorted through the establishment.

The mint at Osaka is one of the most noted enterprises which the government of Japan has undertaken, and likewise one of the most successful. When it was founded it was under foreign supervision, and the most of the employés were from Europe; but year by year the Japanese have learned how to conduct its machinery, and have relieved the foreigners of the labor of managing it. The direction is Japanese, and so are the heads of the departments, and the employés from highest to lowest. When the mint was established, the machinery for it was imported from Europe, but at present it is all made by the Japanese, in their own factory attached to the mint.

"Just to think," said Frank, "that people persist in calling these Japanese 'barbarians!' Here are machines for stamping coin and performing all the work of a mint, and it bears the mark of the Japanese. Here are delicate balances for weighing gold and silver and getting the weight down to the fraction of a grain, and they are just as sensitive and as well made as the best specimens from the French or German makers. If the Japanese can do all this, and they certainly have done it, they deserve to be considered just as good as any other people in the world."

The Doctor took from his pocket some of the coin which was in circulation, and with which the boys had by this time become thoroughly familiar. They had remarked that it was as neatly made as any coin of Europe or America, and, as a matter of curiosity, they were desirous of seeing the machine by which each of the different pieces was stamped.

The director kindly pointed out the various machines, and the boys observed that, with a single exception, they were all of Japanese make. Then they were shown through a factory for the manufacture of sulphuric acid that is attached to the mint, and is run on government account. They were somewhat astonished to learn that all the sulphuric acid used in the mint was made there, and that in the previous year thirteen thousand cases were exported

VIGNETTE FROM THE NATIONAL BANK-NOTES.

to China. For the benefit of his professor of chemistry, Fred made the following memorandum concerning the branch of business he was investigating:

"The sulphur comes from the provinces of Satsuma and Bungo—the most from the latter, and the best from the former; and the product is partly for the use of the mint, and partly for general commerce. The acid is packed in earthen jars which are glazed on the inside, and not in the carboys that are in use with us. Two jars, holding about eight quarts each, are packed in a wooden case; they rest on a bed of lime about three inches thick, and the remainder of the space is filled with coarse ashes and coal cinders. This manner of packing is considered preferable to the old one, and, besides, it enables the Japanese to make their own jars, instead of importing the carboys. The director tells me that thus far the factory has not been able to supply the Chinese demand for acid, and therefore no shipments have been made to other countries. With an increased production, it is quite possible that shipments may be made to America at no very distant day.

"Japan abounds in sulphur, and the supply is said to be inexhaustible. The copper used at the mint for making the Japanese small coins is of native production, and so is most of the silver; but occasionally the supply of the latter metal runs short, and then American silver comes into play. Last year nearly half a million trade-dollars were melted at the mint at Osaka, to be made into Japanese yens, and this year a large number have met a similar fate. The American trade-dollar

IMPERIAL CREST FOR PALACE AFFAIRS.

has not yet become a popular coin for circulation in Japan and China, but is in good demand for the melting-pot. But I suppose we do not care what they do with our silver money so long as they pay for it; and the more they melt up, the better we shall be pleased."

IMPERIAL CREST ON THE NEW COINS.

Having finished their inspection of the mint, our friends thanked the polite director for his kindness and attention, and bade him good-day. They returned to the hotel, where their lunch was waiting for them, and sat down on the balcony, where they had feasted and studied the river scenery the day before. Their morning's excursion naturally led them to talk about the money of Japan, and on this subject the Doctor was ready with his usual fund of information.

"The Japanese currency," said Doctor Bronson, "has had a somewhat checkered career. Previous to the coming of the foreigners, the currency consisted of gold, silver, copper, and bronze coins. The Daimios had money of their own, and some of them had issued paper kinsats, or money-cards.

These were on thick paper, like card-board, and they circulated freely, though sometimes at a discount, owing to the difficulty of redemption or the wasteful ways of the prince by whom they were put forth. The old coins were oval or oblong, and the lower denominations had a square hole in the centre, so that they could be strung on a wire or on a cord. The gold coins were known as 'kobans,' while the silver ones had the general name of 'boos.' There were fractions of each, and they had their names, just as our half and quarter dollars have their distinctive names. The unit of the silver coin was a 'boo,' and it was always called 'ichi-boo,' or one boo. The word *ichi* means *one*, but the early visitors supposed it was a part of the name of the coin. Thus we read in books of twenty years ago that the writer paid 'one ichiboo' or 'two ichiboos' for certain purchases. It is the same as if some one writing of America should say that he paid 'one one-dollar' or 'two one-dollars' for what he had bought.

OLD KINSAT, OR MONEY-CARD.

"All that old currency has been set aside," continued the Doctor, "and the country is now in possession of a decimal system of money. The coins are round, and the general stamp on them is the same, apart from the words and figures showing the denomination and value. The unit is the 'yen,' which is equal to our dollar. In fact, the Japanese currency is assimilated to our own in weight, fineness, and decimal divisions. Here is the table of the values:

10 rin make 1 sen, equal to 1 cent.
100 sen make 1 yen, equal to 1 dollar.

"The coins are stamped with the devices of the coiled dragons and the rising sun (both Japanese symbols), and not with the portrait of the Mikado. Japanese prejudice is opposed to the adoption of the picture of the imperial ruler on the coin of the country, but it will

ICHI-BOO.

probably be overcome in time. It
is less severe than with the Mos-
lems (among whom a true believer
is forbidden to make a picture of
anything that has life), and consequently will be more easy to do
away with.

"The Japanese have ventured
upon that feature of Western civilization known as a national debt,
and how they will get out of it time
alone will determine. At present
they are increasing their indebtedness every year, and their paper
does not show any signs of redemp-

VIGNETTE FROM BANK-NOTE.

tion. They have also, as you have seen, a paper currency like our national issue in America, and so much like ours is it that it is known
as the Japanese greenbacks. They have notes of the same denominations as ours; and they also have a fractional currency, such as we had
during the war of 1861 and the years that followed. The premium on
coin has gone steadily upwards, partly in consequence of the large issue,
and partly owing to the hostility of foreign bankers and others, who have

done all they could to bring
the Japanese credit into dis-
credit."

The dissertation on Jap-
anese money came to an end
with the meal they were eating, and soon after the party
proceeded to take a stroll
through the streets. The
afternoon was spent in this
way and in letter-writing,
and on the following morning the trio started for Kioto, by way of Nara. The
ride was a pleasant one—in
jin-riki-shas — partly along
the banks of the river, where
they saw a goodly number of

VIGNETTE FROM BANK-NOTE.

boats, some descending the stream with the aid of the current, and others making a laborious ascent. The difference of up-stream and down-stream travel was never better illustrated than in the present instance. The Japs who floated with the current were taking things easily and smoking their pipes, as though all the world were their debtor; while the men on the towpath were bending to their toil, evidently giving their whole minds to it, and their bodies as well. Some of the towmen had on their grass coats, while others were without them. Every head was carefully protected from the heat of the sun by the broad hats already described.

MEN TOWING BOATS NEAR OSAKA.

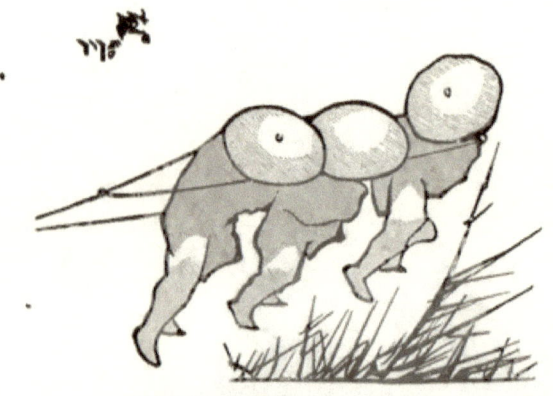

MODE OF HOLDING THE TOW-ROPES.

They saw a native ferry-boat at one point, which was heavily laden with a mixed cargo. According to Fred's inventory, the craft contained a horse and half a dozen men, together with a lot of boxes and bundles, which were, as the auctioneers say, too numerous to mention. The head of the horse was firmly held by the groom who had him in charge, as it

THE FERRY-BOAT.

would have been a serious matter if the beast had broken away and jumped into the stream with all his load about him. A Japanese ferry-boat does not appear the safest thing in the world, but, somehow, one never hears of accidents with it. If any occur, they must be carefully kept out of the papers.

After riding about three hours through a succession of villages and across fields, they reached a hotel, where John suggested they had better halt for lunch. It was a Japanese inn, without the slightest pretence of adapting itself to foreign ideas. There were the usual fish-stew and boiled rice ready, and with these and their own provisions our travellers made a hearty meal, well seasoned with that best of sauces, hunger. There was a stout maid-of-all-work, who bustled about in a manner not altogether characteristic of the Japanese. At the suggestion from the Doctor that he would like to bathe his head in some cool water, she hurried away, and soon returned, bearing a bucket so large and so full that she was forced to bend her body far to one side to maintain her equilibrium. Her powerful limbs and general ruddiness of feature were indicative of the very best condition of robust health, and the boys agreed that she would make a most excellent model for an artist who was endeavoring to represent the best types of the Japanese peasantry.

THE HOTEL-MAID.

Nara is about thirty miles from Osaka, and is famous for some ancient temples and fine groves of trees. The park containing the latter is quite extensive, and supports a considerable number of deer, so tame that they will feed from the hand of a stranger. As they are the stock sights of the place, there are plenty of opportunities to spend a few pennies for cakes to be given to the deer. The cakes are sold by some old women, who call the pets from the shelter of the trees, and bring them bounding to your side. The trees in the park are very old, and among the finest in Japan. There are few lovelier spots in the country than this; and as our friends reclined on the veranda of the little hotel to which John had led the way, and looked upon the smiling valley that spread before them, they pronounced the picture one of the prettiest they had ever seen.

A JAPANESE LANDSCAPE.

The following morning they devoted to the sights of Nara, and were surprised at the number and extent of the temples and tombs. During the eighth century Nara was the capital of Japan, and it had the honor of being the residence of seven different sovereigns. The most famous of its monuments is the statue of Buddha, which was originally cast at the time Nara was the capital, and was afterwards destroyed during an insurrection. It was recast about seven hundred years ago, and has since remained uninjured. Frank applied himself to discovering the dimensions of this statue, and ended by making the following table of figures:

Total height of statue, 53 feet 6 inches; width across shoulders, 29 feet; length of face, 16 feet; width of face, 9 feet 6 inches. It is said to weigh four hundred and fifty tons, and to be made of a bronze composed of gold, mercury, tin, and copper. The head is covered with curls, also of bronze, and there are said to be 966 of them; then there is a halo around the head 78 feet in diameter, and supporting 16 images, each one 8 feet long. The statue is in a squatting posture, like the one at Kamakura, and is covered with a building so small that it is impossible to obtain a good view in consequence of being too near the figure. The expression of the features is not at all equal to that of the great Dai-Boots at Kamakura, and the whole design is far less artistic. But it is the second in the empire in size, and for that reason is worthy of notice as well as for its antiquity.

From Nara the party continued to Kioto, halting for dinner at Uji, which is the centre of an important tea district. Men and women were at work in the fields gathering the leaves from the plants, and other men and women were attending to the drying process which the gathered leaves were undergoing. They were spread out on matting, on paper, or on cloth, where they had the full force of the rays of the sun, and were frequently turned and stirred so as to have every part equally exposed to the solar heat. While the party was at Uji a shower came on, and then there was some very lively hurrying to and fro to save the tea from a wetting. During the afternoon the rain continued, and the rest of the ride to Kioto was not especially cheerful. Part of the route led along the banks of the river, which forms a navigable way for small boats between

DIKES ALONG THE RIVER.

the tea district and Osaka; and at one place, where the bank was broken, Frank had a narrow escape from an overturn into the water. The wheel of his little carriage sank into the soft earth and spilled him out, but, luckily, a friendly tree was in his grasp and saved him from falling down the steep slope of twenty feet or so. "A miss is as good as a mile," he remarked, as he brushed the mud from his clothes, and took his seat again in his vehicle.

"And I know a miss," said Fred, "that is better than any mile we have had to-day."

Frank asked what he meant, and was told—

"Miss Effie."

NIGHT SCENE NEAR FUSHIMI.

He quite agreed with Fred, and said he would gladly exchange that last mile, overturn and all, for one minute of her society. But he had the consolation of knowing he could have her society for a good many consecutive minutes when he got home again, and could keep as long as he liked the recollection of the miles between Nara and Kioto.

They left the river at Fushimi, and followed what seemed to be an almost continuous street for six miles or more. Formerly the great route for travellers and commerce between Osaka and Kioto was by way of the river as far as Fushimi, and thence by the road. The result of this state of affairs for centuries was to build up a long village largely composed of hotels and tea-houses. Their business has somewhat fallen off since the completion of the railway from Kioto to Osaka and Kobe; but there is still enough to maintain a considerable number of them. There is one large hotel, at the foot of the Inari hill, about two miles from the centre of Kioto, where the jin-riki-sha coolies invariably stop for a short rest, and to take tea at the expense of their employers. The custom was carefully observed in the present instance, and our friends were shown to the rear of the hotel, where there was a pretty garden with a little fountain supplied from the hill above. They sipped their tea, and gave side-glances at the black-eyed maids that were moving around the house; and when John announced that the coolies were rested, the journey was resumed.

They passed by several temples, and, after a time, their way led through some narrow streets and up a gently sloping hill. Suddenly they halted and were told that they had reached their stopping-place. There are several hotels at Kioto in the foreign style, but all kept and managed by Japanese. John declared that the one to which he had brought them was the best, but he added, in a quiet whisper, that it was not so good as the hotels at Kobe and Yokohama. After a day's experience of the establishment, Frank suggested that he could make an improvement in John's English.

Fred asked what he had to propose.

"Why," said Frank, "he spoke of this hotel as the best in the place; *best* implies goodness somewhere, and I don't find any goodness in it."

"But, for all that," Fred responded, "the others may be worse than this."

"Quite true," was the answer, "and then let him say so. Instead of calling this the best hotel in Kioto, he should say that it is the least bad. Then he would be making a proper use of language."

Fred retorted that Frank was demanding too much of a boy to whom they only paid

WOMEN OF KIOTO.

19

fifty cents a day, and his expenses, and said he was reminded of the excuse of a soldier who was being censured for drunkenness.

"What was that?" queried Frank.

"His captain asked him what he had to say for himself to escape punishment, and the man replied that it was unreasonable to expect all the cardinal virtues for thirteen dollars a month. The captain told him the excuse was sufficient for that time, but would not do for a repetition of the offence."

They had not been five minutes in the hotel before they were visited by a delegation of peddlers, who had all sorts of wares to offer. Among them were some beautiful embroideries on silk, of a kind they had not seen in Tokio or Yokohama, and there were some exquisite paintings that gave practical evidence of the superiority of the artists of Kioto. The dealers were not at all importunate, and did not seem to care whether the strangers purchased their wares or declined all negotiations. Two or three of them had brought photographs of the scenery around Kioto which they offered to leave for inspection until the next day. This proposal was received with favor, and on a hint that the travellers were tired and wished to be by themselves, each of the itinerant merchants retired, but not till after bowing low and pronouncing a respectful "Sayonara."

Two of the hotels which the foreigners patronize are close to some of the famous temples of Kioto, and thus the process of sight-seeing is greatly facilitated. A third hotel is a considerable distance up the hill-side, and commands a fine view over nearly all the city. The ascent to it is somewhat fatiguing, but the visitor is well paid for the exertion by the remarkable and charming landscape that spreads before his eyes.

CHAPTER XXI.

KIOTO AND LAKE BIWA.

TO tell all that was done and seen by our young friends during their stay in Kioto would be to tell a great deal. They had their time fully occupied from their arrival to their departure, and they regretted much the necessity of leaving when they did. At the Doctor's suggestion, they attempted a new system of relating their adventures to their friends at home, and were so well pleased at the result that they determined to try it again. The new scheme was the preparation of a letter in which both had equal shares, Frank undertaking to write one half of it and Fred the other. They succeeded so well that when they read over their production to Doctor Bronson before sending it away, he was unable to say which was Fred's portion and which was Frank's. We will reproduce the letter and leave our readers to judge how well they performed their self-imposed duty. At the Doctor's suggestion, each of the boys wrote as though speaking for himself, and consequently the letter had a good deal of " I " in it.

" MY DEAR FRIENDS :

" We have seen so many things since we came here that I don't exactly know where to begin in telling the story of our sight-seeing. The names by which this city is known are so numerous that the reader of Japanese history of different dates is liable to be puzzled. Many of the natives speak of it as Miako, or the Capital ; others have called it, and still call it, Saikio, or the Central City, and others know it only as Kioto, or the Western Capital. This last name has become the official one since the removal of the Mikado to Yeddo, which then became Tokio, or the Eastern Capital. But, by whatever name we know it, the city is a most delightful one, and the traveller who comes to Japan without seeing it is like one who goes to New York without visiting Central Park, or a stranger in Boston who does not see the famous Common. In many of its features Kioto is superior to Tokio, and any one of its inhabitants will tell you so. The city stands on a plain of nearly horseshoe shape, the mountains almost encircling it and giving an abundance of charming views. On one side the houses climb a considerable distance up the slopes, so that you may sit on a balcony and see Kioto lying at your feet.

"The streets are almost of chess-board regularity, and generally so clean that you might go out to walk in satin slippers without much danger of soiling them. The people are finer-looking than those of Tokio, and you meet more stalwart men than in the eastern capital. Kioto prides itself on the beauty of its women, and some of the Japanese writers

LADIES OF THE WESTERN CAPITAL.

say that they cause the women of all other parts of the country to despair. They are very proud of their head-dresses, and they have a great many ornaments for the hair; in fact, there are so many of these things, and the trade is so extensive, that you find whole shops devoted to their manufacture and sale.

"Dancing and singing girls are to be counted by the thousand, and they certainly have the most gorgeous toilets I have seen in the country. They are engaged to sing and dance at dinner parties, just as we have bands of music to play for us at large banquets in America, and no Japanese gentleman who was giving a dinner to a friend or friends would think he had done the proper thing unless there were 'geishas' to sing and dance for them. The other evening Doctor Bronson ordered a dinner for us at a Japanese restaurant in the true style of the country; he told the manager to get it up properly, and the answer was that it should be perfect. When we went there, we found the dinner ready; and there were two singing geishas, and two dancing ones, to entertain us. I can't say that I considered it much of an entertainment after the novelty had gone, as the music was monotonous, and we couldn't understand a word of the singing. Their dancing consisted of sliding about the room, and taking a variety of postures with their arms and hands, and it wasn't a bit like what we call dancing. But it was all perfectly proper and nice, and the girls behaved like real ladies. They are educated for dancers or singers, as the case may be, and some of them are great favorites and get high wages. But if I were to have my way, and have them dress to my taste, I should make them put less paint on their faces; they consider that the one who can put the most paint on her face and neck is the prettiest, and so they cover themselves till they look as though they were veneered. One of those that danced for us had her face covered so thickly that she couldn't smile without cracking the varnish, and so she didn't smile at all.

"We are outside of treaty limits, and so we were obliged to have passports to come here. Foreigners may go freely within twenty-five miles of any of the treaty ports without special permission, but Kioto is just beyond the limit, as it is thirty miles from Osaka, and therefore the Japanese permit is needed. We had ours from the consul at Kobe, and had no trouble at all on coming here. A Japanese official called for them soon after we came to the hotel, and he bowed low as he received them. Then he spread the documents on the floor, and as he did so he fell on his hands and knees so as to bring his nose within six inches of the papers, and curve his back into the shape of an arch. He read the passports and copied our names into his note-book; or, at least, I suppose he did so, though I can't say positively. We can stay the time named in the permit without further interference; but if we stopped too long, we should probably be told some morning that a gentleman at Kobe was anxious to see us, and we had better start for there by the first train. The Japanese are so polite that they will never say a rude thing if they can help it, and they will even tell a plump falsehood rather than be uncivil. But the same thing has occurred in America, and so the Japs are not much worse than others, after all.

RESTAURANT AND TEA-GARDEN AT KIOTO.

"Kioto is famous in the rest of the world for its manufactures of porcelain of various kinds, and also for its bronzes and silk goods. There is a large trade in Kioto ware, and everybody says that is is increasing. At any rate, the prices they ask here are as high as in Yokohama for the same kind of articles, and some things are really dearer here than there. Some of the work in bronze is very fine, and I can tell you a funny story about the way the merchants prepare goods for the market. The incident

AN ARTIST AT WORK.

happened yesterday, when we were in a shop with a gentleman from Kobe whom we had met at the hotel.

"This gentleman was admiring a pair of very old vases; there was no doubt about their age, as they were eaten in several places with verdigris, and were covered in spots with dried earth. When he asked the price, he was astonished at the low figure demanded, and immediately said he would take them. Then he asked the shopkeeper if he had any more like them.

LANTERN-MAKER AT KIOTO.

"'I haven't any,' the dealer replied, 'but I can make anything you want to order.'

"The gentleman said he didn't want new vases, but old ones, and thereupon the dealer said,

"'I'll make old vases for you if you want them—will make them just as I made these.'

"We learned how it is that they get up this old ware; at least, we were told so by a man who claims to know. 'Boil the bronzes in strong vinegar,' he says, 'for several hours; and if you want to make them look very old, you must put some acid in the vinegar. You want the strongest vinegar that can be found, and the bronze must be cleaned of all grease before it is boiled.

"'You can buy plenty of old ware of all kinds,' the same man said, 'but you had better have it made, and then you know you are not cheated.' Very sensible advice, I think—don't you?

"They have a great deal of embroidered and figured silk; and when you go into a shop, these are the first things they show you. Some of the work is magnificent; and when you look at it and learn the price, it does not take you long to conclude that the labor of Kioto is not very highly paid. There are many silk-weavers here, and we have visited some of the factories. The largest that we saw contained twenty looms, about half of them devoted to brocades and other figured work, and the rest to plain silks. The looms for ordinary work are quite plain and simple; those for the figured silks are somewhat complicated, and require two persons to operate them. One sits in the usual position in front of the loom, and the other up aloft; each of them has a pattern of the work, and there is a bewildering lot of threads which must be pulled at the right time. The process is very slow; and if these weavers could see a Jacquard loom, I think they would be astonished.

"Kioto is a place of great interest, as has been said already; and we have not been able to exhaust its sights, though we have worked very diligently. It is the most famous city in all Japan for its temples, as it contains altogether about three thousand of them. They are of all sizes and kinds, but the most of them are small and not worth the trouble of visiting. But, on the other hand, there are some magnificent ones, and a charming feature of the temples is the way they are situated. They are nearly all on hill-sides, and in the midst of groves and gardens where you may wander for hours in the shade; and whenever you feel weary you can be sure of finding a tea-house close by, where you may rest and refresh yourself on the fragrant tea of Japan. Children romp and play on the verandas of the temples without thought of harm, and run as they please through the edifices. Outside are the tea-gardens; and the people chatter and laugh as they move to and from the temple, without any of the solemnity of a congregation entering or leaving a church in America. At the hour of worship, the crowd kneels reverently, and pronounces in unison the prayers that are repeated by the priest, and when the prayers are ended, they return to their sport or their work as gayly as ever.

"I must not fail to tell you of a remarkable temple that we have seen; not that any are unworthy of mention, but this one is certainly very curious. It is known as the Temple of Rengenhoin, and contains one thousand idols of large size; then each idol in this lot is surrounded by several smaller ones, and there is one idol larger than all the rest. The whole number is said to be 33,333. We did not count them to make sure that the estimate was correct, but I should think that there must be thirty thousand at least, so that a few odd thousands, more or less, would make no difference. The whole of the inside of the temple is full of them, and each figure is said to have a particular fable connected with it. The temple is nearly four hundred feet long, and is certainly a very fine building; and there is an artificial pond in front of it, which is covered with aquatic flowers in the season for them. There is a veranda that was used in olden times for a shooting-gallery for archery purposes; it is more than two hundred feet long, and there are records of some famous matches that have been shot there. The best on the books took place more than six hundred years ago, when one man is said to have hit the bull's-eye of the tar-

A JAPANESE ARCHER.

get 8,000 times out of 10,000, and another is reported to have done the same thing 8,133 times in 13,053. That was certainly good shooting, and I don't believe that it would be easy to find a bowman to-day who could equal it.

"We have seen one of the famous bells of Japan, or rather of Kioto, for it is this city that has always been celebrated for its bells. The greatest of them lies on the ground just outside of one of the temples, and it is not a piece of property that a man could put in his pocket and walk off with. It is fourteen feet high, twenty-four feet in circumference, and ten inches thick. How much it weighs nobody knows, as the Japanese never made a pair of scales large enough to weigh it with. The Jap-

TEMPLE BELL AT KIOTO.

anese bells have generally a very sweet tone, and to hear them booming out on the evening air is not by any means disagreeable. The art of casting them was carried to a state of great perfection, and stood higher, two or three centuries ago than it does at present.

"If I should name half the temples and public places we have seen I should make you wish, perhaps, that I had not written at all, as the list alone would be tedious, and I could no more give you an idea of the peculiar beauty and attractions of each than I could describe the perfume of each flower in a bouquet from the hands of the florist. One temple had a large cemetery attached to it, and we walked around looking at the inscriptions in a language which we could not read, and studying symbols we could not understand. The temple stands in a grove, as do nearly all the temples of Kioto, and the place reminded us very much of some of our burial-places at home.

"Then we have had glimpses of the way the people spin cotton, and perform other work in the manufacturing line. Their apparatus is very

REELING COTTON.

JAPANESE TEMPLE AND CEMETERY.

simple, and it is rather surprising than otherwise that they can accomplish so much with so little machinery. Then we have walked about the streets, and several times we have had close escapes from being run over by some of the carts that were carrying heavy loads. With two men to push them, and two pulling at the same time, they will move loads that would be no small matter for a pair of horses. They keep up a great shouting, and at first it puzzles you to know why they do it until you remember that it is desirable they should all pull together. You can hear them a long way off, and if you get in their way it is your own fault, as it was ours.

HANDCART FOR A QUARTETTE.

"Well, if we kept on telling you all we have seen in Kioto we should be a long time at it, and so we may as well stop short. Besides, we are going to Lake Biwa, and it is time to be off. If you enjoy this letter half as much as we have enjoyed the material for making it you will have a very pleasant time over it."

The party went to Lake Biwa as they had proposed, and certainly no one should omit it from his excursions in the vicinity of Kioto. The distance is only seven miles, and an excellent road leads there from the city. Along the route they met a dense crowd of people coming and going, for there is a vast amount of business between the city and the lake. There were men on foot and in jin-riki-shas, there were porters with loads and porters without loads, there were pack-horses in great number, and there were wagons with merchandise bound for the interior or for the seaboard. Some of the pack-horses had burdens the reverse of savory, and the boys learned on inquiry that they were transporting liquid manure to the farms near the borders of the lake. Along the roadside they saw little family groups that were always more or less picturesque; fathers were caring for their children, and seemed to take great delight in playing the part of nurse. It is very common in all the Japanese cities to see men thus occupied, and they never appear to be weary of their tasks. In summer both parent and child will be thinly clad, while in winter they will

HORSE CARRYING LIQUID MANURE.

be wrapped against the cold. The summer garments are not always so thick as the rules of polite society require, and even the winter costume is not very heavy.

Lake Biwa is a beautiful sheet of water, surrounded by picturesque mountains and smiling valleys. Steamers ply upon it, so that an excursion may be made on its waters with the utmost ease; and all around it there are picnic booths where parties may sit and enjoy the view. The time of our friends was limited, and so they had only a glimpse of the lake from one of those pleasure resorts, if a couple of hours spent there may be called a glimpse.

THE PATERNAL NURSE.

They returned to Kioto, and proceeded without delay to Kobe. They found the railway journey much more rapid than the one by jin-riki-sha, but it had the demerit of carrying them so fast that very little could be seen of the country. The day after their arrival at Kobe the steamer was ready to take them to Nagasaki and Shanghai, and at the appointed hour they went on board. Practically, they had finished their sight-seeing in Japan, as they were not to break the journey until setting

PICNIC BOOTH OVERLOOKING LAKE BIWA.

foot on Chinese soil. They left it with the most agreeable recollections, and the boys, as they stood on the deck of the steamer slowly moving out of the harbor of Kobe, simultaneously asked the question,

"Wonder if we shall ever see it again?"

A MAKER OF BOWS.

CHAPTER XXII.

THE INLAND SEA AND NAGASAKI.—CAUGHT IN A TYPHOON.

FROM Kobe westward the route lies through the famous Inland Sea of Japan, known to the Japanese as the Suwo Nada. The Inland Sea is more like a lake than an arm of the ocean; and there have been travellers who could not readily believe that it was connected with the ocean, and that its waters were salt instead of fresh. The distance is, in round numbers, about two hundred and fifty miles; and through the entire voyage the land is constantly in sight, and generally close at hand. The islands rise sharply from the water, and a large portion of them are densely wooded and exceedingly picturesque.

THE INLAND SEA NEAR HIOGO.

During the whole of the voyage, as long as the daylight favored them, our young friends remained on deck, and studied the scenery along the route. Sometimes the sea widened out to fifty miles or more, and at others it contracted so that there was no sign of a passage before them, and it was difficult to say which way the steamer would turn. Now and then the islands were so close together that the steamer made her course as though she were tracing the sinuosities of the Mississippi River, and

APPROACHING SIMONESEKI.

it was necessary to keep a sharp lookout to avoid accidents on the numerous rocks that lie sunken in the channel. Mishaps to the steamers are of rare occurrence, as the channel has been carefully buoyed, and the pilots understand their business fully; but it is otherwise with the unwieldy junks, which are often driven by an adverse wind directly into the dangers their captains are seeking to avoid. The traffic through the Inland Sea is very great, both by the steamers and by the junks; and sometimes whole fleets of the latter may be seen waiting in some of the sheltering nooks for a favoring wind. The steamers make the passage from one end to the other of the Inland Sea in less than twenty-four hours; but the junks are frequently a fortnight in covering the same distance. They are never in a hurry, and therefore time is no object.

DANGEROUS PLACE ON THE SUWO NADA.

The Inland Sea is entered soon after leaving Kobe, and it terminates at Simoneseki, where there is a narrow strait leading into the open waters. Our friends wanted to land at Simoneseki, where the steamer made a halt of a couple of hours; but they were informed that the port was not opened to foreigners, and, therefore, their only view of it was a distant one. However, they were consoled by the reflection that they could have plenty of time at Nagasaki, where the ship was to remain a day and a half before continuing her voyage. Nagasaki was the first place opened to foreigners, and there are many points of interest about the city.

Hardly was the anchor down when our trio entered a boat and were rowed to the shore. Nagasaki is prettily situated in a bay that is completely landlocked, and affords secure anchorage to ships even in the severest gales. Doctor Bronson had been in the harbor of Rio Janeiro, in South America, and said that the bay of Nagasaki was a sort of pocket edition of that of Rio Janeiro. The hills rise abruptly from the water, and lie in terraces that seem to lose themselves in the distance. Some of the hills are wooded, while others are cleared and cultivated; and in either case there are evidences of the most careful attention on the part of the inhabitants of the country. Looking seaward the hills gradually separate until the entrance of the bay is reached; here the island of Pappenberg stands directly across the mouth of the bay, and, while seemingly obstructing it, serves as a breakwater against the in-rolling waves.

PAPPENBERG ISLAND.

20

WOMEN OF NAGASAKI.

"That island has a fearful history," said Doctor Bronson, while they were looking at it when the steamer entered the harbor.

"Do you mean the island of Pappenberg?" Frank asked.

"I know," said Fred; "it has a history connected with the establishment of Christianity in Japan more than two hundred years ago."

"I think I have already told you something of the attempt to make Japan a Christian country," the Doctor continued. "The island of Pappenberg is one of the places that witnessed the extinction of the Christian religion in Japan after it had gained a strong footing. Do you observe that one side of the island is like a precipice?"

The boys regarded the point to which their attention was directed; and they regarded it more attentively when they were told that from that steep rock many thousands of men and women were hurled, solely for the offence of being Christians. Those that were not killed by the fall were drowned in the sea, and not one was allowed to escape. Pappenberg is known in history as the Tarpeian Rock of Japan. It is now used as a picnic resort of the foreign inhabitants of Nagasaki, and a more delightful spot for a pleasure excursion could not be easily found.

According to some writers there were nearly a hundred thousand Christians massacred after the discovery of the conspiracy which was to put Japan under the control of Portugal, but the Japanese say that these figures are an exaggeration. It is difficult to get at the truth of the matter, as neither party can be relied on for accuracy, or rather the accounts that have come down to us cannot be considered impartial.

As nearly as can be ascertained the first European who landed on Japanese soil was Mendez Pinto, a Portuguese who combined the occupations of merchant and pirate in such intimate relations that it was not always easy for him to determine where the one ended and the other began. He has been greatly slandered, and his name has an ignoble place in history, as that of a champion liar. The fact is, that the stories he told on his return to Europe, and which caused him to be called "The Mendacious," were substantially correct—quite as much so as those of Marco Polo, and far more than the narrations of Sir John Mandeville. Pinto came with two companions to the island of Tanega-

shima in 1542, and, as might be ex-pected, they were great curiosities. Even more curious were the fire-arms they carried; and they were in-vited to visit the Daimio of Bungo, and bring their strange weapons with them. They did so, and taught the natives how to make guns and pow-der, which soon became generally used throughout Japan. To this day fire-arms are frequently called "Tanegashima," after the island where Pinto landed with the first of these weapons. Christianity fol-lowed closely on the track of the musket. The adventurers returned with a profit of twelve hundred per cent. on their cargo. Their success stimulated others, and in 1549 two Portuguese missionaries, one of them

A CHRISTIAN VILLAGE IN THE SIXTEENTH CENTURY.

being Francis Xavier, landed in Japan, and began the work of converting the heathen. Xavier's first labors were in Satsuma, and he afterwards went to Kioto and other cities. Personally he never accomplished much, as he could not speak the language fluently, and he remained in the coun-try only a few years. But he did a great deal to inspire others; numbers of missionaries flocked to Japan, and it is said that thirty years after Xavier landed on the soil there were two hundred churches, and a hun-dred and fifty thousand native Christians. At the time of the highest success of the missionaries it is estimated that there were not less than half a million professing Christians in Japan, and perhaps another hundred thousand who were nominally so, though their faith was not regarded as

MONUMENTS IN MEMORY OF MARTYRS.

more than "skin deep." Among the adherents of the new religion there were several Daimios, and a great number of persons occupying high social and official positions. Some of the Daimios were so zealous that they ordered their people to turn Christians whether they wished it or not; and one of them gave his subjects the option of being baptized or leaving the country within twenty-four hours.

The Dutch were great traders in the East Indies, and they managed to obtain a footing in Japan during the time of the Portuguese success. They received a concession of the island of Deshima, about six hundred feet square, in the harbor of Nagasaki, and here they lived until our day. When the troubles arose that led to the expulsion of foreigners and the extinction of Christianity, the Dutch were excepted from the operations of the edict, as it could not be shown that they had had any part in the conspiracy. They had been too busy with their commerce to meddle in religious matters; and, if history is true, it is probable that they hadn't religion enough in their small colony at Deshima to go around and give a perceptible quantity to each man.

This little island was in reality a prison, as its inhabitants were not allowed to go outside for any purpose, except once in three years, when a delegation of them made a journey to Yeddo to make presents to the Tycoon. They were compelled to travel the most of the way in closed nori-

A PATH NEAR NAGASAKI.

mons, and thus their journey did not afford them many glimpses of the country. There is a tradition that they were required to go through the ceremony of trampling on the cross in the presence of the Tycoon, and also to intoxicate themselves, as a warning to the Japanese to shun the wicked ways of the foreigners. Whether either account be true I am unable to say; the assertion is very positively made and as positively denied, and therefore I will leave every reader, who has paid his money for the book, to make choice of the side of the story which suits him best.

The first move of our friends on landing was to go to Deshima, as they had a curiosity to see the little island, which was so famous in the history of the foreign relations of Japan with the outer world. The drawbridge leading to the island, and the box where the Japanese sentries stood, were still there, and so were some of the buildings which the Dutch inhabited: but the Dutch were gone, and probably forever. Outside of the historical interest there was nothing remarkable about the island, and the boys wondered how men could voluntarily shut themselves up in a prison like this. Only one ship a year was allowed to come to them, and sometimes, during the wars between Holland and other countries, there were several years together when no ship came. They were permitted to purchase certain quantities of fresh provisions daily, and when they ran short of needed articles they were supplied by the governor of Nagasaki. But no permission could be granted to go outside their narrow limits. How they must have sighed as they gazed on the green hills opposite, and with what longing did they think of a ramble on those grassy or wooded slopes!

HOLLANDER AT DESHIMA WATCHING FOR A SHIP.

The chief use of Deshima, as our friends found it, is to serve as a depository of Japanese wares, and particularly of the kinds for which Nagasaki is famous. Nagasaki vases and Nagasaki lacquer were in such quantities as to be absolutely bewildering, and for once they found the prices lower than at Yokohama. They made a few purchases—their final transactions in Japan—and then turned their attention to a stroll through the city.

There was not much to amuse them after their acquaintance with other cities of Japan, and so they were speedily satisfied. On the hill overlooking the town and harbor they found an old temple of considerable magnitude, then another, and another, and then tea-houses almost without number. In one of the latter they sat and studied the scenery of Nagasaki until evening, when they returned to the steamer.

Another ramble on shore the following morning, and they left the soil of Japan for the deck of the steamer. At noon they were slowly moving down the bay; they passed the island of Pappenberg, and, as they did so, Frank read from a book he had picked up in the ship's cabin the following paragraph:

"In that same year, when the last of the Roman Catholic converts were hurled from the rocky islet of Pappenberg, in the Bay of Nagasaki, a few exiles landed at Plymouth, in the newly discovered continent, where they were destined to plant the seeds of a Protestant faith and a great Protestant empire. And it was the descendants of the same pilgrim fathers that, two centuries later, were the first among Western nations to supply the link of connection wanted, to bring the lapsed heathen race once more within the circle of Christian communion, and invite them anew to take their place in the family of civilized nations."

And while meditating on the mutations of time and the strangeness of many events recorded in history, our friends passed from the harbor of Nagasaki into the open sea.

"Sayonara!" said Frank, raising his cap and bowing towards the receding land.

"Sayonara!" echoed Fred, as he followed his cousin's example. "I say 'Sayonara' now, but I hope that some time in the future I may be able to say 'Ohio.'"

"And so do I," Frank added. "It is a charming country, and I don't think we shall find a more agreeable one anywhere."

The conversation was cut short by the call to dinner, a call that has suppressed many a touch of sentiment before now, on land as well as on the water.

It is a voyage of two days, more or less, according to the speed of the steamer, from Nagasaki to Shanghai. Our friends had hoped to be in Shanghai on the afternoon of the second day from the former port; but their hopes were not destined to be realized. The Japanese gods of Rain, Wind, and Thunder interfered.

THE RAIN DRAGON.

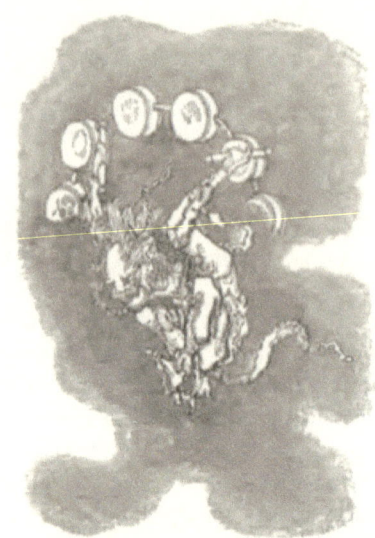

THE WIND DRAGON.   THE THUNDER DRAGON.

The morning after their departure from Nagasaki, Frank went on deck soon after daylight. The wind was so strong that it almost took him from his feet, and he was compelled to grasp something to make sure of remaining upright. The sky was overcast, and every few minutes there came a sprinkling of rain that intimated that the cabin was the better place for any one who was particular about keeping dry. Fred joined him in a few minutes, and soon after Fred's arrival the Doctor made his appearance.

The Captain was on the bridge of the steamer, and appeared much disturbed about something, so much so that the boys asked Dr. Bronson if he thought anything had gone wrong.

The Doctor gave a hasty glance at the sky and the water, and then retreated to the cabin, where a barometer was hanging. A moment's observation of the instrument satisfied him, or, rather, it greatly dissatisfied him, for he returned hastily to the deck and rejoined the boys with the observation,

"We shall have it very lively in a short time, and are not likely to reach Shanghai in a hurry."

"Why? What do you mean?"

"I mean that we are about to have a typhoon."

"I should rather like to see one," Frank remarked.

"Well," the Doctor replied, "you are about to be accommodated, and if we get safely out of it I am very sure you will not want to see another.

"But as we are in for it," he continued, "we must make the best of the situation, and hope to go through in safety. Many a strong ship lies at the bottom of the sea, where she was sent by just such a storm as we are about to pass through, and many another has barely escaped. I was once on a ship in the China seas, when the captain told the passengers that it would be a miracle if we remained half an hour longer afloat. But hardly had he done speaking when the wind fell, the storm abated, and we were safe. The typhoon is to these waters what the hurricane is to the West Indies; it is liable to blow at any time between April and September, and is often fearfully destructive.

"The word typhoon comes from the Japanese 'Tai-Fun,' which means 'great wind,' and the meaning is admirably descriptive of the thing itself. There is no greater wind in the world than a typhoon; the traditional wind that would blow the hair off the back of a dog is as nothing to it. A cyclone is the same sort of thing, and the two terms are interchangeable; cyclone is the name of European origin, while typhoon comes from the Asiatic.

"The typhoon blows in a circle, and may be briefly described as a rapidly revolving wind that has a diameter of from two to five hundred miles. It is a whirlwind on a large scale, and as furious as it is large. A curious fact about it is that it has a calm centre, where there is absolutely no wind at all, and this centre is sometimes forty or fifty miles across. Nearest the centre the wind has the greatest violence, and the farther you can get from it, the less severe is the gale. Mariners always try to sail away from the centre of a typhoon, and I have known a ship to turn at right angles from her course in order to get as far as possible from the centre of a coming tempest. There is a great difference of opinion among captains concerning these storms, some declaring that they have been in the middle point of a typhoon and escaped safely, while others aver that no ship that was ever built can withstand the fury of a storm centre. But I think the weight of evidence is in favor of the former rather than the latter, as I have known captains who have described their situation in such a way as to leave not the slightest doubt in my mind of the correctness of their statements.

"If you have any desire to study the subject fully, I advise you to get 'Piddington's Law of Storms;' you will find it treated very fully and intelligently, both from the scientific and the popular point of view.

A TYPHOON.

"It has never been my fortune," the Doctor continued, "to be farther in a typhoon at sea than the outer edge, but that was quite as much as I wanted. One time on land I saw and felt one of these tempests; it drove ships from their moorings, swamped hundreds of boats, unroofed many houses, tore trees up by the roots, stripped others of their branches, threw down walls and fences, flooded the land, and caused a vast amount of havoc everywhere. Hundreds of people were drowned by the floods, and the traces of the storm will last for many years. The city that has suffered most by these storms is Calcutta. On two occasions the centre of a typhoon has passed over the harbor or within a few miles of it, and the whole shipping of the port was driven from its moorings and the greater part completely or partially wrecked."

While they were listening to the remarks of the Doctor the boys observed that the wind was increasing, and as they looked at the compass they found that the ship's course had been changed. Everything about the vessel that could be made fast was carefully secured, and the party was notified that they might be ordered below at any moment. The waves were not running high, and but for the very severe wind there would have been nothing to cause more than ordinary motion on board the steamer.

After a time the waves broke into what is called a "choppy sea;" the wind was so great that their crests were blown away before they could rise to any height worthy of notice. Mariners say that in a severe typhoon the ocean is quite smooth, owing to the inability of the waves to form against the irresistible force of the wind. It is fortunate for them that such is the case, as they could not possibly survive the combined action of the cyclone and the great waves together.

For three or four hours the wind continued to increase, and the waters to assume the shapes we have seen. The barometer had fallen steadily, and everything indicated that the arrival of the steamer at Shanghai, or at any other port, was by no means a matter of certainty. The order was issued for the passengers to go below, and our friends descended to the cabin. Just as they did so the decks were swept by a mass of water that seemed to have been lifted bodily from the sea by a gust of wind. The order to go below was not issued a moment too soon.

The Doctor took another glance at the barometer, and discovered something. The mercury was stationary!

Ten minutes later it had risen a few hundredths of a degree. The rise was small, but it was a rise. In another ten minutes another gain was perceptible.

The Doctor's face brightened, and he called the boys to observe what he had discovered. He had already explained to them that the barometer falls at the approach of stormy weather, and rises when the storm is about to pass away. Before a storm like a typhoon the fall is very rapid, and so certainly is this the case that mariners rely upon the barometer to give them warning of impending danger.

An hour from the time they went below they were allowed to go on deck again. The wind had abated a little, so that there was no further danger of their being swept from the decks by the water; the clouds were less dense and the rain was not falling so heavily. In another hour there was another perceptible decline in the wind, and a little later the ship was again put on her course. The captain announced the danger over, and said the centre of the typhoon had passed at least a hundred miles to the west of them. "If we had kept our course," said he, "we should have been much nearer to it, and then the storm would have been more dangerous for us."

"How do you know which way to turn?" Frank asked; "it seems to me you are just as likely to run to the centre of the storm as to the circumference."

"There's where you don't understand the science of storms," said the captain smiling. "In the northern hemisphere typhoons, cyclones, and

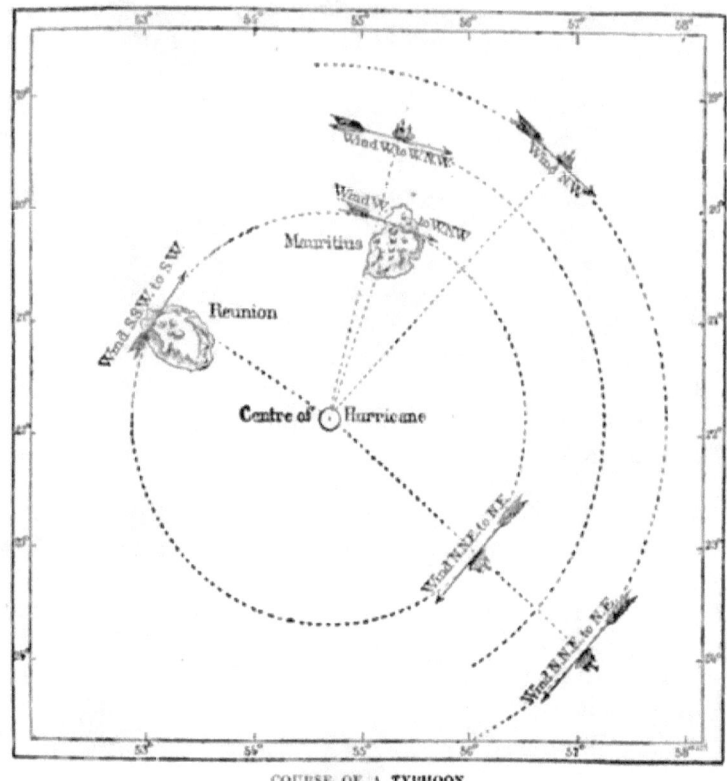

COURSE OF A TYPHOON.

hurricanes—they are all the same—whirl from left to right, that is, they turn like the hands of a watch, while in the southern hemisphere their motion is exactly the reverse. When we think we are in the sweep of a typhoon in these waters, we run with the wind on our starboard, or right hand, and that course will take us away from the centre. In the southern hemisphere we run with the wind on the port, or left hand, with the same result. But we'll go to dinner now and be happy, for the danger is over."

Just as they were rising from table they were suddenly called on deck by the announcement of a wreck. An American bark had been dismasted by the gale and lay helpless on the water; her captain wished to be taken in tow to the mouth of the Yang-tse-kiang, and after some minutes spent in making a bargain, the matter was arranged and a line passed out.

"They were less fortunate than we," the Doctor remarked as they proceeded with their tow.

CAUGHT NEAR THE STORM'S CENTRE.

"Yes," answered the captain, "the poor fellow was nearer the centre of the typhoon than we were. There'll be a job for the ship-carpenters and riggers at Shanghai; it's an ill wind that blows nobody any good."

Frank was looking through the captain's glass at the persons who were moving about the deck of the bark. Suddenly he observed something, and called out to his companions:

"Look, look! here's a familiar face!"

The Doctor took the glass and then handed it to Fred; the latter looked steadily for a minute or more before he had a satisfactory view, and then said:

"It's our old friend, the Mystery!"

CHAPTER XXIII.

FIRST DAY IN CHINA.

IN due time they entered the waters of the great river of Northern China, the Yang-tse. They entered them long before they sighted land, as the vast quantities of earth brought down by the stream make a change in the color of the sea that can be readily distinguished a great distance from the coast. In this respect the Yang-tse is similar to the Mississippi, and the effect of the former on the Yellow Sea is like that of the latter on the Gulf of Mexico. The coast at the mouth of the Yang-tse is low and flat, and a ship is fairly in the entrance of the river before land can be seen. The bar can be passed by deep-draught vessels only at high water, and consequently it often becomes necessary for them to wait several hours for the favorable moment. This was the case with our friends, and they walked the deck with impatience during the delay. But at last all was ready, and they steamed onward in triumph, dropping their tow at Woosung, and waving a good-bye to "the Mystery," who had recognized them from the deck of the disabled bark.

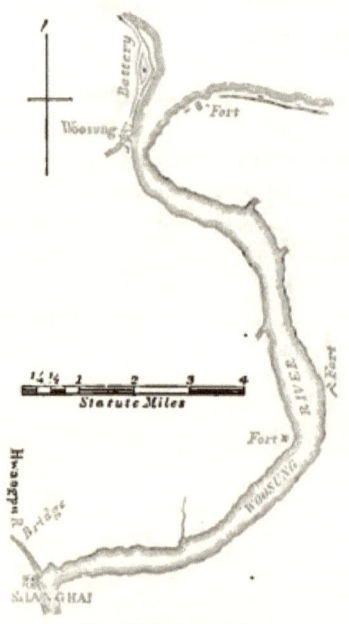

THE WOOSUNG RIVER.

Shanghai is not on the Yang-tse, but on the Woosung River, about twelve miles from the point where the two streams unite. The channel is quite tortuous, and it requires careful handling on the part of a pilot to take a ship through in safety to herself and all others. Two or three times they narrowly escaped accidents from collisions with junks and other craft, and at one of the turnings the prow of their steamer made a nearer acquaintance with a mud-bank than her captain considered desirable; but nothing was injured, and the delay that followed the mishap was for only a few minutes. The tide was running in, and carried them along at good speed; and in less than two hours from the time of their departure from Woosung they were anchored in front

CHINESE TRADING-JUNK ON THE WOOSUNG RIVER.

of Shanghai and ready to go on shore. They had not seen anything particularly interesting on their voyage up the river, as the banks were low and not at all densely settled. Here and there a few villages were thrown together, and it occurred to Frank that the houses were huddling close up to each other in order to keep warm. The most of the ground was clear of timber; but there were some farm-houses standing in little clumps of trees that, no doubt, furnished a welcome shade in the summer season. One mile of the river was very much like another mile, and consequently the monotony of the scenery made the sight of Shanghai a welcome one.

Crowds of sampans surrounded the ship as the anchor-chain rattled through the hawse-hole, and it was very evident that there was no lack of transportation for the shore. The Doctor engaged one of these boats, and gave the baggage of the party into the hands of the runner from the Astor House, the principal hotel of the American section of Shanghai. They found it a less imposing affair than the Astor House of New York, though it occupied more ground, and had an evident determination to spread itself. A large space of greensward was enclosed by a quadrangle of one-story buildings, which formed the hotel, and consequently it required a great deal of walking to get from one part of the house to the opposite side. Our friends were shown to some rooms that were entered from a veranda on the side of the court-yard. They found that on the other side there was a balcony, where they could sit and study the life of the street; and as this balcony was well provided with chairs and lounges, it was a pleasant resort on a warm afternoon. The house was kept by an American, but all his staff of servants was Chinese. Fred regretted that he could not praise the dining-table as earnestly as he did the rooms, and he was vehement in declaring that a breakfast or dinner in the Astor at New York was quite another affair from the same meal in the one at Shanghai. The Doctor and Frank were of his opinion; but they found, on inquiry, that the landlord did not agree with them, and so they dropped the subject.

As soon as they were settled at the hotel, they went out for a stroll through the city, and to deliver letters to several gentlemen residing there. They had some trouble in finding the houses they were searching for, as the foreigners at Shanghai do not consider it aristocratic to have signs on their doors or gate-posts, and a good deal of inquiry is necessary for a stranger to make his way about. If a man puts out a sign, he is regarded as a tradesman, and unfit to associate with the great men of the place; but as long as there is no sign or placard about his premises he is a merchant, and his company is desirable, especially if he is free with his money. A tradesman cannot gain admission to the Shanghai Club, and the same is the rule at Hong-Kong and other ports throughout the East. But there is no bar to the membership of his clerk; and it not infrequently happens that a man will be refused admission to a club on account of his occupation, while his clerk will be found eligible. There are many senseless rules of society in the East, and our boys were greatly amused as the Doctor narrated them.

Shanghai is very prettily situated in a bend of the river, and the water-front is ornamented with a small park, which has a background of fine buildings. These buildings are handsome, and the most of them are large. Like the foreign residences at the treaty ports of Japan, they have a liberal allowance of ground, so that nearly every house fronting on the river has a neat yard or garden in front of it. The balconies are wide, and they are generally enclosed in lattice-work that allows a free circulation of air. Back from the water-front there are streets and squares for a long distance; and the farther you go from the river-front, the less do you find the foreign population, and the greater the Chinese one. The foreign quarter is divided into three sections—American, English, and French—and each has a front on the river in the order here given, but the subjects, or citizens, of each country are not confined to their own national quarter; several Americans live in the French and English sections, and there are French and English inhabitants in the quarter where the American consul has jurisdiction. There is generally the most complete harmony among

SHANGHAI.

21

the nationalities, and they are accustomed to make common cause in any dispute with the Chinese. Sometimes they fall out; but they very soon become aware that disputes will be to their disadvantage, and proceed to fall in again. There is a great deal of social activity at Shanghai, and a vast amount of visiting and dinner-giving goes on in the course of a year.

The Chinese city is quite distinct from the foreign one; it lies just beyond the French concession, or, rather, the French section extends up to the walls of the old city. The contrast between the two is very great. While the foreigners have taken plenty of space for the construction of their buildings and laying out their streets, the Chinese have crowded together as closely as possible, and seemed desirous of putting the greatest number into the smallest area. It is so all over China from north to south. Even where land is of no particular value, as in the extreme north, the result is the same; and there are probably no people in the world that will exist in so small an area as the Chinese. Ventilation is not a necessity with them, and it seems to make little difference whether the air they breathe be pure or the reverse. In almost any other country in the world a system of such close crowding would breed all sorts of pestilence, but in China nobody appears to die from its effect.

At the first opportunity our friends paid a visit to the Chinese part of Shanghai. They found a man at the gate of the city who was ready to serve them as guide, and so they engaged him without delay. He led them through one of the principal streets, which would have been only a narrow lane or alley in America; and they had an opportunity of studying the peculiarities of the people as they had studied in the Japanese cities the people of Japan. Here is what Frank wrote down concerning his first promenade in a Chinese city:

A COOLIE IN THE STREETS OF SHANGHAI.

"We found the streets narrow and dirty compared with Japan, or with any city I ever saw in America. The shops are small, and the shopkeepers are not so polite as those of Tokio or other places in Japan. In one shop, when I told the guide to ask the man to show his goods, they had a long talk in Chinese, and the guide said that the man refused to show anything unless we should agree to buy. Of course we would not agree to this, and we did nothing more than to ask the price of something we could see in a show-case. He wanted about ten times the value of the article; and then we saw why it was he wanted us to agree beforehand to buy what we looked at. Every time we stopped at a shop the people gathered around us, and they were not half so polite as the Japanese under the same circumstances. They made remarks about us, which of course we did not understand; but from the way they laughed when the remarks were made, we could see that they were the reverse of complimentary.

"We went along the street, stopping now and then to look at something, and in a little while we came to a tea-house which stood in the middle of a pond of water. The house was rather pretty, and the balconies around it were nice, but you should have seen the water. It was covered with a green scum, such as you may see on a stagnant pool anywhere in the world, and the odor from it was anything but sweet. Fred said it was the same water that was let into the pool when they first made it. The guide says the house is a hundred years old, and I should think the water was quite as old as the house; or perhaps it is some second-hand water that they bought cheap, and if so it may be very ancient. We went into the house and sat down to take some tea. They gave us some tea-leaves, on which they poured hot water, and then covered the cup over for a minute or two. Each of us had his portion of tea separate from all the others. The tea was steeped in the cup, and when we wanted more we poured hot water on again. Then they brought little cakes and melon-seeds, with salt to eat with the seeds. Our guide took some of the seeds, and we ate one or two each to see how they tasted. I can't recommend them, and don't think there is any danger they will ever be introduced into the United States as a regular article of diet.

"When we rose to go, and asked how much we owed, we were astonished at the price. The proprietor demanded a dollar for what we had had, when, as we afterwards learned, twenty-five cents would have been more than enough. We had some words with him through our interpreter, and finally paid the bill which we had found so outrageous. We told him we should not come there again; and he said he did not expect us to, as strangers rarely came more than once into the Chinese part of Shanghai. He was a nice specimen of a Chinese rascal; and Doctor Bronson says he must have taken lessons of some of the American swindlers at Niagara Falls and other popular resorts. What a pity it is that whenever you find

A TEA-HOUSE IN THE COUNTRY.

something outrageously bad in a strange country, you have only to think a moment to discover something equally bad in your own!

"At one place we looked into a little den where some people were smoking opium. They were lying on benches, and were very close together. The room wasn't more than eight feet square, and yet there were a dozen people in it, and perhaps one or two more. The guide told us it was a mistake to suppose that they smoked opium as we smoke tobacco. We stand, sit, or walk while smoking; but when a Chinese uses opium, he always reclines on a bench or bed, and gives himself up to his enjoyment.

SMOKING OPIUM.

Men go to the shops where opium is sold and lie down on the benches for a period of pleasure. Sometimes two persons go together, and then they lie on the same bench and take turns in filling each other's pipe.

"The opium must be boiled to fit it for use, and when ready it looks like very thick molasses. A man takes a long needle and dips it into the opium, and then he twists it around till he gets a ball of the drug as large as a pea. He holds this ball in the flame of a lamp till it becomes hot and partially burning, and then he thrusts it into a little orifice in the top of the bowl of the pipe. He continues to hold it in the flame, and, while it is burning, he slowly inhales the fumes that come from it. A few whiffs exhaust the pipe, and then the smoker rests for several minutes before he takes another. The amount required for intoxication is regulated and estimated in pipes; one man can be overcome by three or four pipes, while another will need ten, twenty, or even thirty of them. A beginner is satisfied with one or two pipes, and will go to sleep for several hours. He is said to have dreams of the pleasantest sort, but he generally feels weak and exhausted the next day.

"Dr. Bronson says he tried to smoke opium the first time he was in China, but it made him very ill, and he did not get through with a single pipe. Some Europeans have learned to like it, and have lost their senses in

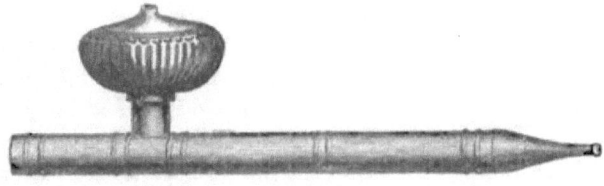

OPIUM-PIPE.

consequence of giving way to the temptation. It is said to be the most seductive thing in the world, and some who have tried it once say it was so delightful that they would not risk a second time, for fear the habit would be so fixed that they could not shake it off. It is said that when a Chinese has tried it for ten or fifteen days in succession he cannot recover, or but very rarely does so. The effects are worse than those of intoxicating liquors, as they speedily render a man incapable of any kind of business, even when he is temporarily free from the influence of the drug. The habit is an expensive one, as the cost of opium is very great in consequence of the taxes and the high profits to those who deal in it. In a short time a man finds that all his earnings go for opium, and even when he is comfortably well off he will make a serious inroad on his property by his indulgence in the vice. A gentleman who has lived long in China, and studied the effects of opium on the people, says as follows:

" ' With all smokers the effect of this vice on their pecuniary standing is by no means to be estimated by the actual outlay in money for the drug.

Its seductive influence leads its victims to neglect their business, and consequently, sooner or later, loss or ruin ensues. As the habit grows, so does inattention to business increase. Instances are not rare where the rich have been reduced to poverty and beggary, as one of the consequences of their attachment to the opium pipe. The poor addicted to this vice are often led to dispose of everything salable in the hovels where they live. Sometimes men sell their wives and children to procure the drug, and end by becoming beggars and thieves. In the second place, the smoking of opium injures one's health and bodily

MAN BLINDED BY USE OF OPIUM.

constitution. Unless taken promptly at the regular time, and in the necessary quantity, the victim becomes unable to control himself and to attend to his business. He sneezes, he gapes, mucus runs from his nose and eyes, griping pains seize him in the bowels, his whole appearance indicates restlessness and misery. If not indulged in smoking and left undisturbed, he usually falls asleep, but his sleep does not refresh and invigorate him. On being aroused, he is himself again, provided he can have his opium. If not, his troubles and pains multiply, he has no appetite for ordinary food, no strength or disposition to labor. He becomes emaciated to a frightful degree, his eyes protrude from their sockets; and if he cannot procure opium, he dies in the most horrible agony.'

" The government has tried to stop the use of opium, but was prevented from so doing by England, which made war upon China to compel her to open her ports and markets for its sale. It is no wonder that the Chinese are confused as to the exact character of Christianity, when a Christian nation makes war upon them to compel them to admit a poison which that Christian nation produces, and which kills hundreds of thousands of Chinese every year.

" We made all our journey on foot, as we could not find any jin-riki-shas, except in the foreign part of Shanghai. They were only brought into use a few years ago, and they cannot be employed in all the cities of

CHINESE GENTLEMAN IN A SEDAN.

China, because the streets are very narrow, and the carriage could not move about. But we saw some sedan-chairs, and one of these days we are going to have a ride in them. It looks as though a ride of this sort would be very comfortable, as you have a good chair to sit in, and then you are held up by men who walk along very steadily. Ordinarily you have two men; but if you are a grand personage, or are going on a long course, three or four men are needed. The chair is quite pretty, as it has a lot of ornamental work about it, and the lower part is closed in with light panelling or bamboo-work. It is surprising what loads the coolies carry, and how long they will walk without apparent fatigue. They are accustomed to this kind of work all their lives, and seem to think it is all right.

"We came back pretty tired, as the streets are not agreeable for walking on account of the dust and the rough places. They don't seem to care how their streets are in China. When they have finished a street, they let it take care of itself; and if it wears out, it is none of their business. I am told that there are roads in China that were well made at the start, but have not had a particle of repair in a hundred years. They must be rough things to travel on."

CHAPTER XXIV.

A VOYAGE UP THE YANG-TSE-KIANG.

THE plans of the Doctor included a journey up the great river, the Yang-tse. There was abundant opportunity for the proposed voyage, as there were two lines of steamers making regular trips as far as Han-kow, about six hundred miles from Shanghai. One line was the property of a Chinese company, and the other of an English one. The Chinese company's boats were of American build, and formerly belonged to an, American firm that had large business relations in the East. The business of navigating the Yang-tse-kiang had been very profitable, and at one time it was said that the boats had made money enough to sink them if it were all put into silver and piled on their decks. But there was a decline when an opposition line came into the field and caused a heavy reduction of the prices for freight and passage. In the early days of steam navigation on

CANAL SCENE SOUTH OF SHANGHAI.

the Yang-tse-kiang a passage from Shanghai to Han-kow cost four hundred dollars, and the price of freight was in proportion. For several years the Americans had a monopoly of the business, and could do pretty much as they liked. When the opposition began, the fares went down, down, down; and at the time our friends were in China the passage to Han-kow was to be had for twenty-four dollars—quite a decline from four hundred to twenty-four.

The boys had expected to find the boats in China small and inconvenient. What was their astonishment to find them like the great steamers that ply on the North River, or from New York to Fall River or Providence. They found the cabins were large and comfortable, though they were not so numerous as on the American waters, for the reason that there were rarely many passengers to be carried. The captain, pilots, engineers, and other officers were Americans, while the crew were Chinese. The managers of the company were Chinese, but they left the control of the boats entirely in the hands of their respective captains. One boat had a Chinese captain and officers, but she was a small affair, and, from all that could be learned, the managers did not find their experiment of running with their own countrymen a successful one.

At the advertised time the three strangers went on board the steamer that was to carry them up the river, and took possession of the cabins assigned to them. Their only fellow-passengers were some Chinese merchants on their way to Nanking, and a consular clerk at one of the British consulates along the stream. The captain of the steamer was a jolly New-Yorker, who had an inexhaustible fund of stories, which he was never tired of telling. Though he told dozens of them daily, Frank remarked that he was not like history, for he never repeated himself. Fred remembered that some one had said to him in Japan that he would be certain of a pleasant voyage on the Yang-tse-kiang if he happened to fall in with Captain Paul on the steamer *Kiang-ching*. Fortune had favored him, and he had found the steamer and the captain he desired.

Frank observed that the steamer had been provided with a pair of eyes, which were neatly carved on wood, and painted so as to resemble the human eye. The captain explained that this was in deference to the Chinese custom of painting eyes on their ships and boats; and if he looked at the first boat, or other Chinese craft, large or small, that he saw, he would discover that it had eyes painted on the bow. This is the universal custom throughout China; and though a native may have a suspicion that it does no good, he would not be willing to fly in the face of old custom. In case he should leave his craft in blindness, and any accident befell her, he would be told by his friends, "Serves you right for not giving your ship eyes to see with."

The steamer descended the Woosung River to its intersection with the Yang-tse-kiang, and then began the ascent of the latter. The great stream was so broad that it seemed more like a bay than a river. This condition continued for a hundred and fifty miles, when the bay narrowed to a river, and the far-famed Silver Island came in sight. It stands in mid-stream, a steep hill of rock, about three hundred feet high, crowned with a pagoda, and covered from base to summit with trees and bushes and rich grass. At first it might be taken for an uninhabited spot, but as the boat approaches you can see that there are numerous summer-houses and other habitations peeping out from the verdure. A little beyond the island there is a city which straggles over the hills, and is backed by a range of mountains that make a sharp outline against the sky. This is Chin-kiang, the first stopping-place of the steamer as she proceeds from Shanghai to Han-kow. She was to remain several hours, and our friends embraced the opportunity to take a stroll on shore. Here is Frank's account of the expedition:

A CHINESE FAMILY PARTY.

"The streets of Chin-kiang are narrow and dirty, and the most of them that we saw seemed to be paved with kitchen rubbish and other unsavory substances. The smells that rose to our nostrils were too numerous and too disagreeable to mention; Fred says he discovered fifty-four distinct and different ones, but I think there were not more than forty-seven or forty-eight. The Doctor says we have not fairly tested the city, as there are several wards to hear from in addition to the ones we visited in our ramble. I was not altogether unprepared for these unpleasant

A GENTLEMAN OF CHIN-KIANG.

features of Chin-kiang, as I had already taken a walk in the Chinese part of Shanghai.

"Everybody says that one Chinese town is so much like another that a single one will do for a sample. This is undoubtedly true of the most of them, but you should make exceptions in the case of Canton and Pekin. They are of extra importance; and as one is in the extreme north, and the other in the far south, they have distinctive features of their own. We shall have a chance to talk about them by-and-by. As for Chin-kiang, I did not see anything worth notice while walking through it that I had not already seen at Shanghai, except, perhaps, that the dogs barked at us, and the cats ruffled their backs and tails, and fled from us as though we were bull-dogs. A pony tried to kick Fred as he walked by the brute, and only missed his mark by a couple of inches. You see that the dumb animals were not disposed to welcome us hospitably. They were evidently put up to their conduct by their masters, who do not like the strangers any more than the dogs and cats do, and are only prevented from showing their spite by the fear that the foreigners will blow their towns out of existence if any of them are injured.

"We bought some things in the shops, but they did not amount to much either in cost or quality. Fred found a pair of Chinese spectacles

CHINESE SPECTACLES.

which he paid half a dollar for; they were big round things, with glasses nearly as large as a silver dollar, and looked very comical when put on. But I am told that they are very comfortable to the eyes, and that the foreigners who live in China, and have occasion to wear spectacles, generally prefer those made by the Chinese opticians. A pair of really fine pebbles will cost from ten to twenty dollars. The glasses that Fred bought were only the commonest kind of stuff, colored with a smoky tint so as to reduce the glare of the sun.

"We went outside the town, and found ourselves suddenly in the country. It was a complete change. Going through a gate in a wall took us from the streets to the fields, and going back through the gate took us to the streets again. We saw a man ploughing with a plough that had only one handle, and made a furrow in the ground about as large as if he had dragged a pickaxe through it. The plough was pulled by a Chinese buffalo about as large as a two-year-old steer, and he was guided by means of a cord drawn through the cartilage of his nose. It was a poor outfit for a farmer; but the man who had it appeared perfectly contented, and did not once turn his eyes from his work to look at us.

"A little way off from this ploughman there was a man threshing grain on some slats; they looked like a small ladder placed on an incline, and the way he did the work was to take a handful of grain and thresh it against the slats till he had knocked out all the kernels and left nothing but the straw. Such a thing as a threshing-machine would astonish them very much, I should think, and I don't believe they would allow it to run.

PLOUGHING WITH A BUFFALO.

Labor is so cheap in China that they don't want any machinery to save it; when you can hire a man for five cents a day, and even less, you haven't any occasion to economize.

THRESHING GRAIN NEAR CHIN-KIANG.

"The man who brought the bundles of grain to the thresher had them slung over his shoulder, as they carry everything in this country; two bundles made a load for him, and they were not large bundles either. Such a thing as a farm-wagon is as unknown as a threshing-machine, and would not be useful, as the paths among the fields are very narrow, and a wagon couldn't run on them at all. Land is very valuable in the neighborhood of the towns, and they would consider it wasteful to have a wide strip of it taken up for a road. And, as I have just said, labor is very cheap, especially the labor of the coolies who carry burdens. All the men I saw at work in the field were barefooted, and probably

CARRYING BUNDLES OF GRAIN.

the wages they receive do not leave them much to spend on boots, after they have supported their families and paid their taxes. They must have a hard time to get along, but they appear perfectly cheerful and contented."

From Chin-kiang the steamer proceeded up the river. The account of what they saw was thus continued by the boys:

"The southern branch of the grand canal enters the river at Chin-kiang; the northern branch comes in some distance below. The river is plentifully dotted with junks, but this condition is not peculiar to the vicinity of the canal. All the way up from Shanghai to Han-kow it is the same, and sometimes twenty or thirty boats will be sailing so closely together as to endanger their cordage and sides. Perhaps you have seen New York Bay on a pleasant afternoon in summer when every boat that could hoist a sail was out for an airing? Well, imagine this great river for hundreds of miles dotted with sails as thickly as our bay on the occasion I have indicated, and you can have an idea of the native commerce of the Yang-tse-kiang. Nobody knows how many boats there are on the river, as no census of them is taken. The mandarins collect toll at the river stations, but do not trouble themselves to keep a record of the numbers. I asked a Chinese merchant who is a fellow-passenger with us how many boats there are engaged in the navigation of the Yang-tse and its tributaries, and he answers,

A RIVER SCENE IN CHINA.

"' P'raps hunder tousand, p'raps million ; nobody don't know.'

" Another says, 'Great many big million,' and he may not be far out of the way, though his statement is not very specific.

" I have heard a curious story of how the foreigners have secured more privileges than are allowed to the native merchants. Every district has the right to tax goods passing through it. At each district there is a barrier, commanded by a petty official, with a military guard, and here each native boat must stop and pay the transit tax. For long distances these taxes amount to a large sum, and frequently are a great deal more than the goods cost originally. These taxes are known as 'squeezes,' and the barriers where they are paid are called 'squeeze stations.' But the foreigners have secured a treaty with China, or, rather, there is a clause in one of the treaties, which exempts them from the payment of the transit 'squeezes;' they only pay the customs duties, and the local tax at the place of destination. Transit passes are issued by which goods belonging to foreigners, though carried in native boats, are exempt from squeezing, but these passes can only be obtained by foreigners.

"Since the law went into operation, many Chinese merchants have gone into partnership with foreigners; the former furnishing the capital and attending to all the business, while the latter obtain the transit passes and give the name to the firm. A gentleman whom we met in Shanghai is associated with some wealthy Chinese; they put in the money, and he furnishes his name and gets the passes, which none of them could do.

"The native junks will always give a free passage to a foreigner who will pretend to own the cargo, since they can escape the squeeze if he plays his part successfully. The captain says that last year a sailor who wanted to join an English gun-boat at a place up the river was carried through for nothing by a junk whose cargo he pretended to own. He passed as a 'foreign merchant,' but the fact was he had never bought anything in his life more valuable than a suit of clothes, and had sold a great deal less than that.

"The river above Chin-kiang is in some places very pretty, and the mountains rise out of the water here and there, making a great contrast to the lowlands farther down. There are several large cities on the way, the most important (or, at all events, the one we know the most about) being Nanking. It was famous for its porcelain tower, which was destroyed years ago by the rebels. Every brick has been carried away, and they have actually dug down into the foundations for more. There is only a part of the city left; and as we did not have time to go on shore, I am not able to say much about it.' But there are several other cities that were more fortunate, since they were able to save their towers, or pagodas, as they are generally called. These pagodas are always built with an odd number of stories, usually five, seven, or nine; but once in a great while there is an ambitious one of eleven stories, or a cheap and modest one of only three. We saw one handsome pagoda of nine stories that had bushes and climbing-plants growing from it. I suppose the birds carried the seeds

there, and then they sprouted
and took root. They make the
pagoda look very old, and certainly that is quite proper, as
they are all of an age that young
people should respect.

"There is a funny little isl-
and—and not so little, after all,
as it is three hundred feet high
—that stands right in the middle of the river at one place.
They call it the Little Orphan
Rock, probably because it was
never known to have any father
or mother. There is a temple
in the side of the rock, as if a
niche had been cut to receive
it. Fred thinks the people who
live there ought not to complain
of their ventilation and drain-
age; and if they fell out of the
front windows by any accident,

A NINE-STORIED PAGODA.

they would not be worth much when picked up. Away up on the top
of the rock there is a little temple that would make a capital light-house,

LITTLE ORPHAN ROCK.

but I suppose the Chinese are too far behind the times to think of turning it to any practical use. Great Orphan Rock is farther up the river, or a little out of the river, in what they call Po-yang Lake.

"Around the shores of Po-yang Lake is where they make a great deal of the porcelain, and what we call 'China ware,' that they send to America. The captain says he has frequently taken large quantities of it down the river to Shanghai, and that it was sent from there to our country. They dig the clay that they want for making the porcelain on the shores of the lake, and they get their fuel for burning it from the forests, not far away. The entrance to the lake is very picturesque; there is a town in a fortress on a hill that overlooks the river, and then there is a fort close down by the water. Probably the fort wouldn't be of much use against a fleet of foreign ships; but it looks well, and that is what pleases the Chinese."

ENTRANCE TO PO-YANG LAKE.

CHAPTER XXV.

THE TAE-PING REBELLION.—SCENES ON THE GREAT RIVER.

THE evidences of a large population along the Yang-tse were easy to see; but, nevertheless, Frank and Fred were somewhat disappointed. They had read of the overcrowded condition of China, and they saw the great numbers of boats that navigated the river, and consequently they looked for a proportionately dense mass of people on shore. Sometimes, for two or three hours at a time, not a house could be seen; and at others the villages were strung along in a straggling sort of way, as though they were thinly inhabited, and wished to make as good a show as possible. There were many places where the land did not seem to be under cultivation at all, as it was covered with a dense growth of reeds and rushes. In some localities the country appeared so much like a wilderness that the boys half expected to see wild beasts running about undisturbed; they began to speculate as to the kind of beasts that were to be found there, and finally questioned Dr. Bronson on the subject.

The Doctor explained to them that this desolation was more apparent than real, and that if they should make a journey on shore, at almost any point, for a few miles back from the river, they would find all the people they wanted. "About thirty years ago," said he, "they had a rebellion in China; it lasted for a long time, and caused an immense destruction of life and property. The rebels had possession of the cities along the Yang-tse, and at one period it looked as though they would succeed in destroying the government."

"Did they destroy the cities that we see in ruins?" Fred asked.

"Yes," answered the Doctor, "they destroyed several cities so completely that not a hundred inhabitants remained, where formerly there had been many thousands; and other cities were so greatly injured that the traces of the rebel occupation have not been removed. I believe there is not a city that escaped uninjured, and you have seen for yourselves how some of them have suffered.

"The rebellion," he continued, "is known in history as the Tae-ping insurrection. The words 'tae ping' mean 'general peace,' and were inscribed on the banners of the rebels. The avowed intention of the leader of the revolt was to overthrow the imperial power, and deliver the country from its oppressors. There were promises of a division of property, or, at all events, the rebels were to have free license to plunder wherever they went; and as there are always a great many people who have everything to gain and nothing to lose, the rebellion gathered strength as time went on. The leaders managed to convince the foreigners that they were inclined to look favorably on Christianity, and the idea went abroad that the Tae-pings were a sort of Chinese Protestants, who wanted to do away with old abuses, and were in favor of progress and of more intimate relations with foreign nations. Many of the missionaries in China were friendly to the rebellion, and so were some of the merchants and others established there.

TAE-PING REBELS.

"So powerful did the rebels become that they had nearly a third of the best part of the empire under their control, and the imperial authorities became seriously alarmed. City after city had been captured by the rebels, and at one time the overthrow of the government appeared almost certain. The rebels were numerous and well officered, and they had the advantage of foreign instruction, and, to some extent, of foreign arms. The imperialists went to war after the old system, which consisted of sound rather than sense. They were accustomed to beat gongs, fire guns, and make a great noise to frighten the enemy; and as the enemy knew perfectly well what it was all about, it did not amount to much. The suppression of the rebellion was largely due to foreigners, and the most prominent of these was an American."

"What! an American leader for Chinese?"

"Yes, an American named Ward, who rose to be a high-class mandarin among the Chinese, and since his death temples have been erected to his honor. He came to Shanghai in 1860, and was looking around for something to do. The rebels were within forty miles of the city, and their appearance in front of it was hourly expected. They were holding the city of Soon-keong, and Ward proposed to take this place by contract, as one might propose to build a house or a railway line."

The boys laughed at the idea of carrying on war by contract, but were reminded that they were in China, where things are done otherwise than in Europe and America.

"The conditions of the contract were that Ward should raise a force of fifty Malays, and undertake the capture of a walled city having a garrison of four thousand rebels. If he succeeded, he was to have a certain sum of money—I think it was ten thousand dollars—and was then to raise a force of one thousand Chinese with twenty-five foreign officers, and was to have command of this army for the purpose of suppressing the rebellion.

"Soon-keong has four gates, and they were opened at a certain hour in the morning. Ward went there secretly one night, and sent fourteen of his men to each of three of the gates, while he himself went with the remaining eight men to the fourth gate. The rebels suspected nothing, and at the usual time the gates were opened. Ward's men rushed in simultaneously at the four gates, made a great noise, set fire to several buildings, killed everybody they met, and pushed on for the centre of the town. In less than ten minutes the enemy had fled, and the battle was over. Ward was in full possession of the place, and a force of the imperial army, which was waiting near by, was marched in, to make sure that the rebels would not return.

GENERAL WARD.

"Ward raised the army that he had proposed, and from one thousand it soon grew to three thousand. It was armed with foreign rifles, and had a battery of European artillery. The officers were English, American, French, and of other foreign nationalities, and the men were drilled in the European fashion. So uniformly were they successful that they received the name of 'the Invincibles,' and retained it through all their career. The American adventurer became 'General' Ward, was naturalized as a Chinese subject, was made a red-button mandarin, and received from the government a present of a large tract of land and a fine house in Shanghai. He was several times wounded, and finally, in October, 1862, he was killed in an attack on one of the rebel strongholds.

"Ward was succeeded by an American named Burgevine, who had been

THE GATE WHICH WARD ATTACKED.

one of his subordinates. Burgevine was quite as successful as Ward had been, and at one time with his army of 5000 trained Chinese he defeated 95,000 of the Tae-ping rebels. This made an end of the rebellion in that part of the country, but it was flourishing in other localities. Burgevine had some trouble with the authorities, which led to his retirement; and after that the Invincible army was commanded by an English officer named Gordon, who remained at the head of it till the downfall of the Tae-pings and the end of the rebellion. The success of this little army against the large force of the rebels shows the great advantages of disci-

GENERAL BURGEVINE.

pline. In all time and in all countries this advantage has been apparent, but in none more so than in China. If the power of Ward and his men had been with the rebels instead of against them, it is highly probable that the government would have been overthrown. A few hundred well-trained soldiers could have decided the fate of an empire."

The conversation about the Tae-ping rebellion and its termination occurred while the steamer was steadily making her way against the muddy waters of the Yang-tse. The party were sitting on the forward deck of the boat, and just as the closing words of the Doctor's remarks were pronounced, there was a new and unexpected sensation.

The day was perfectly clear, but suddenly a cloud appeared to be forming like a thick mist. As they came nearer to it they discovered what it was, and made the discovery through their sense of feeling. It was a cloud of locusts moving from the southern to the northern bank of the river; they had devastated a large area, and were now hastening to fresh woods and pastures new. They filled the air so densely as to obscure the sun, and for more than an hour the steamer was enveloped in them. These locusts are the scourge of China, as they are of other countries. They are worse in some years than in others, and in several instances they have been the cause of local famines, or of great scarcity.

Of course many of the locusts fell on the deck of the steamer, and found their way to the cabins. The flight of the cloud was from south to north, and Frank observed a remarkable peculiarity about the movements of individual members of the immense swarm. He captured several and placed them on the cabin table. No matter in what direction he turned their heads, they immediately faced about towards the north, and as long as they were in the cabin they continued to try to escape on the northern side. After the boat had passed through the swarm, the boys released several of the captives, and found that, no matter how they were directed at the moment of their release, they immediately turned and flew away to the north.

"They've one consolation," Fred remarked — "they have their compasses always about them, and have no need to figure up their reckoning with 'Bowditch's Navigator' to know which way to steer."

"Don't you remember," Frank retorted, "our old teacher used to tell us that instinct was often superior to reason. Birds and animals and fishes make their annual migrations, and know exactly where they are going, which is more than most men could begin to do. These locusts are guided by instinct, and they are obliged to be, as they would starve if they had to reason about their movements, and study to know where to go. Just think of a locust sitting down to a map of China, when there were millions of other locusts all doing the same thing. They wouldn't have maps enough to go around; and when they got to a place they wanted to reach, they would find that others had been there before them and eaten up all the grass."

Frank's practical argument about instinct received the approval of his friends, and then the topic of conversation was changed to something else.

Both the boys were greatly interested in the various processes of work that were visible on shore. Groups of men were to be seen cutting reeds for fuel, or for the roofs of houses, where they make a warm thatch that keeps out the rain and snow. Other groups were gathering cotton, hemp, millet, and other products of the earth; and at several points there were men with blue hands, who were extracting indigo from the plant which produces it. The plant is bruised and soaked in water till the coloring-matter is drawn out; the indigo settles to the bottom of the tub, and the water is poured off; and after being dried in the sun, the cake forms the indigo of commerce. In many places there were little stages about thirty feet high, and just large enough at the top for one man, who worked there patiently and alone. Frank could not make out the employment of these men, and neither could Fred. After puzzling awhile over the matter, they referred it to Doctor Bronson.

"Those men," the Doctor explained, "are engaged in making ropes or cables out of the fibres of bamboo."

"Why don't they work on the ground instead of climbing up there?" Fred asked.

"Because," was the reply, "they want to keep the cable straight while they are braiding it. As fast as they braid it it hangs down by its own weight, and coils on the ground beneath. No expensive machinery is needed, and the principal labor in the business is to carry the bamboo fibre to the platform where it is wanted. This cable is very strong and cheap, and takes the place of hemp rope in a great many ways. It is larger and rougher than a hempen rope of the same strength, but the Chinese are willing to sacrifice beauty for cheapness in the majority of practical things."

The Chinese have a way of catching fish which is peculiar to themselves, and much practised along the Yang-tse. A net several feet square hangs at the end of a long pole, and is lowered gently into the water and then suddenly raised. Any fish that happens to be swimming over the net at the time is liable to be taken in. He is lifted from the large net by means of a small scoop, and the raising and lowering process is resumed. Fred thought it was an excellent employment for a lazy man, and Frank suggested that it would be better for two lazy men than one, as they could keep each other company.

The boys were desirous of seeing how the Chinese catch fish with the aid of cormorants, and were somewhat disappointed when told that these birds were rarely used on the Yang-tse, but must be looked for on some of the lakes and ponds away from the great stream, and particularly in the southern part of the empire. The Doctor thus described this novel mode of catching fish:

"Three or four cormorants and a raft are necessary in this way of fishing. The cormorants are stupid-looking birds about the size of geese, but are of a dark color, so that they cannot be readily seen by the fish. The raft is of bamboo logs bound together, and about three feet wide by twenty in length. The fisherman is armed with a paddle for propelling his raft and a scoop-net for taking the fish after they have been caught by the cormorant, and he has a large basket for holding the fish after they have been safely secured. Each cormorant has a cord or ring around his neck to prevent him from swallowing the fish he has taken, and it is so tight that he cannot get down any but the smallest fish.

FISHING WITH CORMORANTS.

"The birds dive off from the raft, and can swim under water with great rapidity. Sometimes they are not inclined to fish, and require to be pushed off, and, perhaps, beaten a little by their master. If they have been well trained, they swim directly towards the raft, when they rise to the surface; but sometimes a cormorant will go off the other way, in the hope of being able to swallow the fish he holds in his mouth. In such case the fisherman follows and captures the runaway, punishing him soundly for his misconduct. Whenever a bird catches a fish and brings it to the raft, he is rewarded with a mouthful of food. In this way he soon learns to associate his success with something to eat; and a cormorant that has been well trained has a good deal of fidelity in his composition. I am uncertain which to admire most, the dexterity of the fisherman in handling his raft, or the perseverance and celerity of the cormorants."

On her arrival at Han-kow, the steamer was tied up to the bank in front of the portion of the city occupied by the foreigners. Han-kow is on a broad tongue of land at the junction of the Han with the Yang-tse. On the opposite side of the Han is the city of Han-yang, and over on the other bank of the Yang-tse is Wo-chang. Here is the brief description given by the Doctor in a letter to friends at home:

"A hill between Han-kow and Han-yang rises about six hundred feet, and affords one of the finest views in the world, and, in some respects, one of the most remarkable. We climbed there yesterday a little before sunset, and remained as long as the fading daylight and the exigencies of our return permitted. At our feet lay the Yang-tse, rolling towards the sea after its junction with the Han, which we could trace afar, like a ribbon of silver winding through the green plain. Away to the west was a range of mountains, lighted by the setting sun, and overhung with golden and purple clouds; while to the south was an undulating country, whose foreground was filled with the walled city of Wo-chang. The crenelated walls enclose an enormous space, much of which is so desolate that foreigners are accustomed to hunt pheasants and hares within the limits. They say that at one time all this space was covered with buildings, and that the buildings were crowded with occupants. The three cities suffered terribly during the rebellion, and more than three fourths of their edifices were levelled. Looking from the hill, it is easy to see the traces of the destruction, although twenty years have passed since the insurrection was suppressed. The population of the three cities was said to have been four or five millions; but, even after making allowance for the density with which Chinese cities are crowded, I should think those figures were too high. However, there is no doubt that it was very great, and probably more people lived here than on any similar area anywhere else in the world."

Han-kow is a great centre of trade. Frequently the mouth of the Han is so crowded with junks that the river is entirely covered, and you may walk for hours by merely stepping from one boat to another. The upper Yang-tse and the Han bring down large quantities of tea, furs, silk, wax,

A STREET IN HAN-KOW.

and other products, both for home use and for export. There are heavy exports of tea from Han-kow direct to England, and every year steamers go there to load with cargoes, which they take to London as rapidly as possible. Our friends were told that there was a large trade in brick tea, which was prepared for the Russian market; and as the boys were anxious to see the process of preparation, a visit to one of the factories was arranged. Frank made a note of what he saw and wrote it out as follows:

"The dry tea is weighed out into portions for single bricks, and each portion is wrapped in a cloth and placed over a steam-boiler. When it is thoroughly steamed, it is poured into a mould and placed beneath a machine, which presses it into the required shape and size. Some of the machines are worked by hand, and others by steam. Both kinds are very rapid and efficient, and we could not see that the steam had much advantage. Five men working a hand machine, and receiving twenty cents each for a day's labor, were able to press six bricks a minute, as we found by timing them with our watches. The steam press worked only a little faster, and the cost of fuel must have been about equal to that of human muscle.

"Only the poorest kind of tea is made into bricks, and each brick is about six inches wide, eight inches long, and one inch thick. After it has been pressed, it is dried in ovens; and when it is thoroughly dried and ready for packing, it is weighed, to make sure that it is up to the required standard. All bricks that are too light are thrown out, to be mixed up again and done over. Nearly all of this business is in Russian hands, for the reason that this kind of tea is sold only in Russia."

Doctor Bronson arranged that the party should visit Wo-chang and see a famous pagoda that stood on the bank of the river. There was not a great deal to see after they got there, as the place was not in good repair, and contained very little in the way of statues and idols. The stairways were narrow and dark, and the climb to the top was not accomplished without difficulty. Afterwards they went through the principal streets, and visited the shops, which they found much like those of Shanghai and Chin-kiang. The people showed some curiosity in looking at the strangers—more than they had found farther down the river—for the reason, doubtless, that fewer foreigners go there.

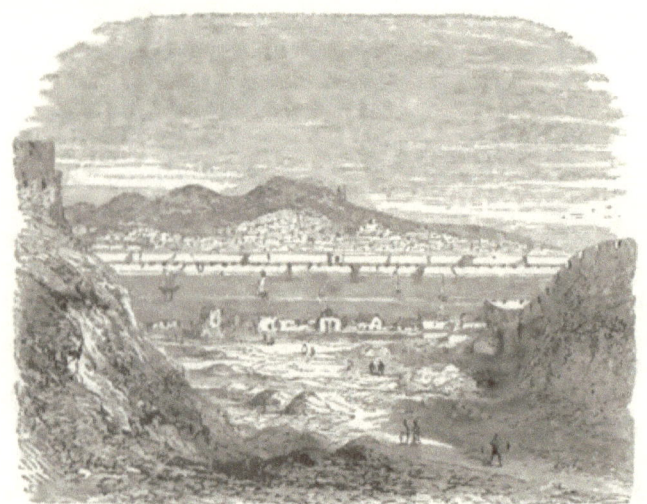

WO-CHANG.

Wo-chang is the capital of the province of Hoo-peh, and the governor-general resides there. Our friends were fortunate enough to get a glimpse of this high official as he was carried through the streets in a sedan-chair, followed by several members of his staff. A Chinese governor never goes out without a numerous following, as he wishes the whole world to be impressed with a sense of his importance; and the rank and position of an official can generally be understood by a single glance at the number of his attendants, though the great man himself may be so shut up in his chair that his decorations and the button on his hat may not be visible.

In a couple of days the steamer was ready for the return to Shanghai. The time had been well employed in visiting the streets and shops and temples of Han-kow, and learning something of its importance as a centre of trade. The return journey was begun with a feeling of satisfaction that they had taken the trouble and the time for the ascent of the Yang-tse and made themselves acquainted with the internal life of the country.

THE GOVERNOR-GENERAL AND HIS STAFF.

CHAPTER XXVI.

FROM SHANGHAI TO PEKIN.

ON their return to Shanghai, the Doctor informed his young companions that they would take the first steamer up the coast in the direction of Pekin.

They had only a day to wait, as the regular steamer for Tien-tsin was advertised to leave on the afternoon following their return. She was not so large and comfortable as the one that had carried them to Han-kow and back; but she was far better than no steamer at all, and they did not hesitate a moment at taking passage in her. They found that she had a Chinese crew, with foreign officers—the same as they had found the river-boat and the steamers from Japan. The captain was an American, who had spent twenty years in China, and knew all the peculiarities of the navigation of its waters. He had passed through two or three shipwrecks and been chased by pirates. Once he was in the hands of the rebels, who led him out for execution; but their attention was diverted by an attack on the town where they were, and he was left to take care of himself, which you can be sure he did. Another time he saved himself by crawling through a small window and letting himself fall about ten feet into a river. The night was dark, and he did not know where to go; but he thought it better to take the chance of an escape in this way, as he felt sure he would have his head taken off the next morning if he remained. Luckily he floated down to where a foreign ship was lying, and managed to be taken on board. He thought he had had quite enough of that sort of thing, and was willing to lead a quiet life for the rest of his days.

They descended the river to the sea, and then turned to the northward. Nothing of moment occurred as the steamer moved along on her course, and on the morning of the third day from Shanghai they were entering the mouth of the Pei-ho River. The Doctor pointed out the famous Taku forts through the thin mist that overhung the water, and the boys naturally asked what the Taku forts had done to make themselves famous.

"There is quite a history connected with them," the Doctor answered.

ATTACK ON THE PEI-HO FORTS.

"They were the scene of the repulse of the British fleet in 1859, when an American commander came to its relief, with the remark, which has become historic, 'Blood is thicker than water!' In the following year the English returned, and had better success; they captured the forts and entered the river in spite of all that the Chinese could do to stop them. Do you see that low bank there, in front of a mud-wall to the left of the fort?"

"Certainly," was the reply.

"Well, that is the place where the sailors landed from the small boats for the purpose of storming the forts, while the gun-boats were shelling them farther up the river."

"But it looks from here as if there were a long stretch of mud," Fred remarked.

"You are right," the Doctor responded, "there is a long stretch of mud, and it was that mud which partly led to the failure at the time of the first attack. The storming force was compelled to wade through it, and many of the men perished. The fire of the Chinese was more severe than had been expected, and the ships of the fleet were badly injured. But when the attack was made the following year, the muddy belt was much narrower, and the sailors passed through it very quickly, and were at the walls of the fort before the Chinese were ready for them.

"The navigation is difficult along the Pei-ho River, and the steamers of the attacking fleet found the passage barred by cables stretched across the stream. They had considerable trouble to break through these obstructions, but they finally succeeded, and the rest of the voyage to Tientsin was accomplished far more easily than the capture of the forts."

As the steamer moved on against the muddy current, and turned in the very crooked channel of the Pei-ho, Frank espied a double-storied building with a wide veranda, and asked what it was.

He was interested to learn that it was known as the Temple of the Sea-god, and had been at one time the residence of the Chinese commander of the Taku forts. It had a handsome front on the river, and a fleet of junks was moored directly above it. Each junk appeared to be staring with all the power of the great eyes painted on its bows, and some of the junks more distinguished than the rest were equipped with two eyes on each side, in order that they might see better than the ordinary craft. Flags floated from the masts of all the junks, and in nearly every instance they were attached to little rods, and swung from the centre. A Chinese flag twists and turns in the breeze in a manner quite unknown to a banner hung after the ways of Europe and America.

TEMPLE OF THE SEA-GOD AT TAKU.

The river from Taku to Tien-tsin was crowded with junks and small boats, and it was easy to see that the empire of China has a large commerce on all its water-ways. The Grand Canal begins at Tien-tsin, and the city stands on an angle formed by the canal and the Pei-ho River. It is not far from a mile square, and has a wall surrounding it. Each of the four walls has a gate in the centre, and a wide street leads from this gate to the middle of the city, where there is a pagoda. The streets are wider than in most of the Chinese cities, and there is less danger of being knocked down by the pole of a sedan-chair, or of a coolie bearing a load of merchandise. In spite of its great commercial activity, the city does not appear very prosperous. Beggars are numerous, and wherever our friends went they were constantly importuned by men and women, who appeared to be in the severest want.

The usual way of going to Pekin is by the road from Tien-tsin, while the return journey is by boat along the river. The road is about

A CHINESE BEGGAR.

SIGNING THE TREATY OF TIEN-TSIN.

ninety miles long, and is one of the worst in the world, when we consider how long it has been in use. According to Chinese history, it was built about two thousand years ago. Frank said he could readily believe that it was at least two thousand years old, and Fred thought it had never been repaired since it was first opened to the public. It was paved with large stones for a good portion of the way, and these stones have been worn into deep ruts, so that the track is anything but agreeable for a carriage. The only wheeled vehicles in this part of China are carts without springs, and mounted on a single axle; the body rests directly on the axle, so that every jolt is conveyed to the person inside, and he feels after a day's journey very much as though he had been run through a winnowing-machine.

The Chinese cart is too short for an average-sized person to lie in at full length, and too low to allow him to sit erect; it has a small window on each side, so placed that it is next to impossible to look out and see what there is along the route. Altogether it is a most uncomfortable vehicle to travel in, and the boys thought they would go on foot rather than ride in one of them.

But it was not necessary to go on foot, as they were able to hire ponies for the journey, and it was agreed all round that a little roughness on horseback for a couple of days would do no harm. So they made a contract with a Chinese, who had been recommended to them by the consul as a good man, to carry them to Pekin. It was arranged that they should take an early start, so as to reach a village a little more than half way by nightfall, and they retired early in order to have a good night's sleep. They had time for a little stroll before they went to bed, and so they employed it in visiting the "Temple of the Oceanic Influences," where the treaty of Tien-tsin was signed after the capture of the Taku forts and the advance of the English to the city. The temple is on a plain outside of the walls, and contains a large hall, which was very convenient for the important ceremonial that took place there. At the time the treaty was signed the British officers were in full uniform, and made a fine appearance, while the Chinese were not a whit behind them in gorgeousness of apparel. Contrary to their usual custom, the Chinese did not think it necessary to hang up any elaborate decorations in the hall, and the attention of the spectators was concentrated on the dignitaries who managed the affair.

There is another way of travelling in China, which is by means of a mule litter. This is a sort of sedan-chair carried by mules instead of men; one mule walks in front, and another in the rear, and the litter is supported between them on a couple of long shafts. The pace is slow, being always at a walk, except at the times when the mules run away and smash things generally, as happens not unfrequently. The straps that hold the shafts to the saddles of the mules have a way of getting loose, and leaving the box to fall to the ground with a heavy thud, which interferes materially with the comfort of the occupant. For invalids and ladies the mule litter is to be recommended, as well as for persons who are fond of having the greatest amount of comfort; but our young friends disdained anything so effeminate, and determined to make the journey on horseback.

They took as little baggage as possible, leaving everything superfluous at Tien-tsin; six horses were sufficient for all the wants of the party—four for themselves and the guide, and two for the baggage. It was necessary to carry the most of the provisions needed for the journey to Pekin, as the Chinese hotels along the route could not be relied on with any certainty. No rain had fallen for some time, and the way was very dusty; but this circumstance only made it more amusing to the boys, though it was not so pleasing to the Doctor. Before they had been an hour on the road, it was not easy to say which was Fred and which Frank, until they had rendered themselves recognizable by washing their faces. Water was scarce, and not particularly good, and, besides, the operation of washing the face was an affair of much inconvenience. So they contented themselves with the dust, and concluded that for the present they wouldn't be particular about names or identity.

At noon they had gone twenty-five miles through a country which abounded in villages and gardens, and had a great many fields of wheat, millet, cotton, and other products of China; the fields were not unlike those they had seen on their voyage up the Yang-tse; and as for the villages, they were exactly alike, especially in the items of dirt and general repulsiveness. The modes of performing field labor were more interesting than the villages: the most of the fields were watered artificially, and the process of pumping water attracted the attention of the boys. An endless chain, with floats on it, was propelled through an inclined box by a couple of men who kept up a steady walk on a sort of treadmill. There were spokes in a horizontal shaft, and on the ends of the spokes there were little pieces of board, with just sufficient space for a man's foot to rest. The men walked on these spokes, and steadied themselves on a horizontal pole which was held between a couple of upright posts. Labor is so cheap in China that there is no occasion for employing steam or wind machinery; it was said that a pump-coolie was able to earn from

MODE OF IRRIGATING FIELDS.

five to ten cents a day in the season when the fields needed irrigation, and he had nothing to do at other times.

The night was passed at a village where there was a Chinese tavern, but it was so full that the party were sent to a temple to sleep. Beds were made on the floor, and the travellers managed to get along very well, in spite of the fleas that supped and breakfasted on their bodies, and would have been pleased to dine there. The boys were in a corner of the temple under the shadow of one of the idols to whom the place belonged, while the Doctor had his couch in front of a canopy where there was a deity that watched over him all night with uplifted hands. Two smaller idols, one near his head and the other at his feet, kept company with the larger one; but whether they took turns in staying awake, the Doctor was too sleepy to inquire.

They were up very early in the morning, and off at daylight, somewhat to the reluctance of the guide, who had counted on sleeping a little longer. The scenes along the road were much like those of the day before, and they were glad when, just at nightfall, the guide pointed to a high wall in front of them, and pronounced the word "Pekin." They were in sight of the city.

"I'm disappointed," said Fred. "Pekin isn't what I thought it was."

THE DOCTOR'S BEDROOM.

" Well, what did you expect to find?" queried Frank.

" Why, I thought it was on a hill, or something of the sort; I had no reason to think so, of course, but I had formed that picture of it."

"Nearly every one who comes to Pekin is thus disappointed," said Doctor Bronson; " he expects to see the city from a distance, while, in reality, it is not visible till you are quite close to it."

The walls were high, and there was nothing to be seen inside of them, as none of the buildings in that quarter were equally lofty. But the effect of the walls was imposing; there were towers at regular intervals, and the most of them were two stories above the level of the surrounding structure. For nearly a mile they rode along the base of one of the walls till they came to a gate that led them into the principal street. Once inside, they found themselves transferred very suddenly from the stillness of the country to the bustling life of the great city.

" I'm not disappointed now," Fred remarked, as they rode along in the direction indicated by the guide; " the streets are so wide in comparison with those of the cities we have seen that they seem very grand, indeed."

"You've hit it exactly, Fred," Doctor Bronson replied, "Pekin is called the 'City of Magnificent Distances' on account of the width of its streets,

PART OF THE WALL OF PEKIN.

the great extent of the city, and the long walks or rides that are necessary for going about in it."

"Evidently they took plenty of room when they laid it out," said Frank, "for it isn't crowded like Shanghai and the other places we have seen."

It was dark when they reached the little hotel where they were to stay. It was kept by a German, who thought Pekin was an excellent place for a hotel, but would be better if more strangers would visit the city. His establishment was not large, and its facilities were not great, but they were quite sufficient for the wants of our friends, who were too tired to be particular about trifles. They took a hearty supper, and then went to bed to sleep away the fatigues of their journey.

Next morning they were not very early risers, and the whole trio were weary and sore from the effect of the ride of ninety miles on the backs of Chinese ponies. Frank said that when he was sitting down he hesitated to rise for fear he should break in two, and Fred asserted that it was dangerous to go from a standing to a sitting position for the same reason.

They determined to take things easily for the first day of their stay in Pekin, and confine their studies to the neighborhood of the hotel. With this object in view, they took short walks on the streets, and in the afternoon ventured on a ride in a small cart; or, rather, they hired two carts, as one was not sufficient to hold them. These carts are very abundant at Pekin, and are to be hired like cabs in European or American cities. They are not dear, being only sixty or seventy cents a day, and they are so abundant that one can generally find them at the principal public places.

The carts, or cabs, are quite light in construction, and in summer they have shelters over the horses to protect them from the heat of the sun.

The driver walks at the side of his team; and when the pace of the horse quickens to a run, he runs with it. No matter how rapidly the horse may go, the man does not seem troubled to keep alongside. The carts take the place of sedan-chairs, of which very few are to be seen in Pekin.

A PEKIN CAB.

Another kind of cart which is used in the North to carry merchandise, and also for passengers, is much stronger than the cab, but, like it, is mounted on two wheels. The frame is of wood, and there is generally a cover of matting to keep off the heat of the sun. This cover is supported on posts that rise from the sides of the cart; but while useful against the sun, it is of no consesequence in a storm, owing to its facility for letting the water run through. The teams for propelling these carts are more curious than the vehicles themselves, as they are indifferently made up of whatever animals are at hand. Oxen, cows, horses, mules, donkeys, and sometimes goats and dogs, are the beasts of burden that were seen by the boys in their rambles in Pekin and its vicinity, and on one occasion Fred saw a team which contained a camel harnessed with a mule and a cow. Camels come to Pekin from the Desert of Gobi, where great numbers of them are used in the overland trade between China and Russia. They are quite similar to the Arabian camel, but are smaller, and their hair is thicker, to enable them to endure the severe cold of the northern winter. In the season when tea is ready for export, thousands of camels are employed in transporting the fragrant herb to the Russian frontier, and the roads to the northward from Pekin are blocked with them.

Walking was not altogether a pleasant amusement for our friends, as the streets were a mass of dust, owing to the carelessness of the authorities about allowing the refuse to accumulate in them. There is a tradition that one of the emperors, in a period that is lost in the mazes of antiquity, attempted to sweep the streets in order to make himself popular with the people; but he found the task too large, and, moreover, he had serious

A COMPOSITE TEAM.

doubts about its being accomplished in his lifetime. So he gave it up, as he did not care to do something that would go more to the credit of his successor than of himself, and no one has had the courage to try it since that time. The amount of dirt that accumulates in a Chinese city would breed a pestilence in any other part of the world. Not only do the Chinese appear uninjured by it, but there are some who assert that it is a necessity of their existence, and they would lose their health if compelled to live in an atmosphere of cleanliness.

One of the most interesting street sights of their first day in Pekin was a procession carrying a dragon made of bamboo covered with painted paper. There was a great noise of tom-toms and drums to give warning of the approach of the procession, and there was the usual rabble of small boys that precedes similar festivities everywhere. The dragon was carried by five men, who held him aloft on sticks that also served to give his body an undulating motion in imitation of life. He was not pretty to look upon, and his head seemed too large for his body. The Chinese idea of the dragon is, that he is something very hideous, and they certainly succeed in representing their conception of him. Dr. Bronson explained that the dragon was frequently carried in procession at night, and on these occasions the hollow body was illuminated, so that it was more hideous, if possible, than in the daytime.

A CHINESE DRAGON.

CHAPTER XXVII.

SIGHTS IN PEKIN.

FROM their own observations and the notes and accounts of travellers who had preceded them, the boys made the following description of Pekin:

"Pekin stands on a great sandy plain, and has a population of about two millions. It consists of two parts, which are separated by a wall; that towards the south is called the Chinese city, and that on the north the Tartar city. The Tartar city is the smaller both in area and population; it is said to measure about twelve square miles, while the Chinese city measures fifteen. There are thirteen gates in the outer walls, and there are three gates between the Tartar and the Chinese city. In front of each gate there is a sort of bastion or screen, so that you cannot see the entrance at all as you approach it, and are obliged to turn to one side to come in or go out. The Chinese city has few public buildings of importance, while the Tartar city has a great many of them. The latter city consists of three enclosures, one inside the other, and each enclosure has a wall of its own. The outer one contains dwellings and shops, the second includes the government offices, and the houses of private persons who are allowed to live there as a mark of special favor; while the third is called the Prohibited City, and is devoted to the imperial palace and temples that belong to it. Nobody can go inside the Prohibited City without special permission, and sometimes this is very hard to obtain; the wall enclosing it is nearly two miles in circumference, and has a gate in each of its four fronts, and the wall is as solid and high as the one that surrounds the whole city of Pekin.

"We had no trouble in going to see the imperial palace, or such parts of it as are open to the public, and also the temples. We could readily believe what was told us—that the temples were the finest in the whole country, and certainly some of them were very interesting. There are temples to the earth, to the sun, the moon; and there are temples to agriculture, to commerce, and a great many other things. There is a very

fine structure of marble more than a hundred feet high, which is called
"The Gate of Extensive Peace." It is where the emperor comes on great
public occasions; and beyond it are two halls where the foreign visitors
are received at the beginning of each year, and where the emperor ex-
amines the implements used in the opening of the annual season of
ploughing. The ploughing ceremony does not take place here, but in
another part of the city, and the emperor himself holds the plough to
turn the first furrow. There are some very pretty gardens in the Prohibited City, and we had a fine opportunity to learn something about the
skill of the Chinese in landscape gardening. There are canals, fountains,
bridges, flower-beds, groves, and little hillocks, all carefully tended, and
forming a very pretty picture in connection with the temples and pavilions that stand among them.

A PAVILION IN THE PROHIBITED CITY.

"We have seen many temples—so many, in fact, that it is difficult to
remember all of them. One of the most impressive is the Temple of
Heaven, which has three circular roofs, one above another, and is said to
be ninety-nine feet high. The tiles on the top are of porcelain of the color
of a clear sky, and the intention of the builder was to imitate the vault of
heaven. On the inside there are altars where sacrifices are offered to the
memory of former emperors of China, and on certain occasions the emperor comes here to take part in the ceremonies.

"Then we went to see the great bell, which is one of the wonders of
the world, though it is not so large as the bell at Moscow. It is said to

weigh 112,000 pounds, but how they ever weighed it I don't know. It is a foot thick at the rim, about twenty feet high, and fifteen feet in diameter; it was cast more than two hundred years ago, and is covered all over, inside and outside, with Chinese characters. There is a little hole in the top of it where people try to throw copper cash. If they succeed, it is a sign that they will be fortunate in life; and if they fail, they must leave the money as an offering to the temple. All of us tried till we had thrown away a double-hand-

TEMPLE OF HEAVEN.

ful of cash, but we didn't get a single one of them through the hole. So if we fail now in anything, you will know the reason.

"The Chinese have a great many gods, and pretty nearly every god has a temple in some part of Pekin. There is a fine temple to Confucius, which is surrounded by some trees that are said to be five hundred years old; the temple has a high roof which is very elaborately carved, and looks pretty both from a distance and when you

PEKIN CASH.

are close by it. But there are no statues in the temple, as the Chinese do not worship Confucius through a statue, but by means of a tablet on which his name is inscribed. . The other deities have their statues, and you may see the god of war with a long beard and mustache. The Chinese have very slight beards, and it is perhaps for this reason that they frequently represent their divinities as having a great deal of hair on their faces, so as to indicate their superiority to mortals. Then they have a god of literature, who is represented standing on the head of a large fish, and waving a pencil in his right hand, while he holds in his left a cap such as is worn by the literary graduates after they have received their degrees.

TRADITIONAL LIKENESS OF CONFUCIUS.   GOD OF WAR.

The god of literature is worshipped a great deal by everybody who is studying for a degree, and by those whose ancestors or other relatives have been successful in carrying away the honors at an examination. Think what it would be to have such a divinity in our colleges and schools

GOD OF LITERATURE.   GOD OF THIEVES.

in America, and the amount of worship he would get if the students really believed in him!

"The Chinese have a god of thieves; but he has no temple, and is generally worshipped in the open air. All the thieves are supposed to worship him, as he is a saint who made their business successful; and, besides this, he is worshipped by those who wish to become wealthy in honest ways. He is said to have been a skilful thief, and very pious at the same time. He was kind to his mother, and the most of his stealing was done to support her.

"One of the interesting places we have visited is the office of the Board of Punishments, which corresponds pretty nearly to our courts of justice. But one great point of difference between their mode of administering justice and ours is that they employ torture, while we do not. Not only is the prisoner tortured after condemnation, but he is tortured before trial, in order to make him tell the truth; and even the witnesses, under certain circumstances, are submitted to the same treatment. We saw some of the instruments that they use, and there was not the least attempt to keep us from seeing them. It is customary to have them piled or hung up at the doors of the courts, so that culprits may know what to expect, and honest persons may be deterred from wickedness through fear. It is the same principle that is followed by some of the school-teachers in America when they hang up in full view the stick with which they intend to punish unruly boys.

"When we went into the court-room, a man had just been sentenced to receive twenty blows of the bamboo, and the sentence was immediately carried out. He was ordered to lie down with his face to the floor; his back was then stripped, and while his legs and arms were held by attendants, the executioner laid on the twenty blows with a bamboo stick about six

A MANDARIN JUDGE DELIVERING SENTENCE.

24

feet long and two inches wide. One side of the stick was rounded and the other was flat; the flesh was blistered at every stroke, or raised in a great puff, and it is certain that the man must be some time in getting well. He did not scream or make the least outcry, but took his punishment patiently, and was raised to his feet at its end. He bowed to the judge, and, perhaps, thanked him for the attention he had received, and was then led away to make room for some one else.

"The Chinese don't seem to have any nerves compared with what we have. They do not suffer so much as we do under tortures, and this is perhaps one of the reasons why they are so much more cruel than the people of Europe and America. For example, it would nearly kill a European to travel a week in carts such as we saw on the road from Tientsin to Pekin. The Chinese don't seem to mind it at all; and the best proof that they do not is that they have never invented any better or more comfortable way of travelling, or tried to improve their roads. And it is the same with their punishments in the courts. They don't care much for whippings, though it is not at all probable that they like them, and the only things that they appear to fear very much are the punishments that are prolonged. There are a good many of these, and I will tell you about some of the most prominent and best known.

"Several times we have seen men with wooden collars three or four feet square, and with a hole in the centre, where the poor fellow's neck comes through. It is made of plank about two inches thick, and you can see that the load is a heavy one for a man to carry. He cannot bring his arms to his head; and if he has no friends to feed him, or no money to pay some one else to do so, he must starve. On the upper surface of the plank is painted the name of the criminal, together with the crime he has committed and the time he has been ordered to wear the collar. This instrument is called a 'cangue,' and is said to be in use all over China from one end of the country to the other.

"There is a mode of torture which is chiefly used to extort confessions from persons accused of crime, and the result of its use is said to be that many a man has been induced to confess crimes of which he was entirely innocent, in order to escape from the terrible pain which is produced. The victim is compelled to stand against a post, and his cue is tied to it so that he cannot get away. His arms are tied to a cross-beam, and then little rods are placed between his fingers in such a way that every finger is enclosed. The rods are so arranged that by pulling a string the pressure on the fingers is increased, and the pain very soon becomes so great that most men are unable to endure it. If you want to know just how a little of it feels, I advise you to put one of your fingers between two lead-pencils and then squeeze the pencils together. You won't keep doing so very long.

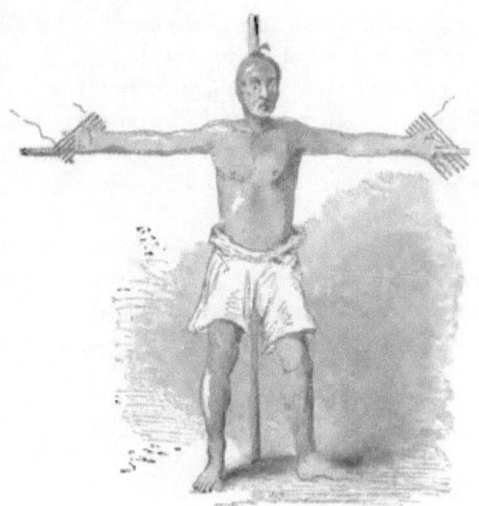

SQUEEZING THE FINGERS.

"They squeeze the ankles in much the same way, by making the man kneel on the ground, with his ankles in a frame of three sticks that are fastened together at one end by a cord like that of the finger-squeezer. Then, when all is ready, they pull at the cord and draw the sticks nearer to each other, so that pressure is brought on the ankles. The pain is intense, and the most demure Chinaman is not able to stand it without shrinking. This mode of torture, like the other, is used to make prisoners confess the crimes of which they are accused, and they generally confess them. It is said that witnesses may be subjected to the ankle torture, but with the modification in their favor that only one ankle can be squeezed at a time. Very kind, isn't it?

"We went near the prison while we were in the Tartar city, and so it was proposed that we should see what there was inside. It was the most

SQUEEZING THE ANKLES.

horrible place I have ever seen, and the wonder is that men can be found inhuman enough to condemn people to be shut up there. There was a large cage so full of men that there was not room on the floor for them all to lie down at once, even if they had been as close together as sardines in a can. We could see through the bars of the cage, as if the captives had been wild animals instead of human beings, and they looked so worn and wretched that we all pitied them very much. If a man is sent to prison in China,

and has no money to pay for his food, he will die of starvation, as the jail-
ers are not required by law to feed the prisoners under their charge.
There were men chained, with iron collars around their necks; and others
tied, with their hands and feet brought close together. The suffering was
terrible, and we were glad to come away after a very few minutes. It is
positive that we do not want to see another prison as long as we stay in
this country.

"In the Chinese prisons they torture men to make them confess, and
also to compel them to tell if they have money, or any relatives or friends
who have it. One of these cruelties is called 'putting a man to bed,' and
consists in fastening him on a wooden bedstead by his neck, wrists, and

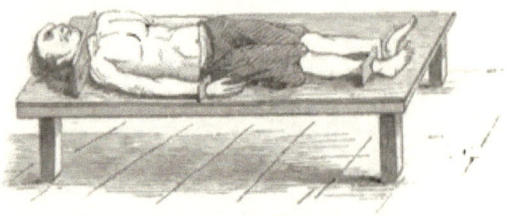

ankles in such a way that
he cannot move. He is
compelled to pass the
night in this position;
and sometimes they give
him a coverlet of a sin-
gle board that presses on
his body, and is occasionally weighted to make it

A BED OF TORTURE.

more oppressive. The next morning he is released and told that he can
be free until night, when he will be again tied up. Generally a man is
willing to do anything in his power rather than pass a second night on
such a bed. If he has money, he gives it up; and, no matter how reluc-
tant he may be to call on his friends, he does so, sooner or later, and throws
himself on their generosity.

"They suspend men by the wrists and ankles; sometimes by one wrist
and one ankle, and at others by all four brought closely together. Then
they place a victim in a chair with his arms tied to cross-sticks, and in this
position he is compelled to sit for hours in the most terrible pain. Another mode is by tying a man's hands together beneath his knees, and then
passing a pole under his arm and suspending him from it. This is called
'the monkey grasping a peach,' and it is frequently employed to compel a
rich man to pay heavily to escape punishment. How it got its name nobody can tell, unless it was owing to a supposed resemblance to the position of a monkey holding something in his paw.

"Just as we were coming out of the prison-yard we saw a man standing in a cage with his head through a board in the top, while his toes just
touched the bottom. Unless he stood on tiptoe, the weight of his body
fell on his neck; and everybody knows how difficult it is to remain on

FOUR MODES OF PUNISHMENT.

tiptoe for any length of time. Sometimes men are compelled to stand in this way till they die, but generally the punishment is confined to a few hours. It is the form most frequently employed for the sentence of criminals who have been robbing on the public highway, and are convicted of using violence at the time of committing their offences.

"I could go on with a long account of the tortures in China, but they are not very pleasant reading, and, besides, some of them are too horrible for belief. I will stop with the torture known as 'the hot-water snake,' which consists of a coil of thin tubing of tin or pewter in the form of a serpent. One of these coils is twisted around each arm of the victim, and another around his body, in such a way that the head of the snake is higher than any other part. Then they pour boiling water into the mouth of the snake, and the flesh of the prisoner is burned and scalded in the most terrible manner. This punishment is said to be used rarely, and only

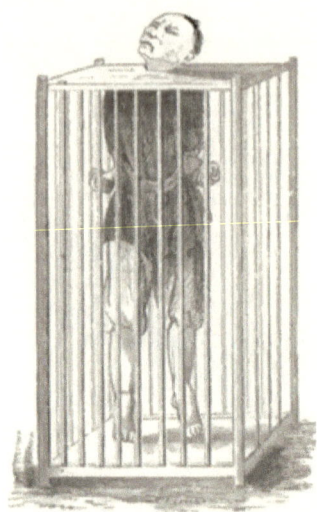

STANDING IN A CAGE.

on persons accused of crimes against the government. It is too horrible to be popular, even among the most cold-blooded people in the world.

"A good many of these punishments precede a much more merciful one, that of decapitation. The victim who is to suffer the loss of his head is carried to the place of execution in a small cage of bamboo, with his hands tied behind him, and the crime for which he is to suffer written on a piece of stiff paper and fastened to his hair. In one corner of the cage is a bucket, which is to hold his head after the executioner has cut it off; and frequently the pail with the head in it is hung near one of the gates of the city or in some other public place. When he reaches the execution-ground, he is required to kneel, and the executioner strikes his head off with a single blow of a heavy sword. The poor fellows who are to suffer death rarely make any opposition, and some of them seem quite willing to meet it. This is said to be due partly to the calmness of the Chinese, and partly to the fact that they have been so tortured and starved in their imprisonment that it is a relief to die. In most of the Chinese prisons the men condemned to death are usually kept until there are several on hand; then a general execution is ordered, and the whole lot of them are taken out to the place of decapitation. During the time of the rebellion they used to have executions by wholesale, and sometimes one or two hundred heads were taken off in a single morning.

"Very great crimes are punished by cutting the body into small pieces before decapitation, or, rather, by cutting it in several places. All the fleshy parts of the body are cut with the sword of the executioner before

HOT-WATER SNAKE.

CARRYING FORTH TO THE PLACE OF EXECUTION.

the final blow; and sometimes this species of torture goes on for an hour or two before the suffering of the victim is stopped by decapitation. There is a story that they have a lottery in which the executioner draws a knife from a basket. The basket is full of knives, and they are marked for various parts of the body. If he draws a knife for the face, he proceeds to cut off the cheeks; if for the hand, he cuts away one of the hands, and so on for all parts of the victim. If he is kindly disposed, or has been properly bribed, he will draw the beheading-knife first of all, and then he will have no occasion to use any other.

JUST BEFORE DECAPITATION.

"Well, we have had enough of these disagreeable things, and will turn to something else. We passed by the place where the candidates for military honors compete for prizes by shooting with the bow and arrow. At the first examination they are required to shoot at a mark with three arrows, and the one who makes the best shots is pronounced the winner of the prize. At the second examination they must practise on horseback, with the horse standing still; and at the third they must shoot three arrows from the back of a running horse. Afterwards they are exercised in the bending of some very stiff bows and the handling of heavy swords and stones. There is a certain scale of merit they must pass to be successful; and when they succeed, their names are sent up for another examination before higher officials than the ones they have passed before. It is a curious fact that a man who does well as an archer is entitled to a degree among the literary graduates, though he may not be able to carry away a single prize for his literary accomplishments alone."

MILITARY CANDIDATES COMPETING WITH THE BOW AND ARROW.

CHAPTER XXVIII.

A JOURNEY TO THE GREAT WALL OF CHINA.

PEKIN is not very far from the famous wall that was built to keep the empire of China from the hands of the Tartars. It is commonly mentioned as " The Great Wall," and certainly it is clearly entitled to the honor, as it is the greatest wall in the world. To go to Pekin without visiting the Great Wall would be to leave the journey incomplete; and, therefore, one of the first things that our friends considered was how they should reach the wall, and how much time they would require for the excursion.

We shall let the boys tell the story, which they did in a letter to their friends at home. It was written while they were on the steamer between Tien-tsin and Shanghai, on their return from Pekin.

" We have been to the Great Wall, and it was a journey not to be forgotten in a minute. We found that we should have to travel a hundred miles each way, and that the roads were as bad as they usually are in most parts of China. We went on horseback, but took a mule litter along for use in case of accidents, and to rest ourselves in whenever one of us should become weary of too much saddle. There are no hotels of any consequence, and so we had to take the most of our provisions from Pekin. We did the same way as when we went from Tien-tsin; that is, we hired a man to supply all the necessary horses and mules for a certain price to take us to the wall and back; and if any of them should fall sick on the road, he was to furnish fresh ones without extra charge. We were advised to make the bargain in this way, as there was a danger that some of the horses would get lame; and if there were no provision for such a case, we should have to pay very high for an extra animal. The Chinese horse-owners are said to be great rascals—almost equal to some American men who make a business of buying and selling saddle and carriage animals. Doctor Bronson says he would like to match the shrewdest Chinese jockey we have yet seen with a horse-dealer that he once knew in Washington. He thinks the Yankee could give the Chinese great odds, and then beat him.

"It was a feast-day when we left Pekin, and there were a good many sports going on in the streets, as we filed out of the city on our way to the north. There was a funny procession of men on stilts. They were fantastically dressed, and waved fans and chopsticks and other things, while they shouted and sang to amuse the crowd. One of them was dressed as a woman, who pretended to hold her eyes down so that nobody could see

WALKING ON STILTS.

them, and she danced around on her stilts as though she had been accustomed to them all her life. In fact, the whole party were quite at home on their stilts, and would have been an attraction in any part of America. Whenever the Chinese try to do anything of this sort, they are pretty sure to do it well.

"Then there were jugglers spinning plates on sticks, and doing other things of a character more or less marvellous. One of their tricks is to spin the plate on two sticks held at right angles to each other, instead of on a single stick, as with us; but how they manage to do it I am unable to say. They make the plate whirl very fast, and can keep it up a long time without any apparent fatigue.

"We passed several men who had small establishments for gambling, not unlike some that are known in America. There was one with a revolving pointer on the top of a horizontal table that was divided into sections with different marks and numbers. The pointer had a string, hanging down from one end, and the way they made the machine work

JUGGLER SPINNING A PLATE.

was to whirl the pointer, and see where the string hung when it stopped. The game appeared to be very fair, as the man who paid his money had the chance of whirling the pointer, and he might do his

GAMBLING WITH A REVOLVING POINTER.

own guessing as to where it would stop. If he was right, he would win eight times as much money as he had wagered, since the board was divided into eight spaces. If he was wrong, he lost all that he put down, and was obliged to go away or try his luck again. The temptation to natives seems to be very great, since they are constantly gambling, and sometimes lose all the money they have. Gambling is so great a vice in China that a good many of its forms have been forbidden by the government. The case is not unusual of a man losing everything he possesses, even to his wife and children, and then being thrown naked into the streets by the proprietor of the place where he has lost his money.

"We stopped to look at some fortune-tellers, who were evidently doing a good business, as they had crowds around them, and were taking in small sums of money every few minutes. One of them had a little bird in a cage, and he had a table which he folded and carried on his back when he was moving from one place to another. When he opened business, he spread his table, and then laid out some slips of paper which were folded, so that nobody could see what there was inside. Next he let the bird out of the cage, which immediately went forward and picked up one of the slips and carried it to his master. The man then opened the paper and read what was written on it, and from this paper he made a prediction about the fortune of the person who had engaged him.

FORTUNE-TELLING BY MEANS OF A
BIRD AND SLIPS OF PAPER.

"There was another fortune-teller who did his work by writing on a plate. He had several sheets of paper folded up, and from these he asked his customer to select one. When the selection was made, he dissected the writing, and showed its meaning to be something so profound that the customer was bewildered and thought he had nothing but good-fortune coming to him. We tried to get these men to tell our fortunes, but they preferred to stick to their own countrymen, probably through fear that they would lose popularity if they showed themselves too friendly with the strangers.

"The Chinese are great believers in fortune-telling, and even the most intelligent of them are often calling upon the necromancers to do something for them. They rarely undertake any business without first ascertaining if the signs are favorable; and if they are not, they will decline to have anything to do with it. When a merchant has a cargo of goods on its way, he is very likely to ask a fortune-teller how the thing is to turn out; and if the latter says it is all right, he gets liberally paid for his information. But in spite of their superstition, the Chinese are very shrewd merchants, and can calculate their profits with great accuracy.

FORTUNE-TELLING BY DISSECTING CHINESE CHARACTERS.

"Well, this is not going to the Great Wall. We went out of Pekin by the north gate, and into a country that was flat and dusty. Fred's pony was not very good-natured, and every little while took it into his head to balance himself on the tip of his tail. This was not the kind of riding we had bargained for, as it made the travel rather wearisome, and interfered with the progress of the whole caravan. We thought the pony would behave himself after a little fatigue had cooled his temper; but the more we went on, the worse he became. When we were about ten miles out, he ran away, and went tearing through a cotton-field as though he owned it, and he ended by pitching his rider over his head across a small ditch.

"Then we found how lucky it was we had brought along a mule litter, as Fred rode in it the rest of the day. Next morning he made our guide change ponies with him. In half an hour the guide was in a mud puddle, and saying something in Chinese that had a very bad sound, but it didn't help dry his clothes in the least. On the whole, we got along very well with the ponies in the north of China, when we remember the bad reputation they have and the things that most travellers say about them.

"We stopped at the village of Sha-ho, about twenty miles from Pekin; and as we had started a little late, and it was near sunset, we concluded to spend the night there. There was not much to see at the village, except a couple of fine old bridges built of stone, and so solid that they will evidently last a long time. A barber came around and wanted to shave us, but for several reasons we declined his proposal, and satisfied ourselves by seeing him operate on a native customer. The Chinese razor is a piece

CHINESE RAZOR.

of steel of a three-cornered shape, and is fastened to a handle about four inches long. It is kept very sharp, as any well-regulated razor should be, and a barber will handle it with a great deal of dexterity. The Chinese haven't much beard to shave off, but they make up for it with a very thick growth of hair, which is all removed every ten or twelve days, with the exception of a spot on the crown about four inches in diameter. The hair on this spot is allowed to grow as long as it will, and is then braided into the cue or pigtail that everybody knows about.

BARBER SHAVING THE HEAD OF A CUSTOMER.

"After we left Sha-ho the country became rough, and the road grew steadily worse. Our ponies were pretty sure-footed, but they stumbled occasionally, and Frank narrowly escaped a bad fall. The pony went down all in a heap and threw Frank over his head. He fell on a soft spot, and so was not injured; but if the accident had happened six feet farther on, or six feet farther back, it would have thrown him among the rough stones, where there were some very ugly points sticking up.

"We found another fine bridge on this part of the road, and our guide said it was called the 'Bridge of the Cloudy Hills,' because the clouds frequently hung over the hills in the distance. The Chinese are very fond

BRIDGE OF THE CLOUDY HILLS.

of fanciful names for their bridges and temples, and frequently the name has very little to do with the structure itself. I am told that there is a bridge in the south of China with exactly the same name as this, and not far from it is another called the 'Bridge of the Ten Thousand Ages.' We have seen the 'Temple of Golden Happiness' and the 'Bridge of Long Repose.' We shall be on the lookout for the 'Temple of the Starry Firmament,' and probably shall not be long in finding it. Strange that a people so practical as the Chinese should have so much poetry in their language!

"We came to the village of Nan-kow, at the entrance of the Nan-kow Pass, and stopped there for dinner. Our ride had given us a good appetite, and though our cook was not very skilful in preparing our meal, we did not find fault with him, as we did not wish to run the risk of waiting while he cooked the things over again. The Chinese inn at Nan-kow is not so good as the Palace Hotel at San Francisco; in fact, it is as bad as any other hotel that we have seen. They don't have much pleasure travel in this part of the world, and therefore it does not pay them to give much attention to the comfort of their guests.

"The Nan-kow Pass is about thirteen miles long, and the road through it is very rough. The mountains are steep, and we saw here and there ruins of forts that were built long ago to keep out the Tartar invaders of China. Our animals had several falls, but they got through without accident, and, what was more, they brought us to a village where there was an inn with something good to eat.

"What do you suppose it was? It was mutton, which is kept boiling in a pot from morning till night; and as fast as any is taken out, or the soup boils down, they fill the kettle up again. Mutton is very cheap here, as sheep are abundant and can be bought at the purchaser's own price, provided he will keep himself within reason. Great numbers of sheep are driven to Pekin for the supply of the city, and we met large flocks at several points on the road. Their wool has been exported to England and America; but it is not of a fine quality, and does not bring a high price.

THE GOD OF THE KITCHEN.

"We passed the ruins of forts and towers every few miles, and our guide pointed out some of the towers that were formerly used for conveying intelligence by means of signal-fires. They are now falling to pieces, and are of no further use.

"This is the road by which the Tartars went to the conquest of China, and there is a story that the empire was lost in consequence of a woman. The Chinese were very much afraid of the Tartars, and they built the Great Wall to keep them out of the country. But a wall would be of no use without soldiers to defend it, and so it was arranged that whenever the Tartars were approaching, a signal should be sent along the towers, and the army would come to Pekin to defend it.

"One day a favorite lady of the emperor's palace persuaded the emperor to give the signal, to see how long it would take for the generals and the army to get to Pekin. He gave the signal, and the army came, but the generals were very angry when they found they had been called together just to amuse a woman. They went back to their homes, and the affair was supposed to be forgotten.

"By-and-by the Tartars did come in reality, and the signal was sent out again. But this time no army came, nor did a single general turn his face to Pekin. The city fell into the hands of the invaders, and they are there to-day. So much for what a woman did; but it sounds too much like the story of 'The Boy and the Wolf' to be true.

"At the last place where we stopped before reaching the Great Wall we found the people very insolent, both to us and to the men in our employ. They said rude things to us, and perhaps it was fortunate that we did not understand Chinese, or we might have been disposed to resent their impudence, and so found ourselves in worse trouble. Our guide said something to a lama, or priest, and he managed to make the people quiet, partly by persuasion and partly by threats. Some of the men had been drinking too freely of sam-shoo, which has the same effect on them as whiskey has on people in America. It is not unusual for strangers in this part of China to be pelted with stones; but the natives are afraid to do much more than this, as they would thereby get into trouble.

"At the place where we reach the Great Wall there is a Chinese city called Chan-kia-kow; but it is known to the Russians as Kalgan. It is the frontier town of Mongolia, and the Russians have a great deal of commerce with it. It stands in a valley, and so high are the

A LAMA.

mountains around it that the sun does not rise until quite late in the forenoon. Doctor Bronson said there is a town somewhere in the Rocky

25

THE HILLS NEAR CHAN-KIA-KOW.

Mountains of America which is so shut in that the sun does not rise there until about eleven o'clock next day; and we thought it might possibly be a relative of Chan-kia-kow. There is an odd sort of population here, as the merchants who trade with the Russians are from all parts of China; and then there are Mongols from the Desert of Gobi, and a very fair number of real Russians.

"One curious article of trade consisted of logs from the country to the north. They are cut in lengths of about six feet, and are intended for coffins for the people of the southern part of the empire. Wood is scarce in the more densely inhabited portions of China, and must be carried for great distances. It is six hundred miles from the Great Wall to where these logs are cut, and so they must be carried seven hundred miles in all before they reach Pekin. The carts on which they are loaded are very strong, and have not a bit of iron about them.

"We are now at the Great Wall, which comes straggling over the hills that surround the city, and forms its northern boundary. It is very much in ruins, but at the town itself there is a portion of it kept in good repair, and one of the gates is regularly shut at night and opened in the morning. Some of the old towers are still in their places; but the weather is slowly wearing them away, and in time they will all be fallen.

"The Great Wall is certainly one of the wonders of the world, and it was very much so at the time of its construction. It was built two thousand years ago, and is about twelve hundred miles long. It runs westward from the shores of the Gulf of Pe-chi-li to what was then the western frontier of the Chinese Empire. For the greater part of the way it consists of a wall of earth faced with stone or brick, and it is paved on the top with large tiles. It is about twenty-five feet wide at the bottom, and diminishes to fifteen feet wide at the top, with a height of thirty feet. In many places it is not so substantial as this, being nothing more than a wall of earth faced with brick, and not more than fifteen feet high. At varying intervals there are towers for watchmen and soldiers. They are generally forty or fifty feet high, and about three hundred feet apart.

"The wall follows all the inequalities of the surface of the earth, winding over mountains and through valleys, crossing rivers by massive archways, and stretching straight as a sunbeam over the level plain.

"Think what a work this would be at the present day, and then remember that it was built two thousand years ago, when the science of engineering was in its infancy, and the various mechanical appliances for moving heavy bodies were unknown!

"We spent a day at the Great Wall. We scrambled over the ruins and climbed to the top of one of the towers, and we had more than one tumble among the remains of the great enterprise of twenty centuries ago. Then we started back to Pekin, and returned with aching limbs and a general feeling that we had had a hard journey. But we were well satisfied that we had been there, and would not have missed seeing the Great Wall for twice the fatigue and trouble. They told us in Pekin that some travellers have been imposed on by seeing only a piece of a wall about thirty miles from the city, which the guides pretend is the real one. They didn't try the trick on us, and probably thought it would not be of any use to do so.

"We did not stay long in Pekin after we got back from the Great Wall, as we had to catch the steamer at Tien-tsin. Here we are steaming down the coast, and having a jolly time. We are on the same ship that took us up from Shanghai, and so we feel almost as if we had got home again. But we are aware that home is yet a long way off, and we have many a mile between us and the friends of whom we think so often."

CHAPTER XXIX.

FROM SHANGHAI TO HONG-KONG.—A STORY OF THE COOLIE TRADE.

THE party reached Shanghai without accident, and on their arrival at that port the boys had a welcome surprise in the shape of letters from home. Their first letters from Japan had been received, and read and reread by family and friends. To judge by the words of praise that they elicited, the efforts of the youths at descriptive composition were eminently successful. Frank's mother said that if they did as well all through their journey as they had done in the beginning, they would be qualified to write a book about Japan and China; and a similar opinion of their powers was drawn from Fred's mother, who took great pride in her son. Mary and Effie composed a joint letter to Frank, to tell how much pleasure he had given them. They were somewhat anxious about the purchases, but were entirely sure everything would be correct in the end. Fred began to be a trifle jealous of Frank when he saw how much the latter enjoyed the communication from the girl who came to the railway station to see them off. He vowed to himself that before he started on another journey he would make the acquaintance of another Effie, so that he would have some one to exchange letters with.

The letters were read and reread, and their perusal and the preparation of answers consumed all the time of the stay in Shanghai. The delay, however, was only for a couple of days, as the weekly steamer for Hong-kong departed at the end of that time, and our friends were among her passengers. Another of the ship's company was our old friend "the Mystery," who told Doctor Bronson that he had been travelling in the interior of Japan, and had only recently arrived from there. He was going to Canton, and possibly farther, but could not speak with certainty until he had arranged some business at Hong-kong.

The steamer on which our friends were travelling was under the French flag, and belonged to the line popularly known as "the French Mail." The service between Europe and China is performed alternately by two companies, one of them English and the other French; and by means of these two companies there is a weekly ship each way. The French steamers are preferred by a great many travellers, as they are generally larger than the English ones, and are admirably arranged for comfort. They make the voyage from Shanghai to Marseilles in about forty days, calling at the principal ports on the way, and going through the Suez Canal. The English steamers follow very nearly the same route as the French ones, as long as they are in Eastern waters; but when they reach the Mediterranean Sea, they have two lines, one going to Venice and the other to Southampton. The official names of the two companies are " The Peninsular and Oriental Steam Navigation Company " (English), and " La Compagnie des Messageries Maritimes " (French).

There were not many passengers, perhaps a dozen in all, and they were mostly merchants and other residents of Shanghai on their way to Europe or to some of the southerly ports of Asia. Two of the passengers were accompanied by their Chinese servants, and the boys were greatly amused to hear the efforts of the latter to speak English. They had already heard the same kind of thing during their movements in China, but had not paid much attention to it in consequence of their occupation with other matters. Now, however, they had some leisure for investigation, and Fred suggested that they had better take a glance at the Chinese language.

A few glances were all they wanted, as Frank was not long in ascertaining that it would require years of study to acquaint himself with enough of the language to be able to converse in it. Fred learned, about the same time, that there was a written language and a spoken one, and the two were so unlike that a man can read and write Chinese without being able to speak it, and can speak without being able to read and write. They found that very few foreigners who came to China to stay for years ever troubled themselves to learn the language, but were contented with " pidgin English." Then the question very naturally arose, " What is pidgin English ?"

SPECIMEN OF CHINESE WRITING.

In a small book entitled " John, or Our Chinese Relations," Frank found something relating to pidgin English, which he copied into his note-book for future reference. When he had done with the volume, it was borrowed by Fred for the same purpose, and the boys gave a vote of thanks to the author for saving them the trouble to hunt up the information by asking questions of their friends. What they selected was as follows:

"In attempting to pronounce the word 'business,' the Chinese were formerly unable to get nearer to the real sound than 'pidgin' or 'pigeon;' hence the adoption of that word, which means nothing more nor less than 'business.' Pidgin English is therefore business English, and is the language of commerce at the open ports of China, or wherever else the native and foreigner come in contact. A pidgin French has made its appearance in Saigon and at other places, and is steadily increasing as French commerce has increased. On the frontier line between Russia and China there is an important trading-point—Kiachta—where the commerce of the two empires was exclusively conducted for a century and a half. A pidgin Russian exists there, and is the medium of commercial transactions between the Russian and Chinese merchants.

"Long ago the Portuguese at Macao had a corresponding jargon for their intercourse with the Chinese; and it may be safely stated that wherever the Chinese have established permanent relations with any country, a language of trade has immediately sprung into existence, and is developed as time rolls on and its necessities multiply.

"The decline in Portuguese trade with China was accompanied with a corresponding decline in the language, but it left its impress upon the more recent pidgin English, which contains many Portuguese words. Pidgin English is a language by itself, with very little inflection either in noun, pronoun, or verb, and with a few words doing duty for many. The Chinese learn it readily, as they have no grammatical giants to wrestle with in mastering it, and the foreigners are quite ready to meet them on the road and adapt their phraseology to its requirements. The Chinese has only to commit to memory a few hundred words and know their meaning; the foreigner (if he be English-speaking) has less than a hundred foreign words to learn, together with the peculiar construction of phrases. The Chinese have printed vocabularies in which the foreign word and its meaning are set forth in Chinese characters, and thus they have no occasion to trouble themselves with the alphabet of the stranger. These books are specially intended for the use of *compradores* and servants in foreign employ, and are so small that they can be readily carried in the pocket.

"In pidgin English the pronouns *he, she, it*, and *they* are generally expressed by the single pronoun *he*. All the forms of the first person are included in *my*, and those of the second person in *you*. When we come to the verbs, we find that action, intention, existence, and kindred conditions are covered by *hab, belongey*, and *can do*. Various forms of possession are expressed by *catchee* (catch), while *can do* is particularly applied to ability or power, and is also used to imply affirmation or negation. Thus: 'Can do walkee?' means 'Are you able to walk?' If so, the response would be 'Can do,' while 'No can do' would imply inability to indulge in pedestrianism. *Belongey* comes from 'belong,' and is often shortened to a single syllable, *b'long*. It is very much employed, owing to the many shades of meaning of which it is capable. Thus: 'I live in Hong-kong' would be rendered 'My belongey Hong-kong side,' and 'You are very large' would be properly translated 'You belongey too muchee big piecee.'

"The Chinese find great difficulty in pronouncing r, which they almost invariably convert into *l*. They have a tendency to add a vowel sound (*o* or *e*) to words ending with a consonant. Bearing these points in mind, we readily see how 'drink' becomes *dlinko*, and 'brown' *blowner*. Final *d* and *t* are awkward for them to handle, and *th* is to their lips an abomination of first-class dimensions. 'Child' becomes *chilo*, and 'cold' is transformed to *colo*, in pidgin English. 'That,' and other words beginning with *th*, generally lose the sound of *h*, though sometimes they retain *h* and drop the *t* before it. 'Side' is used for position, and the vocabulary contains *inside*, *outside, bottom-side* (below), and *top-side* (above). *Chop-chop* means 'fast,' 'quick,' 'immediately;' *man-man* means 'slowly,' 'slower,' 'gently,' in the south of China; while at Han-kow, on the Yang-tse, it means exactly the reverse. At Canton or Swatow, if you say *man-man* to your boatmen, they will cease rowing or will proceed very lightly; say the same thing to your boatmen at Han-kow or Ichang, and they will pull away with redoubled energy."

" As we have learned the principles of this new language," Frank remarked, "we ought to be able to understand some proverbs in it. For instance, here are four that contain whole heaps of good advice, besides showing us how to read pidgin English:

'Who man swim best, t'hat man most gettee dlown;
Who lidee best he most catch tumble down.'

'One piecee blind man healee best, maskee;
One piecee deaf man makee best look-see.'

'One man who never leedee,
Like one dly inkstand be;
You turn he top-side downey,
No ink lun outside he.'

'Suppose one man much bad—how bad he be,
One not'her bad man may be flaid of he.'"

" Those will do," Fred answered, "and here is Longfellow's famous poem 'Excelsior,' which every schoolboy knows, or ought to know. It was done into pidgin English by somebody who lived in the country and evidently knew what he was about:

'TOP-SIDE GALAH!

'T'hat nightee teem he come chop-chop
One young man walkee, no can stop;
Maskee snow, maskee ice;
He cally flag wit'h chop so nice—
            Top-side Galah!

'He muchee solly; one piecee eye
Lookee sharp—so fashion—my:
He talkee large, he talkee stlong,
Too muchee culio; allee same gong—
            Top-side Galah!

'Insidee house he can see light,
And evly loom got fire all light;
He lookee plenty ice more high,
Insidee mout'h he plenty cly—
            Top-side Galah!

'Olo man talkee, " No can walk,
Bimeby lain come, velly dark;
Have got water, velly wide!"
Maskee, my must go top-side—
            Top-side Galah!

'"Man-man," one girlee talkee he:
"What for you go top-side look-see?"
And one teem more he plenty cly,
But alla teem walk plenty high—
                    Top-side Galah!

'"Take care that spilum tlee, young man,
Take care that ice, must go man-man."
One cooiie chin-chin he good night;
He talkee, "My can go all light"—
                    Top-side Galah!

'That young man die: one large dog see
Too muchee bobbly findee he.
He hand b'long coldee, all same like ice,
He holdee flag, wit'h chop so nice—
                    Top-side Gulah!'"

"But does every Chinese who goes to a foreign country understand how to talk pidgin English?" Frank asked of Doctor Bronson.

"Not by any means," was the reply; "thousands of them are not able to speak a word when they go abroad, but they gradually pick up the language of the country to which they go. Not all of them go to America or other English-speaking lands; many have gone to Cuba, Peru, and Brazil, where there was no need of a knowledge of English. Spanish and Portuguese are the only tongues in use there, and many an emigrant never took the trouble to learn a word of them."

Their old acquaintance "the Mystery" had joined the party while the conversation just recorded was going on. When the Doctor made allusion to the emigration to Cuba and Peru, "the Mystery" opened his eyes a little wider than was his custom, and said he was well aware that many had gone to those countries who knew nothing but Chinese, and never learned a word of any other language. As the boys showed a desire to hear more on the subject, he proposed to tell them something about the coolie-trade; and it was arranged that they should assemble in the smoking-saloon after dinner, where they could talk at their leisure.

After dinner they met as agreed, and "the Mystery" seated himself comfortably for the story he was about to tell.

"The coolie-trade," said he, "does not exist any more. It was very much like the slave-trade, of which you have read; in fact, it was nothing more than the slave-trade with the form changed a little. In the African slave-trade the slaves were bought as one might buy sheep and cattle. In the coolie-traffic the men were hired for a term of years at certain stipu-

T'hat nightee teem he come chop-chop
One young man walkee, no can stop.

"Take care that spilum tlee, young man,
Take care that ice, must go man-man."

"Man-man," one girlee talkee he:
"What for you go top-side look-see?"

T'hat young man die: one large dog see
Too muchee bobbly ündee he.

lated wages, and were to be returned to their homes at the end of that term, provided all their debts had been discharged. The plan was all right on its face, but it was not carried out. When the period for which he was engaged was up, the coolie was always made to be in debt to his employer; and, no matter how hard he might work, he was not allowed to free himself. He was a slave to his master just as much as was the negro from Africa, and not one coolie in a thousand ever saw his native land again.

"Not only were the men hired on contracts that they could never cancel, but they were stolen, just as slaves are stolen in Africa. Boats were sent up the rivers in the southern part of China to bring back loads of coolies. They would land an armed party at a village, seize all the men in the place, and bring them to the port, where they would be transferred to the dealers, who would send them to the places where their labor was needed. Macao was the great port for the coolie trade, and the Portuguese had large sheds there, which they called *barracoons*, for holding the coolies in prison till they were ready to ship them away. These barracoons were sometimes so crowded that thousands of coolies died there in the course of a single year. The natives called them '*chu-tze-kuan*,' or 'pig-pens,' and they were so filthy that they richly deserved the name.

BARRACOONS AT MACAO.

COOLIES EMBARKING AT MACAO.

"The name 'coolie' belongs properly to a tribe of natives on the northern coast of Africa, but it is applied to a laborer of any part of the East, and this is its meaning in Japan and China.

"The laborers who were to be taken to Cuba or Peru were received on board the ships, and counted as they came over the side, like so many boxes or bales of merchandise; in fact, they were nothing but merchandise, and the receipts were made out for a certain number of coolies without the least record of their names and residences. I was once in a ship that took a cargo of these people to Peru, and I don't believe that anybody on board felt otherwise than if he had been in the slave-trade. And we had a narrow escape from having our throats cut by our cargo and our bodies thrown into the sea."

ENRAGED COOLIE.

"Please tell us about that," said Fred. Frank echoed the request, and their informer nodded his consent.

"The ship had taken its cargo at Macao, and we went out to sea with a fine breeze. We had over a thousand 'passengers' in the hold, and only a small number were to be allowed on deck at one time, as several ships had been captured by the coolies, and we did not intend to be taken if we could help it. Two days after we started there was trouble among the coolies, and several of them ran about the space below-deck and threatened to set the ship on fire. They did build a fire of some of the dry boards used for making their sleeping-berths; but we covered the hatches with tarpaulins, and held the smoke down there, so that the coolies were nearly smothered and compelled to put the fire out themselves.

"The hatchways were covered with gratings to admit of a free circulation of air, and they were so firmly fastened that the coolies could not disturb them. Several men were on deck when the trouble began, and one of them tried to get through the grating to join his companions. He managed to squeeze his body through the opening, and then discovered too late that he had a fall of nearly thirty feet before him, as the hatch of the lower deck was open. He struggled a moment, then dropped to the lower hold, and was killed by the fall.

"It became necessary to fire on the mutineers, and for this we raised the tarpaulins over one of the hatches. The smoke poured out in a dense mass and almost smothered us, and we could only see the forms of the men very dimly, like a ship in a fog. We fired, and continued to fire till

A DEADLY FALL.

FIRING DOWN THE HATCHWAY.

several of them had been shot down, and all their efforts to get at us were of no avail. There were about sixty men in the crew, and, as we had over a thousand coolies on board, we had numbers against us fearfully. But they had no fire-arms, while we had a good supply of rifles and pistols, with plenty of ammunition. At the time of the outbreak there were not far from a hundred coolies on deck; but we drove them forward, and kept so large a guard over them that they could not have done anything to help their friends below if they had been disposed to do so.

"We got out of water, and the only way to reach what we had on board was by going down through the hold. Of course anybody who ventured there would be killed instantly; but we had the consolation of knowing that they could not get water any more than we could, as the place where it was stowed was fastened too securely for the coolies to open it with any tools they had on hand. We had a small condenser in the cook's galley, and with this we procured enough water to save us from death by thirst; but we refused to give a drop to the mutineers.

"They held out for two days, and during all that time hardly a man of us slept more than a few minutes at a stretch. Many of the coolies were suffering terribly with thirst and hunger, and they asked to have their wants supplied while they were making negotiations for peace. The captain refused anything but the most unconditional surrender, and the only concession he would grant was to have the dead bodies passed up to be thrown overboard. Of course the coolies were very glad of this, as they were suffering from the fearful condition of the narrow space where they were confined. When this work was completed, they asked for half

THE WRITING IN BLOOD.

an hour's time to make a proposal for surrender, which was allowed them.

"Looking through the hatch, we could see them grouped together and engaged in earnest conversation. Two were dead or dying, and from one of them there was a stream of blood slowly oozing. A coolie who appeared to be a ringleader among them dipped his pen in the blood and wrote on a sheet of paper:

"'We want three hundred coolies to be allowed on deck at a time. The ship must go back to the coast, and allow us to land at Whampoa, below Canton. We promise to make no trouble if this be done, but will burn the ship at once unless the captain agree to it.'

"We knew that any promise they made would not amount to anything when they were once in possession of the deck, and, besides, to go back to China would be a complete surrender of the voyage. The captain did not hesitate a moment in his answer to this demand.

"He opened one of the hatches just enough to allow one man to descend at a time, and through this hole he compelled all the coolies who were then on deck to pass. Then he told the interpreters to say that they might burn the ship as soon as they liked, and the crew would leave in the boats. The boats were made ready for lowering; and, as we were not far from the coast, and the wind was fair, there was not much doubt of our getting safe to Hong-kong. Not a coolie would escape, and we should take good care that the fire would be so far advanced before we left that it could not be put out.

"In an hour we received another message, written in blood, like the first. It promised to deliver the ringleaders of the mutiny, to be kept in irons till we arrived at our destination, and also promised that there should be no more attempts to set fire to the ship. The captain was to fix the number of men to be on deck at one time, and they were to obey his orders without question. In fact, the surrender was complete.

"We had no trouble after that; but we only allowed fifty men on deck at one time, and those under a strong guard. You can be sure we were in a hurry to finish the voyage, which we did without accident. I had had all I wanted of the coolie-trade, and never went on another voyage like that."

THE INTERPRETERS.

CHAPTER XXX.

HONG-KONG AND CANTON.—CHINESE PIRATES.

THE story of the coolie-trade and some of the conversation that followed cleared the mystery that surrounded the narrator and had given him the name by which he was known. He had been an active participant in the peculiar commerce of the East, which includes the violation of laws whenever they prove inconvenient, such as the smuggling of opium and the shipment of coolies to the countries where they are in demand. His latest venture was one that required considerable secrecy, as it involved the purchase of arms for the rebels in Japan. For this reason he had been very cautious in his movements around Yokohama and during his whole stay in Japan, and he had found it judicious to leave the country on the vessel that came so near being wrecked in the typhoon that overtook our friends. He was safely away from Japan now, and the arms that he had purchased for the rebels were in the hands of the government. He had made money by the operation, and was on the lookout for something new.

"That man belongs to a class which is not at all rare in the far East," said Doctor Bronson to the boys when the subject of the conversation had left them. "A great many adventurers find their way here, some of them being men of ability which borders on genius, while the others are not far removed from rascals. Ward and Burgevine were of the better sort; and there are others whom I could name, but they are not so numerous as the other and worse variety. They are very often men of good manners, and not at all disagreeable as travelling companions, but it is not advisable to be intimate with them. Travelling, like poverty, makes us some strange acquaintances. We can learn a great deal from them if we proceed properly; and if we know where the line of familiarity should be drawn, we are not in any danger of suffering by it."

The morning after the above conversation the steamer arrived at Hong-kong, and dropped anchor in the harbor. She was immediately surrounded by a fleet of small boats, which competed eagerly among themselves for the patronage of the passengers. Our friends selected one which was rowed by a couple of women, and had a group of children in a little pen at the stern. Doctor Bronson explained to the boys that in Southern China a great deal of the boating is done by women, and that entire families live on board the little craft on which they earn their existence. The boat population of Canton numbers more than sixty thousand persons. They are not allowed to live on shore, and their whole lives, from birth to death, are passed on the water. The most of the boatmen and boatwomen at Hong-kong come from Canton, which is only ninety miles away; and as they have privileges at the former place which are denied them in the latter, they are quite satisfied to stay where they are.

HONG-KONG.

Hong-kong is a rocky island on the coast of China, and has an excellent harbor, sheltered from most of the winds that blow. The town of Victoria is built at the edge of this harbor, and the streets that lead back from the water are so steep that the effort of climbing them is liable to throw a stranger from the North into a violent perspiration. Fortunately, there is an abundance of sedan-chairs, and any one who wishes to take a promenade may do his walking by hiring a couple of chair-coolies to do it for him. The chairs are everywhere, and it is generally desirable to hire one in order to be rid of the continual applications from those that are unemployed. At the wharf where they landed the Doctor

26

engaged porters to carry the baggage to the hotel, and then took chairs for the transportation of himself and the boys. As they had the afternoon before them, the chairs were kept for making the ascent of the mountain just back of the town, and as soon as the rooms were secured, and a slight lunch had been served, they started on their excursion.

At the highest point of the mountain—about eighteen hundred feet above the water-level—there is a signal-station, where all vessels coming into port are announced by means of flags. Our friends were carried along a zigzag road to this station, the coolies stopping every few minutes to rest from the fatigue of ascending a steep road with a burden on their shoulders. At the station they had a view extending a long distance out to sea and over the coast of China, and the mountain was so nearly perpendicular that it seemed as if they could toss a penny on the town or into the harbor. Fred tried it, and so did Frank; but after throwing away several ounces of copper, and finding they only went a short distance, they abandoned the experiment. They returned well satisfied with the excursion, and agreed that no one who visits Hong-kong should omit the journey to the top of the mountain.

Hong-kong, being an English colony, is governed after the English form, and consequently the laws enforced in China do not necessarily prevail on the island. The population includes four or five thousand English and other European nationalities, and more than a hundred thousand Chinese. The number of the latter is steadily increasing, and a very large part of the business of the place is in their hands. The money in circulation is made in England for the special use of the colony. It has the head of the Queen on one side, and the denomination and date on the other; and, for the accommodation of the Chinese, the denomination is given in Chinese characters. The smallest of the Hong-kong coins is made to correspond with the Chinese cash, and it takes ten of them to make a cent, or one thousand for a dollar. It has a hole in the centre, like the Chinese coins generally, to facilitate stringing on a wire or cord, and is so popular with the natives that it is in free circulation in the adjacent parts of the empire.

There was not a great deal to be seen in the town, and so the next morning the three travellers started for Canton. There is a boat each way daily, and the journey is made in seven or eight hours; the boys found that the boat in which they went was of American construction, and had an American captain, and so they felt at home, as they had felt on the Yang-tse under similar circumstances.

Soon after they left the dock, Frank observed that the gangway leading to the lower deck was covered with a grating fastened with a padlock,

FAC-SIMILE OF A HONG-KONG MILLE.   FAC-SIMILE OF A HONG-KONG DIME.

FAC-SIMILE OF A HONG-KONG CENT.

and that a Malay sailor stood over it with a sword in his hand and a pistol at his belt. He called Fred's attention to the arrangement, and as soon as they found the captain at leisure they asked what it meant.

"It's a very simple matter," said Captain B——, "when you know about it. The fact is, that we were once very near losing our lives by Chinese pirates, and we don't propose to have another risk like it."

"Why, what could pirates have to do with this boat, I wonder?" said Frank.

"We didn't know at the time," was the reply, "but we found out."

"How was that?"

"Well, it seems that some Chinese pirates determined to capture this boat, murder all the foreigners on board, rob the Chinese passengers, and then get away on a junk that was to be ready to receive them. They made their plans, and on a certain day fifty of them took passage from Canton to Hong-kong. When about half way, they were to meet a junk with more men; and as the junk hung out her signal and came near, the fellows were to fall upon us with their knives, and capture the boat. They intended to kill us all, but their scheme failed, as there were four ships at anchor that day close by the spot where the junk was to meet them, and so the junk took the alarm and left. There was no disturbance, and we did not have a suspicion of anything wrong. Finding they had failed with us, they went the next day and captured the steamer *Spark*, which runs between Canton and Macao. They killed the captain and officers and the only European passenger who happened to be on board, plundered all the native passengers, and got away. Some of them were afterwards captured, and confessed to their part in the affair, and then the whole story came out that they had intended to rob this boat. Since then we always have the gratings down, so that the third-class passengers cannot come on deck; and we keep plenty of rifles and revolvers in the pilot-house and captain's cabin ready for use. They may never try it on us again, and we don't intend to give them a chance to do so."

FORT IN CANTON RIVER.

The captain went on to say that there were many pirates in the waters around Canton, and all along the southern coast. The government tries to suppress them, but it is not easy to do so, and hardly a day passes without the report of a robbery somewhere. All trading-junks are obliged to go heavily armed, and out of this fact comes a great deal of the piracy, as a junk may be a peaceful trader at one o'clock, a pirate at two, and a peaceful trader again at three. It takes very little to induce a Chinese captain to turn pirate when he sees a rich prize before him, and he has no trouble in winning over his crew. It is impossible to distinguish the pirate from the trader; and as the coast is seamed with island passages and indented with bays, it is easy for a junk to escape after she has committed a robbery.

The voyage from Hong-kong to Canton is partly among islands and through a bay, and partly on the Pearl River. The navigation is easy in the first part of the course, but after the steamer has reached the narrower portion of the river the great number of junks and other craft compels a sharp lookout on the part of the pilots, to avoid accidents. They passed the famous Whampoa Anchorage, where the ocean-bound ships used to receive their cargoes before Hong-kong assumed its present importance. A few miles farther on, the great city of Canton was brought into sight as the steamer swung around a bend in the river. In front was the island of Ho-nan, with its temple bowered in trees, and on the surface of the river there were thousands of boats of many kinds and sizes. The boys remembered what they had heard of the boat population of Canton, and now they realized that they had reached a city where sixty thousand people make their homes on the water.

Before the steamer stopped she was surrounded by dozens of the smaller boats, and, as soon as they could do so, many of the boatwomen came on board. The captain recommended one of them who was known as "American Susan," and the trio were confided to her care for transfer to the hotel on Ho-nan Island. Susan and her attendant women shouldered the valises which the travellers had brought from Hong-kong, and led the way to her boat. The gallantry of the boys received a shock when they saw their baggage carried by women, while their own hands were empty; but the Doctor told them it was the custom of the country, and by carrying their own valises they would deprive the women of an opportunity of earning a few pennies. To this view of the matter they yielded; and before they had recovered their composure the boat was gliding across the river, propelled by the powerful arms of her feminine crew. Susan proposed to be in their employ during their stay at Canton, and a bargain was speedily concluded; for fifty cents at day, the boat was to be at their disposal from morning till night to carry them over the river, or to any point they wished to visit along its banks. Frank thought they would be obliged to look a long time to find a boat with two men at the oars for a similar price in New York, and Fred thought they would have to look still longer to find one rowed by two women.

They had three or four hours to spare before sunset, and at once set about the business of sight-seeing. Their first visit was to the temple on the island, and they were followed from the landing by a crowd of idle people, who sometimes pressed too closely for comfort. There was an avenue of trees leading up to the temple, and before reaching the building they passed under a gateway not unlike those they had seen at the

GATEWAY OF TEMPLE NEAR CANTON.

temples in Kioto and Tokio. The temple was not particularly impressive, as its architectural merit is not of much consequence, and, besides, it was altogether too dirty for comfort. There was quite a crowd of priests attached to it, and they were as slovenly in appearance as the building they occupied. In the yard of the temple the strangers were shown the furnaces in which the bodies of the priests are burned after death, and the little niches where their ashes are preserved. There were several pens occupied by the fattest pigs the boys had ever seen. The guide explained that these pigs were sacred, and maintained out of the revenues of the temple. The priests evidently held them in great reverence, and Frank intimated that he thought the habits of the pigs were the models which the priests had adopted for their own. Some of the holy men were at their devotions when the party arrived, but they dropped their prayer-books to have a good look at the visitors, and did not resume them until they had satisfied their curiosity.

From the temple they proceeded to a garden, where they had an opportunity of seeing some of the curious productions of the Chinese gardeners in the way of dwarfing trees and plants. There were small bushes in the shape of animals, boats, houses, and other things, and the resemblance was in many cases quite good. They do this by tying the limbs of the plants to little sticks of bamboo, or around wire frames shaped like the objects they wish to represent; and by tightening the bandages every morning, and carefully watching the development of the work, they eventually accomplish their purpose. If they represent a dog or other animal, they generally give it a pair of great staring eyes of porcelain, and sometimes they equip its mouth with teeth of the same material. Many of the Chinese gardens are very prettily laid out, and there are some famous ones near Canton, belonging to wealthy merchants.

On their return from the garden they stopped at a place where eggs are hatched by artificial heat. They are placed over brick ovens or furnaces, where a gentle heat is kept up, and a man is constantly on watch to see that the fire neither burns too rapidly nor too slowly. A great heat would kill the vitality of the egg by baking it, while if the temperature falls below a certain point, the hatching process does not go on. When the little chicks appear, they are placed under the care of an artificial mother, which consists of a bed of soft down and feathers, with a cover three or four inches above it. This cover has strips of down hanging from it, and touching the bed below, and the chickens nestle there quite safe from outside cold. The Chinese have practised this artificial hatching and rearing for thousands of years, and relieved the hens of a great deal of the monotony of life.

On the river, not far from the hatching establishment, they saw a man engaged in the novel occupation of herding ducks. A hundred or more ducks were on the water, and the man was near them in a small boat and armed with a long pole. The ducks were very obedient to him, but occasionally one would show a little opposition to the herder's wishes, and endeavor to stray from his companions. A rap from the pole brought him speedily to his senses, and back to the herd, and he was pretty certain not to stray again till the blow had been forgotten. Geese were herded in the same way, and both they and the ducks managed to pick up a good part of their living from the water. Ducks are an important article of food among the Chinese, and the rearing of them gives occupation to a great many persons in all parts of the empire.

CHAPTER XXXI.

SIGHTS AND SCENES IN CANTON.

THE party remained three days at Canton. They rose early every
morning, and went on excursions through and around the city, and
it is fair to say that they did not have a single idle moment. Each of the
boys made careful notes of what he saw and heard, and by the end of
their stay both had enough to fill a small volume. They returned to
Hong-kong on the fourth day, and on the morning after their return
they sat down to write the story of their adventures. But before they
began writing the projected letter a discussion arose between them, which
was about like this:

They expected the steamer to arrive from America in a day or two,
and it would doubtless bring letters for them, which would determine
their future movements. They expected to return home by way of San
Francisco, as they had come; but it was by no means improbable that they
would keep on to the westward, and so go around the world by way of
India and Europe.

"What is the use of writing up our Canton experiences," said Frank,
"till we know what we are to do? If we go home by San Francisco, we
will have plenty of time on the steamer; and if we go on to the west, we
will have to go by steamer too; and then we will have time enough between Hong-kong and the first port we stop at. Why should we be in a
hurry to write up our account, when, in any case, we shall have the time
to do so while we are at sea?"

Fred admitted the force of the argument, but thought there would
be an advantage in writing while the subject was fresh in their minds.
While they were debating the pros and cons of the case, the Doctor came
into the room, and the question was appealed to him. After careful de-
liberation, he rendered a decision that covered the case to the perfect satisfaction of both the disputants.

"It will be several days, at any rate," said he, "before we can leave
Hong-kong, whether we go east or west. Now, I advise you to take an

hour each day for writing up your story of Canton, and you will then have plenty of time for sight-seeing. You will have ended your writing before we leave, and then can devote your time at sea to other things which the voyage will suggest."

His suggestion was adopted, and they at once set about their work, determined to write two hours daily till they had described Canton so fully that their friends would know exactly what was to be seen there. They divided the work, as they had done on previous occasions, one of them making a description of a certain part of their route, and the other taking another portion of it. When they were through with it, they put the two stories together, and found that they fitted to perfection. Here is what they wrote:

"Canton is the capital of the province of Kwang-tung, and its name in English is a corruption of the Chinese one. The people who live there call it 'Kwang-tung-sang-shing,' and the Portuguese call it Kam-tom, and they write it that way. It is called the City of Rams, just as Florence is called the Beautiful City, and Genoa the Haughty; and the Chinese who live there are very proud of it. The climate is warm, the thermometer rising to 85° or 90° in the summer, and rarely going below 50° in winter. Occasionally ice forms to the thickness of heavy paper, and once in five or ten years there will be a slight fall of snow, which astonishes all the children, and many of the older people.

"The population is said to be about a million, on land and water. Those who live in boats are about sixty thousand. The city was founded more than two thousand years ago, according to the Chinese historians, but it was not surrounded with a wall until the eleventh century. The wall to-day is the same that was first built, but it has been repaired and changed a good deal in the time it has stood, and some new parts have been added. The circuit of the walls is about seven miles, but there are suburbs that now form a part of the city, so that it is a journey of not less than ten miles to go around Canton.

"There are sixteen gates to the city, and each has a name that designates its position. There are two pagodas near the West Gate, and there are a hundred and twenty-four temples, pavilions, and halls inside the walls of Canton. Then there are four prisons, and there is an execution ground, where many a poor fellow has lost his head. The prisons are like all such establishments in China, and a great many men would prefer death to incarceration in one of these horrible places.

"We don't know positively whether there are a million people in Canton or not. We took the figures from the guide-book, just as everybody else takes them, and we want to acknowledge our indebtedness to it. The guide-book is very useful in a strange country, as it tells you in a few minutes what you might spend hours or days in learning. It gives you an outline which you must fill in for yourself by practical observation; and

STREET SCENE IN CANTON.

unless you have it with you, there is a great deal that you may miss, if your time is limited, and you are compelled to do your sight-seeing rapidly.

"When we came in sight of Canton, we saw some buildings that rose far above all others, and very naturally we asked what they were. We were somewhat taken aback when told that they were pawnbrokers' establishments, and of course they were among the things we went to look at. They were filled from top to bottom with clothing and other things, and our guide explained to us that the Chinese are in the habit of pawning everything they are not using, for the double reason that they get money which they can use, and at the same time they save the trouble of taking care of the property. At the beginning of winter they pawn their summer clothes, and at the beginning of summer they pawn their winter clothes. All other things on which they can borrow money they take to the pawn-shop, even when they are not obliged to have the cash. It saves the trouble of storing the goods themselves, and running the risk of having them stolen.

"We went through one of the pawn-shops, climbing stairway after stairway, and being almost stifled in the narrow and musty places we were obliged to go through. The goods were done up in packages, each one of them being labelled and ticketed, and there was a register down-stairs, so that any desired package could be found when wanted. Diamonds and other articles of great value were kept in safes near the basement, and the least costly goods were near the roof. There must have been many thousands of things stowed away in this pawn-shop. The building was said to be fire-proof, and its great height was intended to secure it against thieves.

"Close by the door of this establishment there was an opium den, where a dozen or more men were intoxicating themselves with opium, or sleeping off the effects of what they had already taken. We just looked in for a moment; it was so much like the place of the same kind that we saw in Shanghai that we did not care to stay, and, besides, the smell was very bad and the heat almost stifling. The Cantonese are said to be just as inveterate smokers of the deadly drug as the people of the North; in fact, it is about the same all over China, and with all classes that can afford to indulge in the vice. Only the middle and poorer classes go to the shops to smoke opium. The rich people can enjoy the luxury at home, and some of them have rooms in their houses specially fitted up for it.

"We saw a good many temples, and went through some of them, but, on the whole, they were rather disappointing, as they were not so fine as those at Pekin, and far behind those of Japan. The most interesting of the pagodas is the one known as the 'Five-storied Pagoda,' so called be-

FIVE-STORIED PAGODA.

cause it is five stories high. It stands on a hill that overlooks the whole city on one side, and a large cemetery on the other; and when you have climbed to the top, the view is very fine. The roofs of the houses are of all shapes and kinds, and the streets are so narrow that you can see very few of them as you look down from the top of the pagoda. On the one hand you have a densely peopled city of the living, and on the other an equally densely peopled city of the dead. Our guide said the cemetery had more inhabitants than the city; and when we asked him how many people lived there, he said 'Many millions.' You have to come to China to learn that the people in a cemetery are supposed to live there.

"And yet the guide was not so far out of the way, according to the Chinese idea. The Chinese bring food to the graves of their friends, and leave it there as an offering. The spirits of the dead are believed to linger around the spot and to eat this food, but it is really devoured by the priests and others who stay around the cemetery, and what they do not eat or carry away is consumed by the birds. At certain seasons they have grand festivals, when many thousands of people go to the cemeteries with offerings for the dead, and good things for themselves. The affair is more like a picnic than a ceremony of mourning; and when it breaks up, the mourners go to the theatre or some other place of amusement. The best burial-place is on a hill-side, and the tomb is made in the form of a terrace, or rather of three terraces, with steps leading up to them. As you look at it

HORSESHOE OR OMEGA GRAVE.

from a little distance, the tomb has the shape of a horseshoe, or, better still, of 'Omega,' the last letter of the Greek alphabet.

"Our guide said that not only do they make offerings in the cemeteries to the spirits of the dead, but they have shrines in their houses where the dead are worshipped. To prove what he said was true, he took us into a house and showed one of these shrines with bowls of rice and fruit, cups of tea, and other things, on a table. He explained that when the offerings were made they sent for a priest, who came with two men to assist him; and while the priest stood behind the table and repeated his prayers, one of his attendants pounded on a drum, and the other rang a bell. There was a fire in front of the shrine, and during the time the priest was performing the man who gave the feast knelt before the fire and burned some mock money, made out of silver paper in imitation of real coin. When the affair was over, the priest took all that he wanted from the table, and the remainder was eaten by the company who had been invited.

"Not a great distance from the five-storied pagoda we saw the leper hospital, where the unfortunate people who suffer from leprosy are compelled to live, and soon to die. The sight was a horrible one, and we did not want to stay long among the sufferers. We had expected to find a large

PRESENTING FOOD TO THE SPIRITS OF THE DEAD.

building, like a hospital in America, but instead of this there were several small buildings, grouped together in a little village, some of the houses having garden patches near them. The people were lying or sitting around

A LEPER.

in the sun, and some few of them were at work in the gardens. The most were not able to do anything, as they were suffering from the disease, which was slowly killing or crippling them.

"The guide said there were two kinds of leprosy, the 'wet' and the 'dry.' In the wet leprosy the body of the victim abounds in running sores, while in the dry there is nothing of the sort, and the appearance of the skin is not greatly different from what it is in health. The disease generally attacks the joints of the hands or feet, particularly those of the former, and the sufferer loses the first joint of the fingers and thumbs at about the same time. Then, in a few months, he loses the second joints, and in two or three months more the third joints go. We saw lepers in all the stages of the disease—some with the first joints of the hands gone, others who had lost the second joints, and others the third; while others, again, had lost the hands at the wrists. There seems to be no cure for most of the forms of the leprosy; and when a man is attacked with it, he must go at once to the hospital, no matter whether he is rich or poor. And when he has gone there, he generally remains till death relieves him from his sufferings.

A LITERARY STUDENT.

"One of the curious places we saw was the Hall of Examinations. This is a large enclosed space, having rows on rows of little cells, where the candidates for the literary degree are examined once in every three years. There are eleven thousand of these cells, and each cell is just large enough for one man to occupy. The candidates are put in these cells, and each man is furnished with a sheet of paper and a pen. He must write on the paper any given page of the Chinese books called 'The Classics' without mistake or alteration, and he is not allowed to try a second time until the next examination comes round. There are men who keep on trying all their lives for the degree, and they tell of one man who succeeded after he was eighty years old. The candidates try all sorts of tricks to smuggle in copies of the books on which they are to be examined, and also extra sheets of paper; but they are carefully searched, and everything of the sort is taken away from them.

A LITERARY GRADUATE IN HIS ROBES OF HONOR.

"There is a story in Pidgin-English verse of how a Chinese student befriended an American, who was a photographer by profession. The American believed that one good turn deserved another, and so, when the

A SEDAN-CHAIR WITH FOUR BEARERS.

examination time came round, he photographed 'The Classics' on the finger-nails of his Oriental friend. The student was allowed to wear spectacles during his examination, and so he bought a pair of magnifying-glasses that enabled him to read every word that he wanted. He came out at the head of his class, and was no doubt very thankful that he had done a kindly action towards a stranger.

"But the great sights of Canton we have not yet mentioned. These are the streets, and they are by all odds the finest we have seen in the country. They are very narrow, few of them being more than six or eight feet wide, and some of them less than the former figure. Not a single wheeled carriage can move in all Canton, and the only mode of locomotion is by means of sedan-chairs. We had chairs every day with four bearers to each, and it was strange to see how fast the men would walk in the dense crowds without hitting any one. They kept calling out that they were coming, and somehow a way was always made for them. Several times, when we met other chairs, it was no easy matter to get by, and once we turned into a side street to allow a mandarin's chair to pass along. We did knock down some things from the fronts of stores, and several times the tops of our chairs hit against the perpendicular sign-boards that hung from the buildings. There are great numbers of signs, all of them perpendicular, and they are painted in very gaudy colors, so that the effect is brilliant. Sometimes, as you look ahead, the space between the two sides of the street is quite filled with these signs, so that you cannot see anything else.

"The streets are not at all dirty, and in this respect are vastly different from those of any other city we have seen in China. The authorities evidently pay some attention to keeping them clean and preventing the accumulation of dirt. The fronts of many shops are fully open to the street, and the merchants know how to arrange their wares in the most tempting manner. You see lots of pretty things, and are constantly tempted to buy, and it was very well for us that we agreed not to buy anything till the last day, which we were to devote to shopping.

"Nearly all the vast crowd in the streets consisted of men; now and then a woman was visible, but only rarely, except near the river-side, where there were some of the class that live on the water. We met some of the small-footed women, and it was really painful to see them stumping about as if they were barely able to stand. Double your fist and put it down on the table, and you have a fair resemblance of the small foot of a Chinese woman; and if you try to walk on your fists, you can imagine how one of these ladies gets along. Some of them have to use canes to balance themselves, and running is quite out of the question. The foot is compressed in childhood, and not allowed to grow much after five or six years of age. The compression is done by tight bandages, that give great pain at first, and sometimes cause severe inflammation.

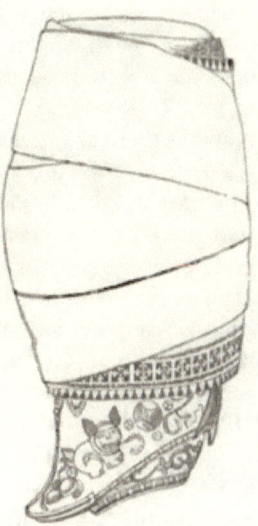

A SMALL FOOT WITH A SHOE ON IT.

"We were rather impatient for the last day, when we could do our shopping and buy the things for our friends at home. There are so many fine things for sale in Canton that it is hard to determine where to begin and where to leave off. A great many people keep on buying till their money is all gone, and some of them do not stop even then.

"The first things we looked at in our shopping tour were silks, and we found them of all kinds and descriptions that you could name. There were silks for dresses and silks for shawls, and they were of all colors, from snowy white to jet-black. Some people say that white and black are not colors at all; but if they were turned loose among the silks of Canton, perhaps they might change their minds. It is said that there are fifty thousand people in Canton engaged in making silk and other fabrics, and these include the embroiderers, of whom there are several thousands. Chi-

PEASANT WOMAN WITH NATURAL FEET.

nese embroidery on silk is famous all over the world, and it has the advantage over the embroidery of most other countries in being the same on one side that it is on the other. We have selected some shawls that we think will be very pretty when they are at home. They are pretty enough now, but there are so many nice things all around that the articles we have selected look just a little common.

"One good thing about going on a shopping excursion in Canton is that most of the establishments for the sale of different articles are grouped together, just as they are said to be in the bazaars of Cairo and Damascus. Thus we find most of the silk-dealers in Silk Street, those who sell mirrors and similar work are in Looking-glass Street, and the workers in ivory are in a street by themselves. Then there is Curiosity Street (or Curio Street, as it is generally called), where you can buy all sorts of odds and ends of things, old and new, which come under the head of Chinese curiosities. Lacquered ware and porcelain have their especial quarters; and so when you are in the region of any particular trade, you do not have to walk about much to make your purchases. In the vicinity of the river there are several large concerns where they have a general assortment of goods, and you may buy lacquer and porcelain, silk and ivory, and nearly everything else that is produced in Canton, under one roof.

"We have already described lacquer and cloisonné work in writing from Japan. The Chinese productions in the same line are so much like the Japanese that a description of one will do for the other. Some of the shapes are different, and it is not difficult, after a little practice, to distinguish the Chinese from the Japanese; but the modes of working are essentially the same. All things considered, we like the Japanese lacquer better than the Chinese, as it has more variety, and the Japanese seem to be more cunning than the Canton people in making those bewildering little boxes with secret drawers and nooks and a great variety of shapes. But when it comes to ivory carvings, we have something else to say.

"You can hardly have dreamed of the beautiful things we found in Canton cut out of ivory. There were combs and brooches so delicate that it seemed as if they could be blown to pieces by a breath; and there were boxes and card-cases with representations of landscapes, and men and animals on them so small that we needed a microscope to see them distinctly. In one shop we saw the whole tusk of an elephant carved from one end to the other so closely that you could hardly put a pin on it without hitting some part of the work. They told us that the tusk had been sent there by the gentleman who killed the elephant in India, and he was having it carved to keep as a trophy. The carving had cost six hundred dollars; and if it had been done in America, it would have cost nearer six thousand. Skilled labor is cheap in China, just as unskilled labor is, and it is astonishing for how little a man can be employed on the kind of work that would bring a high price in Europe or America.

"Then there were carvings in tortoise-shell of a great many kinds, and all the forms you could think of, together with many you could not. The Chinese tortoise-shell work used to be the best in the world; but those who know about it say that it is now equalled by the productions of Naples and Florence, both in fineness and cheapness. Then they had some beautiful things in silver filigree and in bronzes, and we bought a few of each, so as to show what Canton can do in this line.

"But such fans! such fans! They were so pretty that we couldn't keep our eyes off them, and we bought more of them, perhaps, than we needed. In one shop we would find something so nice that we couldn't see how it could be surpassed, and so we

A TABLET CARVED IN IVORY.

would buy it; and in the next we found something nicer yet, and so we had to buy that. Anybody who has a liking for fans, and hasn't a mint of money, had better keep out of the stores of Canton, or he will run a risk of being ruined. The varieties are so great that we cannot begin to name them. There were fans on silk, and fans on paper; fans carved in ivory, tortoise-shell, sandal-wood; fans of feathers from various birds, with rich paintings right on the surface of the feathers; and a great many other fans besides. There was one with frame and sticks of sandal-wood, beautifully carved, while the body was of painted silk. There were groups of figures on each side of the fan, and each figure had a face painted on ivory which was afterwards glued to the silk. It was the prettiest thing to be found for any price we could afford, and you can be sure that it was secured for somebody at home.

"We had a long search among the porcelain shops for some blue china plates of what is called 'the willow pattern.' We must have gone into twenty shops at least before we found them; and, finally, when we did get them, the dealer was as anxious to sell as we were to buy. He said he had had those plates on hand a very long time, and nobody wanted them. We did not tell him how rare they are at home, and how anxious people are to get hold of them.

"The variety of porcelain in the Canton shops is very great, and a simple list of what there is would fill several pages. They showed us some of what they call egg-shell porcelain. It was so thin that you could almost see through it, and so delicate that it had to be carefully handled. The varieties of cups and saucers we could not begin to tell; they make them suited to every market in the world, and it is said that the greatest part of what they make is of the shapes that are not used in China. Of vases there was no end, and they were of all sizes, from a tiny cone for a small bouquet up to a huge one capable of holding a barrel of water, with plenty of room to spare. The trade in vases must be very great, if we are to judge by the quantities and variety that we saw. Many of them were very elaborate, and must have cost a great deal of money.

"But there is danger that you will get tired if we keep on much longer about the sights of Canton, and particularly the shopping part of it. Besides, we want to go out and see what there is in Hong-kong, and perhaps we may run across something new in the Chinese part of the city that we shall want to buy. A good many people say that you can buy Canton goods just as cheaply in Hong-kong as in the city they come from. That may be so; but then it is more satisfactory to get them there and have the pleasure of buying them on the spot.

"We'll stop now and say good-bye. We have seen China and Japan, and had a splendid time. We think we have learned a great deal about the two countries, and hope that what we have written about them has been interesting to those for whom it was intended. We have tried to see things, and think of them without partiality or prejudice. We believe that the people of the East have the same claims to respect that ours have, and that it is only a narrow mind that sneers at the ways of others because they are not like its own. We know that there are many things in which we are superior to the Orientals, but we also know that we have our weak points, and might be profitably instructed by those whom some of us affect to despise. And the more we know these patient and industrious people, the more we shall be likely to respect them. We are soon to leave China, perhaps never to see it again; but both China and Japan will always be pleasant recollections to both

"FRANK AND FRED."

"GOOD-BYE!"

INTERESTING BOOKS FOR BOYS.

HOW TO GET STRONG, AND HOW TO STAY SO. By WILLIAM BLAIKIE. With Illustrations. 16mo, Cloth, $1 00.

THE BOYS OF '76. A History of the Battles of the Revolution. By CHARLES CARLETON COFFIN. Illustrated. 8vo, Cloth, $3 00.

THE STORY OF LIBERTY. By CHARLES CARLETON COFFIN. Illustrated. 8vo, Cloth, $3 00.

FRED MARKHAM IN RUSSIA; or, The Boy Travellers in the Land of the Czar. By W. H. G. KINGSTON. Illustrated. Small 4to, Cloth, 75 cents.

THE ADVENTURES OF A YOUNG NATURALIST. By LUCIEN BIART. Edited and Adapted by PARKER GILLMORE. With 117 Illustrations. 12mo, Cloth, $1 75.

THE LIFE AND SURPRISING ADVENTURES OF ROBINSON CRUSOE, OF YORK, MARINER; with a Biographical Account of Defoe. Illustrated by Adams. Complete Edition. 12mo, Cloth, $1 00.

ROUND THE WORLD; including a Residence in Victoria, and a Journey by Rail across North America. By a Boy. Edited by SAMUEL SMILES. Illustrated. 12mo, Cloth, $1 50.

CHARACTER. By SAMUEL SMILES. 12mo, Cloth, $1 00.

SELF-HELP. By SAMUEL SMILES. 12mo, Cloth, $1 00.

THRIFT. By SAMUEL SMILES. 12mo, Cloth, $1 00.

THE SWISS FAMILY ROBINSON; or, Adventures of a Father and Mother and Four Sons on a Desert Island. Illustrated. 2 vols., 18mo, Cloth, $1 50.

THE SWISS FAMILY ROBINSON—Continued: being a Sequel to the Foregoing. 2 vols., 18mo, Cloth, $1 50.

THE BOYHOOD OF MARTIN LUTHER; or, The Sufferings of the Little Beggar-Boy who afterward became the Great German Reformer. By HENRY MAYHEW. Illustrated. 16mo, Cloth, $1 25.

THE STORY OF THE PEASANT-BOY PHILOSOPHER; or, "A Child Gathering Pebbles on the Sea-Shore." (Founded on the Early Life of Ferguson, the Shepherd-Boy Astronomer, and intended to show how a Poor Lad became acquainted with the Principles of Natural Science.) By HENRY MAYHEW. 16mo, Cloth, $1 25.

YOUNG BENJAMIN FRANKLIN; or, The Right Road through Life. A Story to show how Young Benjamin learned the Principles which raised him from a Printer's Boy to the First Ambassador of the American Republic. A Boy's Book on a Boy's own Subject. By HENRY MAYHEW. With Illustrations by John Gilbert. 16mo, Cloth, $1 25.

THE WONDERS OF SCIENCE; or, Young Humphry Davy (the Cornish Apothecary's Boy who taught himself Natural Philosophy, and eventually became President of the Royal Society). The Life of a Wonderful Boy, written for Boys. By HENRY MAYHEW. 16mo, Cloth, $1 25.

SCIENCE FOR THE YOUNG. By JACOB ABBOTT. Illustrated. 4 vols. now ready: *Heat.—Light.—Water and Land.—Force.* 12mo, Cloth, $1 50 each.

THE BOYHOOD OF GREAT MEN. By John G. Edgar. Illustrated. 16mo, Cloth, $1 00.

THE FOOTPRINTS OF FAMOUS MEN. By John G. Edgar. Illustrated. 16mo, Cloth, $1 00.

HISTORY FOR BOYS; or, Annals of the Nations of Modern Europe. By John G. Edgar. Illustrated. 16mo, Cloth, $1 00.

SEA-KINGS AND NAVAL HEROES. A Book for Boys. By John G. Edgar. Illustrated by C. Keene and E. C. Johnson. 16mo, Cloth, $1 00.

THE WARS OF THE ROSES. By John G. Edgar. Illustrated. 16mo, Cloth, $1 00.

STORIES OF THE ISLAND WORLD. By Charles Nordhoff. Illustrated. 12mo, Cloth, $1 00.

POLITICS FOR YOUNG AMERICANS. By Charles Nordhoff. 12mo, Half Leather, 88 cents.

STORIES OF THE GORILLA COUNTRY. By Paul B. Du Chaillu. Illustrated. 12mo, Cloth, $1 50.

THE COUNTRY OF THE DWARFS. By Paul B. Du Chaillu. Illustrated. 12mo, Cloth, $1 50.

WILD LIFE UNDER THE EQUATOR. By Paul B. Du Chaillu. Illustrated. 12mo, Cloth, $1 50.

MY APINGI KINGDOM: with Life in the Great Sahara, and Sketches of the Chase of the Ostrich, Hyena, &c. By Paul B. Du Chaillu. Illustrated. 12mo, Cloth, $1 50.

LOST IN THE JUNGLE. By Paul B. Du Chaillu. Illustrated. 12mo, Cloth, $1 50.

OUR CHILDREN'S SONGS. Illustrated. 8vo, Ornamental Cover, $1 00.

THE THOUSAND AND ONE NIGHTS; or, The Arabian Nights' Entertainments. Translated and Arranged for Family Reading, with Explanatory Notes, by E. W. Lane. **600 Illustrations** by Harvey. 2 vols., 12mo, Cloth, $3 50.

THE HISTORY OF SANDFORD AND MERTON. By Thomas Day. 18mo, Half Bound, 75 cents.

THE HISTORY OF A MOUTHFUL OF BREAD, and its Effect on the Organization of Men and Animals. By Jean Macé. Translated from the Eighth French Edition by Mrs. Alfred Gatty. 12mo, Cloth, $1 75.

THE SERVANTS OF THE STOMACH. By Jean Macé. Reprinted from the London Edition, Revised and Corrected. 12mo, Cloth, $1 75.

YOUTH'S HEALTH-BOOK. 32mo, Paper, 25 cents.

Published by HARPER & BROTHERS, New York.

☞ *Any of the above works sent by mail, postage prepaid, to any part of the United States, on receipt of the price.*

www.ingramcontent.com/pod-product-compliance
Lightning Source LLC
Chambersburg PA
CBHW030811110726

47900CB00006B/1593